THE POPULAR AND
THE POLITICAL

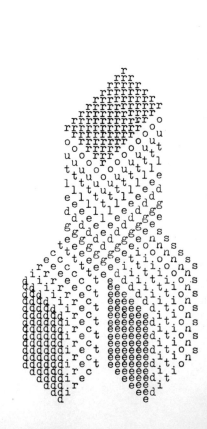

THE POPULAR AND THE POLITICAL

Essays on socialism in the 1980s

edited by
MIKE PRIOR

ROUTLEDGE DIRECT EDITIONS

Routledge & Kegan Paul
London, Boston and Henley

First published in 1981
by Routledge & Kegan Paul Ltd
39 Store Street,
London WC1E 7DD,
9 Park Street,
Boston, Mass. 02108, USA and
Broadway House,
Newtown Road,
Henley-on-Thames,
Oxon RG9 1EN
Printed in Great Britain by
Thomson Litho Ltd

British Library Cataloguing in Publication Data

The popular and the political.
1. Socialism - History
I. Prior, Mike
335'.009   HX21   80-41467

ISBN 0 7100 0627 6

The essays in this book are all dedicated to the memory of Bill Warren who helped us in many ways, intellectually and personally. He died in 1978, suddenly and before his contribution to British Marxism could be fully recognised. We hope that this work is a tribute to him.

CONTENTS

INTRODUCTION

The last year of the decade has, since the war, marked low points for the British left. In 1949, 1969 and 1979, one saw tired and compromised Labour governments trying, without success, to hang on to power; 1959 saw a massive electoral victory by the Conservatives.

The cycle of hope followed by disillusion has now swung around three times in thirty-five years and cannot be said to be diminishing. In 1949, there was at least some record of solid achievement in health care and social welfare. In 1969, a backdrop of a rejuvenated socialist movement could give promise of new ideas and fresh social forces entering British politics. In 1979, the most conservative of all post-war governments allowed many of the objectives even of social democracy, such as full employment and extending social services, to dribble away before going down before an onslaught based on an open appeal to individual greed.

This failure was all the more marked because of the election in 1974 of a Labour Party which had, in principle, a clearer strategic programme for advancing socialism than any previous Labour government. This should not be taken as a major compliment, since previous Labour administrations had almost no preconceived strategy. However, the policy of coupling overall economic planning to the development of genuine areas of working-class power via the use of compulsory planning agreements, the National Enterprise Board, and a range of increased trade union rights, whatever its defects, did at least begin to approach the central problem of British socialism; how to prise power away from an entrenched and complex system of capitalist control in the context of a highly developed framework of political democracy.

The actual process whereby this ambitious policy was neutered by the civil service, right-wing Labour politicians and all the apparatus of capitalist resistance is a story for a future historian to unravel. One factor is apparent, however, that the British left contributed to the failure by not comprehending the links between strategic policy and popular movements. They adhered to the long-standing socialist weakness of confusing stating a thing with putting it into practice.

Faced with the problem of forcing the implementation of the

spirit of the 1974 Labour manifesto by the Labour government, in a way that would actually shift the balance of power in Britain, the left, whether in the Labour Party or the Marxist groups, too often retreated to their accustomed positions as political Jeremiahs, attacking, usually with justification, the increasingly reactionary policies of Wilson and Callaghan, but offering little alternative other than the usual mixture of short-term militancy and long-term utopia.

The essays in this book are an attempt by a group of British socialists to come to terms with this failure and to establish British socialist policy on a more coherent footing. Although they differ in particular political commitment, they share a common position in the use of a Marxist analysis within the framework of a democratic transition to socialism. The development of this political perspective has been one of the more positive, if ambiguous, aspects of socialist thought in the 1970s. In continental Europe, the general tendency is conveniently, if misleadingly, characterised as Eurocommunism, but in Britain its sources are much more fragmented. One strand does lie with intellectuals within the British Communist Party and the discovery, by some, of the political philosophy of Gramsci. A number of new and important currents have grown up within the Labour Party during the same period. The one with the most support within the labour movement is the tendency around Tony Benn. This has been criticised for theoretical weaknesses, but other currents, perhaps more sophisticated at the theoretical level, have made themselves known within the constituency and student sections of the Labour Party.

Although fairly coherent, at least in political philosophy, these groups would be of little significance if it were not for a much larger, though less easily identifiable, move towards redefining socialism in a more flexible and complex fashion than the old, rather utopian dogmas. One major part of this trend has been the women's liberation movement, which has focused on the actual nature of human oppression under capitalism by insisting that it is not possible to reduce exploitation to a simple boss/worker dichotomy, and directed attention instead to the whole social framework, including the family, education, culture, and sexuality as a vehicle for human repression.

Another, though separate, thread is the move by industrial workers to offer much more precise strategies for their working future, to resist threatened redundancy by advancing new investment programmes and changes in industrial strategy. The best known of these is the Lucas Aerospace shop stewards' initiative, but other, less ambitious schemes have been proposed. Community and environmental activities have also forced a detailed and multifaceted analysis of social problems which offer few easy solutions and require positive alternatives.

This growth of wide-ranging but unfocused social pressure gave the politics of the 1970s a hazy feel, as though the surface movement of party politics was hardly touching the real pressures building up underneath. One aspect of this, on the left, was an increasing confusion as to what socialism actually represented, let alone the best way to achieve it. The politics of an alternative culture faded after a brief florescence, but they raised, and be-

queathed, concern with one of the oldest problems of socialism,
which had been largely submerged for decades, the conflict between
socialism as liberation for the individual and as a system of extended state control. The solution which dominated left thinking
from 1917, that the conflict could be wished away by running together the concepts of state ownership and communal ownership,
foundered on the rocks of experience both in the Soviet Union and
in the extended areas of state control in post-war Britain. An old
debate was reopened but with new ground-rules and new perceptions.

The key to many of the movements mentioned is the idea of
'community', of some way of living, whether at work or home, in a
relationship to others which is, in some sense, communal or social.
This is a pervasive concept in socialist thought, though one that
is often difficult to pin down. Yet in the 1970s, it entered many
popular movements in very concrete ways. Workers' control, co-
operatives, production for social use, are expressions of this in
work-place activity. The women's movement, environmental and community action and many other groups, such as professionals in education, law and medicine, have all attempted to develop communal
interest, a way for people to live and work together rather than in
isolation, a sense of social rather than individual responsibility.

Yet at the level of what is normally termed politics, that is the
deliberate attempt to construct social alliances in an organisational form to promote particular national programmes, there has been
little overt recognition of this change. That the Conservative
Party should win power essentially by appealing to blatant self-
seeking is not surprising; it remains one possible, though false,
path in a country so lacking in a national dynamic as Britain. What
is more surprising is the failure of the British socialist left to
take any real advantage of the conspicuous failings of the social
democratic leadership of the Labour Party and remain so committed to
the policies of a 'statist' socialism, something of which even committed Labour supporters have become suspicious.

The idea of statism and its relationship with socialism forms a
central theme in these essays. Although used before, particularly
by Jugoslav Marxists in discussing Eastern Europe, it has never been
so directly applied to trends in Western countries as in the essay
by Phil Leeson. His argument is that statism forms a recognisable
and, in certain circumstances, desirable intermediary between capitalism and socialism. It is not the same as socialism, however, and
cannot be pushed in that direction simply by the exertion of more
central state activity. This theme is picked up in other essays:
on housing, where the failure of socialists to grasp the nettle of
'municipalisation' has led council housing into a dead-end with no
effective answer to a back-lash of demands for the sale of council
properties; on medicine, where the gulf between an elitist medical
profession and community health care has never been bridged; on
work-place activity and free collective bargaining, where detailed
arguments by Paul Hirst and Dave Purdy demonstrate the limits of
wage-bargaining and the need for alternatives in the form of extended workers' control and a socialist incomes policy.

Other essays consider the kind of alternatives that socialism has
to offer, both in terms of ethical values and organisational forms,
and the kind of relationship which must exist between national

economic policies, political bodies and popular movements. As David
Fernbach notes, socialism has to offer an objective which is not
only practical but also to be desired. It has to stand as a bridge
which straddles both material needs and the ideals of humanity,
which have always motivated socialist activists, but which have
played less and less part in their popular images.

Although different in their emphases and some of their basic assumptions, all the essays share a sense of socialism as being a
series of practical steps aimed towards reversing, or at least minimising, the lack of control, the alienation, which is one of the key
popular attitudes with which a socialist movement must harmonise.
The suspicion with which state bureaucracies are regarded, a suspicion often encouraged by the left, sits uneasily with a constant
emphasis on greater state regulation. In one respect this common
element derives from the fact that all the essays were written to
commemorate the death, in 1978, of Bill Warren, who made an influential contribution to Marxist economics and political theory in the
previous two decades. Bill was born in 1935, and studied at Glasgow
and Cambridge Universities. He took up a post at the School of
Oriental and African Studies in 1964, which he held until his death
from kidney failure. He joined the Communist Party in the early
1950s and worked actively for it, though increasingly uneasily,
until 1974. Then, despairing partly of its policies, but also of
its monolithic lack of democracy, he left and joined the British and
Irish Communist Organisation. One of his main political activities
in the last three years of his life was as co-editor of the journal,
'Problems of Communism', which he tried to develop as a discussion
forum for the left.

He made a number of pioneering studies on various topics, all
centred on the current realities of capitalist development. He was
among the first British Marxists to analyse the role of planning and
conscious state control on the functioning of advanced capitalist
economies. He recognised the importance of inflation as an endemic
symptom of class struggle within such countries and discussed, with
great force, the kinds of political responses which the left had to
make in this situation. He put great emphasis on the practical need
for advanced forms of workers' control and a socialist incomes
policy.

He also made substantial, though controversial, analyses of the
theory of imperialism, refusing to accept much of the conventional
wisdom of left theory, preferring instead to look carefully at what
was actually happening in developing countries. This work is
shortly to be published in a book on Imperialism.

His work was, in many areas, preliminary, as any innovatory work
is likely to be, and British Marxism is weakened by his early death.
It would be wrong to suggest that all the contents of this book represent things in ways with which he would have agreed, for much of
what he wrote was at the forefront of controversy about socialist
policy. He took part in many debates, at times with some of the
authors in this book. Nevertheless, there is a discernible link
which they would acknowledge. The book is dedicated to his memory
as a kind and brave man as well as a good comrade.

Chapter 1

CAPITALISM, STATISM AND SOCIALISM

Phil Leeson

State action has grown rapidly everywhere in the course of this
century. The spectacle of an advanced capitalism operating alongside a minimal state apparatus, observed briefly in Britain and the
USA during the nineteenth century, has not become the normal pattern
of development since that time. Marx was, of course, writing
'Capital' during the period of Britain's capitalist heyday, and
'Capital' was based on a model of a pure capitalist system. He did
not live to write his volume on the state. Had he done so he would,
by that time, have found plenty of material with which to modify
Volume III, far more than Volume III in fact modified Volume I.

Since Marx's day Marxist writers have produced a great diversity
of theoretical writings on the state in attempting to encompass the
new phenomena. I do not intend to survey the literature in this
essay. I am concerned with the general problem implicit in the
notion of 'the capitalist state'. Both in the literature and in the
image of the state carried around by most of us as rank and file
socialists, there is a spectrum of emphases in which at the one extreme the state is seen as acting directly, narrowly and inevitably
on behalf of the capitalist class, or its dominant fraction, and at
the other extreme the state is accorded a degree of 'relative
autonomy' so that 'only in the last instance' does it act in the
interests of the system.

Some degree of dependence of the state on the capitalist class,
or system, has been judged to be necessary for Marxist theory. Yet
the state keeps escaping and we find ourselves considering state
activities which are only in the long-run, or most indirect,
interests of the system, which may in fact be opposed by the
capitalist class, and which may amount to no more than actions to
preserve social cohesion, to preserve the social and economic fabric
within which capitalism operates.

It seems to me that whilst the 'relative autonomy' end of the
spectrum is the more realistic, and the more relative autonomy that
we envisage the more realistic do our accounts become, nevertheless
this position is still inadequate, both as analysis and in its capacity to generate fruitful political lines of action. It doesn't
avoid the danger of tautological thinking in which the state's actions are deemed, ultimately, by definition, to be in the interests

of capitalism, and it creates the difficulty of explaining the
mechanisms whereby the state can be both relatively autonomous and
ultimately dependent. The greater the degree of relative autonomy
allowed in the name of realism, the more problematic becomes the
link implied by the phrase 'the capitalist state'. 'Relative
autonomy', in fact, constitutes an invitation to conduct analysis
without any theoretical underpinnings at all.

We are witnessing the growth of a phenomenon, in the shape of
extended state activity, which probably cannot be successfully analysed in this way. I propose, at least in the hope of provoking
argument (perhaps phrased in a clearer manner than is common in the
opaque language often used in this sort of discussion), to put forward an extreme version of state autonomy. I shall assert that the
activities of the state in modern society cannot be reduced to dependence on the capitalist system. To emphasise the independence,
I shall refer to the complex of state activities observed in the
twentieth century as 'statism'.

The state, of course, has been with us for a long time. And many of
the state's current activities are simply extended forms of traditional state roles. Nevertheless, just as it is usual to refer to
the last part of the nineteenth century as the beginning of the era
of imperialism, even though empires have existed for thousands of
years, so also there is a justification for regarding the present
century as an era when state activity became something both quanti-
tatively and qualitatively different from that of previous periods.
(In fact the era of statism and the era of imperialism have close
connections with one another.)

Compared with the weakly developed state apparatuses of the
nineteenth century, governments nowadays spend large proportions of
their nations' national incomes for military and police purposes,
for social programmes, and on the provision of economic services.
Many productive enterprises are set up under public ownership, or
have become so through acts of nationalisation. The state is a
major purchaser from firms and farms. It is sometimes the major
employer of labour. State fiscal, monetary, trade and planning
policies seek to control the level and direction of economic activity. State policies have results, intended and unintended, which
cause the pattern of output in the private sector, and the prices
at which that output is traded, to be very different from what would
otherwise have been the case.

Thus the activities of the modern state amount to an intensifi-
cation of its traditional forms of activity, police, military, di-
plomatic etc.; to the development of many new functions in the attempt to control the level and direction of private economic activity; and, perhaps most distinctive of the modern era, to the entry
of the state into the actual production of goods and services,
through central and local government and through state-owned semi-
autonomous enterprises.

A major reason for the phenomenon of statism, and one to which
Marxist writers have, of course, drawn attention, has been that it
is a response to the contradictions and inadequacies of the capitalist system. Inside each country where capitalism has developed
there has arisen the need for the social provision of the technical,

educational, transport, energy etc., infrastructure of the production process; for social investment where private profitability is uncertain or absent; for management of demand, of the price level and of the external balance in order to avert crises; to deal by concession or coercion with those manifestations of class struggle which threaten stability; to maintain those for whom capitalism finds no useful employment; for a collectivist answer to the socially disintegrating effects of the capitalist system.

But as state action grows so does the pressure of sectoral demands by all the numerous interest groups intent on achieving their aims via state patronage. This results in further growth of state activity and of the state apparatus. As the state apparatus grows, the various groups of employees within it acquire the strength to preserve and extend their own power, income and numbers.

The growth of statism is also very much a result of the development of international relationships. Uneven development leading to the consciousness of relative backwardness induces statist responses. Even before the nineteenth century was over, the state was playing a major role in the emergence from relative backwardness of such countries as Russia and Germany. That Britain in the mid-nineteenth century operated with a minimal state apparatus was very much connected with the fact that the country was not at that time very conscious of the threat of economic competition. As soon as she was, state action intensified, though the period left a legacy of laissez-faire ideology which has been influential long after it has ceased to be practically relevant. The consciousness of the need to catch up induces spending on education and economic infrastructure, subsidies to industry, protectionism in trade, etc.

Closely related to all this has been the rise in military budgets during this period. The close connection between imperialism and statism was noted above. The increase in capitalist world competition via trade and investment was accompanied by state action. Increasingly *all* powers felt an insecurity akin to the consciousness of relative backwardness mentioned above, and the state was involved whether the country was one whose capitalists were making incursions into new areas, or was one which was the recipient of these incursions. Marxists have often been criticised by non-Marxist historians for assuming too direct a link between economic expansion and colonial expansion. There is no need to incur this charge if we place the growth of statism within the chain of causes and effects. The development of capitalism led to economic expansion *and* the growth of statism. Colonial expansion was sometimes a direct function of economic expansion and called forth an increment of statism. But on the other hand colonial expansion was sometimes a product of statism, whether or not it involved direct economic gain.

The two world wars again involved statist responses to economic frictions and also reflected the direct impact of the growth of statism acting independently of economic necessity. The world-wide growth of nationalist ideology, with fascism as its extreme form, is also closely allied to the development of statism. And whatever the initiating factors in the two world wars, there is little doubt that the intervening and regulating functions of the state received their greatest impetus during those periods.

In effect, the spread of statism throughout the world has been at least as dramatic as the spread of capitalism. Statism in one country calls forth statism in another. It has been experienced in countries where capitalism has developed fully and in countries where indigenous capitalism has gained only a weak footing, and nowadays constitutes a tremendous impulse on a world scale.

As examples of the ramifications of statism we may quote both Britain, the oldest capitalist country, and the countries of the Third World at the other extreme. In Britain the contradictions felt internally, with a labour movement strong enough to combat capitalism but which has made little effort to bring capitalism to an end, and externally, as the sense of developing backwardness deepens, have been productive of state action on a large scale. Capitalist enterprises have become dependent on state orders, tax policies, subsidies, incomes policies etc. Capitalists and workers both look to the state for a bigger share of the national cake. The power of the various professional and bureaucratic groups within the state apparatus has grown. The various interest groups in the country see their raison d'être in the light of their relationship to the state structure, national or local. The peculiar nature of the labour movement in this country with a strong trade union movement oriented almost solely towards traditional trades union aims and with political action concentrated in the Labour Party, with an extremely weak revolutionary presence, is surely a product of the emergence of statism from the balance of class forces. And through its growth statism made more feasible the kind of programme on which the Labour Party has always based itself.

The countries of the Third World have a weakly developed indigenous capitalism, but they experience the sense of relative backwardness and the incursion of international capital. They have a state structure often still conditioned by the colonial legacy through which state apparatuses developed in advanced countries were imposed on them. They are involved in international relationships which foster the growth of statism. The aid relationship requires that a state apparatus be in existence to handle the funds, and in the process often causes the state machine to expand. The incursion of the multinational company, intent on setting up productive enterprises instead of merely trading, results in the growth of state power, since the multinationals have to relate to the public authorities in the territory concerned. 'Slush funds' are a manifestation. It is even the case that in some ways multinationals are a creation of statism. They set up branches abroad because they must do so in order to overcome tariff barriers and to be positioned so as to obtain state concessions as against potential rivals. The incursion of international capital may or may not stimulate, or inhibit, local capitalism, but it certainly stimulates the growth of statism. None of this is to be taken to imply that the presence of international capital and the consequent dependent status of the Third World countries are not of fundamental importance. But neither should it be concluded that the internal factors, especially the power of the state (for instance in bargaining with the multinationals), are to be ignored. What is at stake is how the power of the state is used, not whether that power exists.

Of the two kinds of industrialisation proceeding in the Third

World, import substituting industrialisation has been very much a
matter of the interplay between the multinationals and local state
power, with local capitalism often playing a subsidiary role. This
form of industrialisation, for the home market, depends very much
on state policies, protection, licensing, etc. But also the modern
show-cases of capitalist growth in South-east Asia, South Korea,
Taiwan, etc., whose expansion is very much export-orientated, have
certainly not been based on classical laissez-faire principles. The
capitalist development in those countries has very much depended on
state policies there.

The incursion of capitalism dissolves the traditional way of life
in replacing subsistence production by cash transactions and
bringing modern consumer goods to remote areas. This brings about
the incorporation of the population into the monetary economy. It
also brings the population into the area of state control, or at
least of state interference, especially where village people migrate
to urban areas. This process, whereby 'subsistence' provision
through the family and local community is replaced by cash transactions but also by state supplied welfare, education, coercion,
etc., is still proceeding in the 'advanced' countries as well.

Finally it is possible to detect, with the rise of state action
in the Third World countries, the elements of a statist ideology.
One reason why the state is involved so directly is recognised to
be the weakness of local capitalism. The production of development
plans has become the symbol of the cult of state direction of
economic activity (as well as a means of attracting aid). There
has been in these countries a great upsurge of nation-building,
nationalist ideology. Many of the regimes are, in fact, military.
The elite come to acquire their careers, income and status through
state employment. There is a great deal of use of socialist rhetoric, with the multinational company the target of political attack.
But the reality is nationalistic, technocratic, modernising,
elitist.

Assuming that the existence of the phenomenon is recognised, the
question arises of how to explain statism. Those writers who assume
an absence of any functional dependence of state action on the capitalist class or system (thinking of the state as disembodied,
benevolent, above class, or subject equally to pressure groups of
all kinds, or narrowly bureaucratic) have usually been outside the
Marxist tradition. They certainly would not stimulate those who
already base themselves on that tradition to abandon the search for
an adequate Marxist theory.

If, within the Marxist framework, we regard the state as a part
of the superstructure, then the traditional notion of the dependence
of the superstructure on the economic base is called into question.
It is true that many of us, whilst admiring the vision contained in
the Preface to 'A contribution to the critique of political economy'
have nevertheless regarded it simply as the background framework to
our reading of history. We didn't expect that Marx, or anyone else,
would provide us with an infallible guide to the whole complex of
human society. We were prepared to allow all the scope in the world
for history to decide whether at a given moment the forces of production were enforcing changes in the relations of production, or

vice versa, whether changes in the superstructure were or were not
lagging behind, to what extent the superstructure could re-act back
on to the base, etc.

The connections between the tenets of historical materialism and
the reality of political practice have also been fairly loose.   As
capitalism arose during the period of crisis of feudalism so it was
believed that the crisis of capitalism would bring socialism on to
the agenda.   But whereas capitalism arose spontaneously within the
womb of feudalism, the transition to socialism required conscious
political action and a more or less abrupt break between systems.
The mere perception by the socialist pioneers that socialism would
resolve the contradictions of capitalism did not suffice to bring
socialism about.   Naturally, therefore, and although the enterprise
may make historians wince, a good deal of Marxist thinking in this
century has been devoted to the attempt to spell out the relationships between the economic, political and cultural-ideological
levels of society.   It may be that this work, of which some of the
writings on the state referred to above form a part, will lead to
an adequate theorisation of the problem.

What follows here however is based on scepticism concerning the
basic concept embodied in the Marxist theory of the capitalist
state.   At the same time the rather eccentric alternative proposed
does claim to be within the spirit of historical materialism.

As asserted earlier, a crucially important part of statism is the
phenomenon of state production.   State production is in general
organised on different lines from capitalist production.   It could
therefore be referred to as a separate mode of production.   All that
is necessarily entailed by this statement is that state production
of goods and services involves a sufficiently different method of
economic organisation to require that it be conceived of separately
from the capitalist mode, or the petty commodity mode, etc.   In
this sense the existence of a state mode of production is a fairly
obvious statement of fact.   It might nevertheless be a very useful
statement of fact if it led us towards a study of the characteristics of state production, its rules of operation, its relationships with capitalist production, etc. - all very necessary since
our existing models of the workings of the economy are mostly
models of private capitalist production.   It would seem to be un-
Marxist to ignore such basic questions to do with the organisation
of production.

Hence there would seem to be some point in using the term 'mode
of production' in this limited sense to call attention to the
characteristics of state production which differ in a significant
way from those of the capitalist process.   Nothing more fundamental
would be implied.   State production would simply be regarded as a
part of the complex of state activities operating within a capitalist society.

However, in Marxist discourse the concept of a mode of production
usually conjures up far more than this.   Although it is commonly
accepted that more than one mode of production may be in existence
at a given time, especially in transitional periods, in due course
one of them will predominate over the other, and will come to
exercise a determining influence over the whole social formation,
superstructure as well as economic base.

Hence the use of this category in connection with state activities inevitably leads on to wider (or wilder) speculation as to the
historical sequence of epochs. The state mode *may* be of such a
character that it will come to predominate over the capitalist
mode. It is clear that state production has fairly close connections with other state activities, with events in the political
and ideological spheres. These connections would again repay close
study – the extent to which a statist ideology develops, the relationships between politicians and civil servants, the law concerning public bodies etc. It *may* be the case that the state mode
will come to exercise a predominant influence over the superstructure.

In order to present as extreme a version as possible of state
autonomy, I shall dabble in the rest of this essay with the larger
notion that what I have termed statism has a status for Marxism on
a par with capitalism, feudalism or socialism. This does not mean
that I am asserting the historical inevitability that statism will
supplant capitalism. It seems quite possible in fact that statism
and capitalism will advance together in the world at large, though
at differing rates in individual countries, for a prolonged period.
Whatever may happen in the future there do seem to be good historical reasons for the emergence and growth of statism in the recent
period. And the manner of its emergence and growth – out of the
contradictory aspects of capitalism, spreading internationally, in
a state of tension with capitalism but capable of an accommodation
with it – is analogous to the manner in which Marxists have, for
instance, argued that capitalism emerged out of feudalism. That
the growth of statism results from the contradictions of capitalism
does not of course imply any great departure from much Marxist
writing on 'the capitalist state'. What is necessary for present
purposes is the proposition that statism can develop along lines
which are antagonistic to capitalism.

If, however, readers find the discussion of the state mode of
production to be a red herring, I hope that they will nevertheless
agree that there is a phenomenon – whether called statism or not –
which has certainly not been theorised in the corpus of Marxist
literature adequately enough for it to be coped with successfully
in political practice.

The question of what is covered by the term production is an arbitrary question of definition. If we look at production from the
point of view of the capitalist system then we think of what is produced for a profit and for exchange via the market. In that case
the state certainly produces to the extent that state enterprises
such as the nationalised industries exist and sell their product.

Even in the case of the nationalised industries, however, there
are many differences between state and capitalist production. State
enterprises may sell at prices, dictated by state policy, which
differ from those indicated by normal profitability criteria. They
may produce kinds of output which private firms would not attempt to
produce. They may be able to recoup losses by state subsidy or
their profits may be used for purposes other than capital accumula-
tion. Their internal rules of behaviour differ in some ways from
those of capitalist concerns. Still, they often do attempt to copy
capitalist rules of profitability, regarding this rather than

service to the community as the test of success. And if they were
the sum of state production then we would hardly be justified in
talking of a separate mode.

However, in addition to state enterprises which sell their output
via the market there is the whole gamut of tax-financed services
provided by central and local government. The production of education, health care, street cleanliness, etc., is manifestly organised
on lines different from those of capitalist enterprise (though in
principle and in a small way in practice capitalist firms do produce
some of these things). The method of finance, the objectives of
production, the internal organisation of work are all very different.

It is a sterile way of looking at the modern economy to start
from the proposition that the only productive workers are those who
produce surplus within the capitalist system, and then either define
government workers as unproductive or get into contortions as to
their status. Moreover, the notion that state employees are unproductive, existing out of the surplus produced within the capitalist
sector, leads to politically unacceptable conjunctions of Marxist
jargon and Tory rhetoric. The need, at least in the case of by far
the greater part of total employment, for this categorisation of
productive and unproductive work disappears as soon as we accept
that there are two modes of production in operation. What is produced in the one mode should not be defined from the standpoint of
the other.

We could, if we wished, proceed to abolish conceptually the distinction between state production and other state activity altogether. Just as the concept of production is arbitrary and depends
solely on what is considered to be the most fruitful way of looking
at social reality, so, by the same token, there is an element of
arbitrariness in the Marxist distinction between basis and superstructure. We could regard the 'production' of law and order, stability, ideology, etc., as part of the output of the state mode.

However, a great deal to do with the analysis of a class society
is clarified by the maintenance of a distinction in this regard,
even though it is clear that there are close connections between
state production and state 'superstructural' activity, the analysis
of which is of great importance both for 'mixed' social formations
such as ours, and for those where statism might be the sole mode.
But even though a distinction, arbitrary or otherwise, is maintained, there is still a great and growing volume of output of goods and
services which can be agreed to be a component of the standard of
living (the social wage, etc.) and which emanates from the state
mode.

If statism constitutes (or contains) a mode of production, are state
employees a class (or classes)?

State officials are unlike capitalists in that although their positions may give them high incomes, those incomes are not used as
capital in the exercise of their state functions. (They may, and in
many countries do, acquire wealth through their positions, and proceed to become capitalists, but that is not the immediate point.)
Even though they do not own the means of production, however, they
do, through their positions, acquire the means to high consumption,
prestige, power and security. In this sense they are like any other

ruling class throughout history. They are, in fact, more typical
than capitalists since ruling classes and state apparatuses have
normally been fused in function and in personnel, whereas this is
not the case with the capitalist system. (Clearly many parallels
could be drawn with the so-called 'Asiatic' mode of production, and
also with the feudal system.)

Marxist theories of the state have usually found space for upper
state officials within the ruling class, assuming them to be paid
out of the surplus generated by capitalist production. But if we
are envisaging statism as a mode of production then something else
must be implied.

Where there are two modes co-existing then part at least of the
surplus may be generated by the exploitation of one mode by another.
In addition to extracting a surplus from their own workers, capitalists may, for instance, increase that surplus through the favourable
terms at which they trade with peasants. The capitalist mode and
the state mode trade with one another. There have been many arguments over whether or not the nationalised industries sell to capitalist firms at prices which represent a subsidy to them. There is
also discussion over whether capitalists derive a net surplus from
the balance between the taxes they pay and the services provided by
the state which are of direct economic value to them.

But in general the output of the state mode is 'sold', paid for
in taxes or via the market, partly to state employees themselves and
partly to capitalists and their employees. In addition, extra taxes
have to be raised to pay for those other state activities not regarded as part of state production. If the output of the state
sector is sold then there are state workers who produce it. If we
envisage that there is also a statist controlling or ruling class
then the incomes of this group must either come from the additional
taxes mentioned above, or from exploitation of the capitalist mode
by 'trade', or from exploitation of state workers.

The amount of surplus extracted from state workers depends on
their rates of pay, their productivity, and the 'prices' at which
their product is sold. They may, in fact, work the same number of
hours as workers in capitalist industry, whilst being paid at somewhat lower rates, though casual observation indicates that the intensity of work may be lower too. But we cannot compare prices.
Hence we are left with an indeterminate picture in which a state
ruling class might be financed by exploitation of state workers
whilst capitalist industry nevertheless does quite well out of the
'trade', i.e., also shares in the state surplus. But, especially
when we take into account the assumption that additional taxes are
raised for state 'non-productive activities', then several other
combinations are possible.

The attempt to construct a picture of two groups, controllers and
producers, within the state mode is not an absolute necessity. We
could have a mode of production without a controlling class at all.
Much more to the point is that class structures have usually been
hierarchies rather than simply bi-polar. And within the state
structure there are not two polarised groups but hierarchies in
which the upper shades into the lower.

Where hierarchies are concerned the notion of 'intermediate
strata' is unsatisfactory. And the concepts of productive and unproductive labour are just as much a positive hindrance to analysis

of activities within the state sector as they are to analysis of the
interrelations between the capitalist and the state sectors. We are
obliged to use some notion of the 'collective labourer', in which
employees at all levels are regarded as contributing to the product.
But a complementary requirement is that we recognise that in hierarchies employees exploit those beneath them and are exploited by
those who are above them.

The difficulty of quantifying exploitation in cash terms where
the state mode is concerned has been pointed out above. This difficulty is compounded when we recognise the existence of hierarchies.
In any case, there are many instances where the attempt to see exploitation in these terms would not assist in understanding actual
situations. Exploitation in the state sector is not normally of a
kind in which a state official can directly enhance his own income
by depressing those of his subordinates or increasing their intensity of work. In fact, the rules of operation might well mean that an
official has little incentive to reduce the staff under him, or to
fail to spend to the limit the cash allowed him for the year.
(Nevertheless when cuts do occur in public expenditure it is common
for the axe to fall at the level of the reduction in the numbers of
lower level producers (teachers, dustmen, nurses) rather than at the
level of higher officials.)

More generally if it is remembered that what is at stake in acquiring a privileged class position is authority, influence, promotion, prestige, immunity from unfavourable consequences of actions,
rather than just the amount of cash surplus commanded, then it is
easy to see that there are many ways in which a superior officer ex-
ploits and derives his standing from the work of those beneath him
(as many secretaries could testify) and is in turn exploited by
those above him.

It has been asserted that statism is growing within the context of
capitalism. But it has not been claimed that it will oust capitalism, unless of course it is given a dramatic push in a revolutionary
direction. On the contrary, capitalism has continued to expand
during the period when statism has been developing. What are the
dynamics of the interaction between these modes?

That the co-existence of modes results in modifications in the
workings of each is something which is, or certainly ought to be,
accepted by Marxists. It was noted above that state enterprises may
attempt to copy the capitalist manner of operation. Capitalist
operations are also affected by the statist environment within which
they are situated. At a trivial level they develop bureaucratic
characteristics in response to state legal, tax, and information demands. But more importantly, capitalist firms become dependent on
the state for orders, infrastructure, subsidies, protection, etc.

There is nothing to imply that statism seeks the destruction of
capitalism. Statism is hardly more conscious of any such historical
role than were previous modes. Statism is not in most countries in
a position to organise the whole economy, and statism needs the revenue which can be obtained from capitalist operations. State officials may well be imbued with capitalist ideology and may try to
foster capitalist growth. (2) Capitalists will, of course, cease-
lessly attempt to dominate the state decision-making centres and to
use for their own benefit state resources. There is nothing new

about an accommodation between an old and a new ruling class.

Nevertheless, so far from the state being the handmaiden of capitalism, its operations are, in fact, leading to a profound weakening of the system. Statist measures which have benefited the working class, the income maintenance of the unemployed for instance, strike at the heart of the capitalist need for a reserve army of labour. Many of the most significant improvements in living standards in this century have come about by statist interference with the capitalist system, have resulted in redistribution away from property income, and have usually been resisted by the capitalist class.

It is true that it might be claimed that without these actions (and many others) the capitalist system would have collapsed long ago and that therefore the state's actions are in the interest of capitalism. It may well be the case that the existence of statism has prolonged the life of the capitalist system. But to survive in a dependent client role is hardly the picture of the relationship between capitalism and the state intended to be conjured up by theories of 'the capitalist state'. The fact that capitalism has continued to expand on a world scale at the same time as statism has expanded merely means that both have grown at the expense of pre-capitalist modes, and is quite compatible with a weakening of capitalism relative to statism in any given country.

It is not being asserted here that the state, whilst retaining co-existence with the capitalist system, *can* actually resolve the contradictions generated by that system. The belief that state action is a growing force does not imply the holding of illusions (Keynesian, social democratic, or otherwise) that the state has the capacity to ensure harmonious development. So long as a substantial part of economic activity is via the market and is directed by private investment decision then it will not be possible, except partially, for the state to resolve the ensuing contradictions – unless, that is, the fact that the state succeeds in preventing capitalism from destroying itself is regarded as sufficient. Attempts to impose state policies will continually be frustrated. A good deal of state activity will perforce be *reactive,* that is by way of attempting to clear up the mess created by the individualistic operations of capitalism, in the sphere of contra-cyclical policy, in the cause of dealing with the social and environmental effects of capitalist production processes and capitalist consumption products. Under capitalism, investment decisions are taken without regard to social consequences, and the effects are unforeseen or ignored. In this blind way market operations continually change the social structure. A large part of state action is a necessary response to this, but not necessarily a successful response.

Not only will the state only partially be able to control capitalist anarchy and its effects, but in certain cases the state may actually compound the anarchy, since to capitalist decentralisation will be added the confusion, competition and conflict of aims which stem from the numerous decision centres within the state apparatus and the many pressure groups operating on them. The existence of a state apparatus is no guarantee that the state can forecast future events, or that it will demonstrate an adequate interest in them.

One could list many examples of state provision - tower-block council housing, social security payments, large schools, motorways, nuclear power, slum clearance, North Sea oil - where either the results have not been predicted, or complementary action has not been taken, or an intended social policy has not been adhered to with enough determination.

But none of this necessarily implies that the state may not be, or become, the dominant partner. The power of the state is the power to intervene and dictate, not the power to do so successfully (if success is taken to mean the solution of social problems). Whether successful in this sense or not the state will continue to grow in size and power.

Apart from questions arising from the co-existence of capitalism and statism, what can be said of the internal characteristics of statism, discernible as it operates in mixed economies? Does it generate contradictions which cause it to run into crisis?

Statism clearly has progressive attributes which capitalism does not possess. It is able to expand production in certain spheres which capitalism finds it difficult to cope with. It tends to lead towards a stability and predictability of economic activity. It has led to an improvement in the distribution of income, to the eradication of absolute poverty, and, as noted above, has been very much involved in this century's rise in living standards. The step by step increase in state action implies *some* degree of understanding of social processes, or at least the possibility of acquiring it, and the power to act on that understanding, all of which are denied to the capitalist system as such. Probably statism has succeeded in preserving social cohesion when otherwise capitalism would have destroyed it.

On the other hand, statism generates bureaucratic ways of behaving. The rules of bureaucracy, the impulse to play safe, bring about a lack of dynamism so far as economic growth is concerned. The lack of dynamism does not, however, mean lack of tensions between sections of the bureaucracy and between the bureaucracy and other groups. Nor does it mean that no growth of any other sort proceeds. Bureaucratic empire building proceeds, and can be socially very expensive.

The state is vulnerable to being pulled in many directions by the various pressure groups for whom access to the social surplus is via state patronage. The combination of pressure groups and bureaucratic vested interests means that it is difficult for the state to acquire the unification of aims and the conscious co-ordinated decision-making capacity which are necessary if the full potentialities of the system are to be achieved.

A particular set of problems emerges from the relationships between state officials and the politicians. The existence of the state apparatus leads in election periods to exaggerated claims as to what can be achieved. But the realities of the location of power in the state structure result in a convergence of political action in practice whichever party is elected. Yet on the other hand the necessity for decisions to be taken formally at the political level means an inability to take decisive action on the more deep-seated long-term problems.

Statism engenders a pauperisation, a growing dependence on the
state, on the part of individuals and groups. At the same time its
remoteness and paternalistic characteristics make it unpopular even
with those who benefit from its actions. The system finds it difficult to achieve an adequate level of motivation on the part of its
workers to increase production. The capitalist whip cannot be fully
utilised, and the (hoped for) socialist motivation is absent. The
provision of services by professionals (medics, police, social
workers, teachers, etc.), whilst being a great step forward beyond
the provision of no services, means that opportunities to seek community solutions of problems are missed. For instance, a great deal
of the problem of crime could be resolved by community action, far
more successfully than by the enrolment of more policemen.

A tendency for the state to run into crisis ensues. In many
countries the state has responded to its crisis by dictatorial, repressive solutions, sometimes involving military governments. This
kind of response is often ineffective at the level of production.
And the resort to military regimes reproduces the tensions within
the military units themselves.

By no means all states, however, respond in this way. The traditions and level of development of the country concerned help to
determine whether such measures are resorted to. And (as is the
case with capitalist crisis) the crisis of the state can proceed a
long way before the patient dies. In fact the crisis does not
prevent the growth of the various components of the state apparatus.
The power of the various sections of the bureaucracy grows with the
pauperisation process. Rather than the competing claims for resources leading to a sudden breakdown, the nature of the system and
its method of finance is such that inflation can become an endemic
phenomenon in a mixed society. Ultimately the crisis of the state
could become of such a magnitude that the system would be unable to
provide the necessary largesse to groups within and outside the
state apparatus for it to continue. But it may be that its capacity
for preserving some level of stability, its ability to prevent
actual breakdown, might mean that whilst it does not, even in its
better periods, have any great success in terms of dynamic growth,
it can survive a prolonged period of chronic crisis.

The question of the relationship between statism and socialism is,
of course, as vital to the discussion as the question of the relationship between statism and capitalism. In the Marxist sequence
of epochs the assumption and the hope has been that socialism will
succeed capitalism. It has not usually been envisaged that this
will happen as a result of a gradual development within capitalism
but rather as a result of a drastic break with it accompanied by a
gigantic arousal of political consciousness on the part of the
workers. The record indicates that this has not so far occurred
except fitfully in revolutionary situations at certain moments and
in certain places.

Whilst socialist transition in the Western world remains but a
hope, it has been argued here that there are endogenous mechanisms
at play which make it realistic to expect the growth of statism
within the womb of capitalist society, a growth which displays a
much clearer analogy with the emergence of capitalism within the

womb of feudal society than does the scenario for the transition
to socialism. Not that it would be correct to overstate the element
of spontaneity in the development of statism. Each act of statism
requires some conscious move on the part of a public body, some
effort to interfere with the existing order, and very often involves
extensive political campaigning. But it does happen piecemeal and
gradually, and there are good reasons to believe that once begun the
process will continue.

It has been argued that it is inadequate for Marxists to analyse
the activities of the state as just functions of the necessities of
the capitalist system. But as much confusion is caused on the
other hand by the equation of statist measures with the socialist
system. This has been a habit of both supporters and opponents of
statist policies. We need not concern ourselves too much with the
'Daily Telegraph' readers for whom any act of statism is a socialist
measure, though, in anticipation of later discussion, it may be said
that sometimes ultra-Tories have an instinctive grasp of the social
process which has eluded the Marxists. But the left has also always
confused the two.

It would not, in fact, be easy to identify a distinctive statist
ideology separate from that which is commonly thought of as
socialist - though bits of one might be pieced together from a
variety of sources appearing in the last hundred years. Many
statist measures have been achieved as a result of campaigns run
under socialist banners. Though there are many differences between
the reformist and the revolutionary wings of the socialist movements, both by and large have traditionally equated the achievement
of public ownership and control with the building of socialism.
Socialism largely *was* 'the common ownership of the means of production, distribution and exchange'. Nowadays, after the experience
of a number of Labour governments there is perhaps less confusion,
though much sadness, amongst labour supporters who now recognise
that statist measures may be intended more for the better regulation
of capitalism than for the building of socialism. But the confusion
is still manifest in the decline in overt support for socialism
alongside the growing unpopularity of many aspects of statism.

All this certainly implies that the aspirations of those who have
worked and suffered for socialism in the past hundred years or so
have been thwarted, not just because capitalism has not been ended
but because their efforts have contributed to the growth of statism
rather than to the achievement of socialism. It is of course
nothing new in history for the efforts of those who struggle for the
emancipation of mankind to be rewarded with something very different
from that for which they fought. It must be said, however, that in
so far as the working-class movement as a whole has been engaged it
has usually been a series of specific demands, health services,
education, etc., which have been at stake - demands which involved
an extension of statism, not the achievement of socialism.

Socialism was certainly the aspiration of those who, by revolution or military victory, took power in the Soviet Union, China and
elsewhere. This essay has discussed the growth of statism in the
West and in the Third World. It has had nothing so far to say about
the 'Second World'. Here it must be said that just as Western
social democracy adopted political programmes which were well at-

tuned to the potentialities of Western statism, so the political
theory of Leninism, developed before the revolution, was quite well
adapted to the rapid build up of statist structures. But whatever
the initial theory with which socialist regimes have taken power,
their experience shows that the same statist imperatives which
operate elsewhere have operated in these countries with even greater
force. For them the acute situation of relative backwardness whilst
under external military threat, the enforced co-existence in the
world at large with an expanding capitalism, the lack of an educated
population, the enormity of the initial problems, readily turned the
socialist impulse into an extreme form of statism with nationalist
ideology predominating over socialist aspirations, and with all the
ensuing tragedies which we have discussed so incessantly over the
years. It may be that statism explains the career of J.V.Stalin as
well as those of Lloyd George and Clement Attlee.

In the previous section it was simply assumed that socialism was
different from statism in spite of all the confusion over it.
Socialists have always maintained that socialism would resolve the
contradictions of capitalism. The question for present discussion
is whether socialism would resolve the contradictions of statism.
Clearly if socialism involves the abolition of capitalism, or at
least its demotion to a minor role in the economy, then the inadequacies of statism which are a function of its co-existence with
capitalism would cease to be relevant (except, of course, to the
extent that capitalism is still rampant in the rest of the world,
then some of the problems of co-existence remain and with them the
danger of a relapse into statism).
    Abstracting from the issues arising from the presence of capi-
talism, if that is possible, what are the ways in which socialism
ought to differ from statism, and do they carry the promise that
they would cure the endogenous ailments to which statism is prone?
Here it is difficult to avoid the temptation simply to portray a
utopian society in which socialism is defined as that state of
affairs in which all the contradictions observed in the real world
are resolved. Discussion is only sensible if it stresses both the
feasibility of what is envisaged and at the same time the difficulties of achieving it.
    An interpretation of what most socialists would hope for from the
socialist mode of production would say that on the basis of public
property there would be the maximum development of the forces of
production by technical advance and by education. The relations of
production would be such as to require the thoroughgoing democratisation of all aspects of public life via the development of popular
participation at all levels and in all aspects of economic and
political affairs. In this way socialism would remove the class
antagonisms of a stratified society, and be free from the stagnation
and lack of motivation to which statist societies are prone.
    The implication is that socialism can arouse within people a far
deeper sense of responsibility to the community and for public property than exists in capitalist or statist or capitalist-statist societies, that it can arouse a heightened sense of the extent to
which a full life derives from the milieu created by the community
rather than simply from the acquisition of personal possessions.

There have been, and still are, many societies where the individual is very much subordinated to the dominant social pressures,
both local and national. After the experience of capitalist indi-
vidualism and the limited but genuine advances in democracy and
freedom thereby attained, there could be no going back to such an
atmosphere. What is required for the successful operation of a
socialist society, therefore, would seem to be that the human race
should develop a new faculty, the ability to recognise in any situation what is the proper territory within which individual freedom
reigns supreme, and what is the sphere within which the potentialities deriving from social action can be brought into play. The
balance has to be struck at all levels from the consideration of
matters of high policy down to the thousand and one daily instances
where individuals and crowds are involved.

At present the two facets of life are a source of painful tension
with social action often appearing as a threat to the individual,
who may only have a very indistinct notion of the extent to which he
or she depends on such action. Since small communities and groups
(and not only neighbourhood and work-place groups are relevant - a
football crowd, or a group of bus passengers are, momentarily, communities as well) have not yet learned to develop the almost in-
finite potential of social action, much necessary social action is
undertaken by remote statist professional bodies, and on to them
falls the odium of the felt infringement of liberty.

The development of socialist consciousness clearly involves an
attack on statism. Those involved in bureaucratic hierarchies would
not welcome such an extension of democracy, in which public property
is handled and managed by users and producers. The status as a ruling group of state officials and of many professional workers would
be undercut by the development of participation and life-long education, with the distinction between amateur and professional,
teacher and pupil, becoming blurred along with the distinction
between ruler and ruled.

Nevertheless if socialist programmes are not to be purely utopian
it seems clear that socialism, as well as involving an attack on
statism, must also involve the completion of statism. The ending or
emasculation of capitalism can only be achieved by the extension of
social ownership and control. All kinds of solutions to the problem
of the balance between centralisation and decentralisation, and many
different kinds of ownership or stewardship of property (co-operative forms for instance) might emerge, but statism would have to be
pushed a long way first. No recognition of, or campaigning against,
the blemishes of statism could be allowed to obscure the fact that
statism is a step forward. Socialism involves the completion and
the truncation of the stage of statism.

As opposed to the hope that socialism might be achieved as a result
of the crisis of capitalism it has been posed as hard reality that
statism develops within capitalism. If we were then left simply
with the hope that political action might turn statism into socialism, we would not be much further forward. However, there seem
to be good grounds for believing that just as statism grows within
capitalism so the conditions for socialism grow within statism.

State activity involves a growth, however imperfect, in the

understanding of social processes and in the acceptance that social problems can be dealt with by social action. Each activity involves some reference to social policy, some awareness of the possibility of the public taking an attitude. Many of these activities are piecemeal, reactive affairs but their multiplication places more thoroughgoing, long-term, questions on to the agenda for public discussion.

It is true that the situation is ambiguous, with negative features as well as positive ones. For instance many public bodies, the health service for instance, have a participatory element built into them. But the reality may be just a very pale reflection of what participation ought to be. On the one hand the existence of public bodies creates the possibility of public participation, whilst on the other hand the remoteness and paternalism of statist bodies induces passivity amongst the recipients of social benefits.

The great growth of popular pressure groups in recent years - at least partly a product of statism - is evidence of a growing capacity for social action. Again the record is ambiguous. Some of these groups are making sectional demands which would be a very troublesome problem for a socialist regime to cope with. Others are making demands which must be considered reactionary and anti-socialist. Yet others are limited by the statist context, i.e., they are demands that the state do this or that rather than that there be popular involvement in decision-making. But many, for instance the environmentalist groups, have developed a responsible approach to long-term social policy. And others, notably the women's movement, seek to change the whole climate within which social relationships have been conducted.

The most prominent of all the people's organisations, the trade unions, are hampered in playing a role in the democratisation of statism by the fact that their main task, the fight for better wages and conditions of work, stems from the struggle with capitalism, and by itself does not engender a socialist consciousness. However, the weakening of capitalism concurrently with the extension of statism, and the consequent growth of state intervention in industrial affairs, means that trade unions now are increasingly involved in political policy matters.

That the conditions for socialism should grow within statism seems a realistic proposition. It is saying no more than that an educated population, with a high degree of public provision of services, and a high degree of government intervention in the economy, must develop some of the necessary attitudes and attributes. That this process should happen prior to the advent of a socialist regime is also highly necessary for the future success of that regime. With a completely unprepared population the attempt at socialism would relapse into a not very inspiring statism and the subsequent learning process would be very painful and costly.

However, it would be totally incorrect to talk of the spontaneous emergence of the conditions for socialism within statism as if no overt political struggle is called for. The level of ambiguity in the situation, with negative as well as positive features abounding, amply demonstrates that. In fact at the purely political level one of the results of statism is that the appeal of socialism has never

been weaker. The development of the conditions for socialism means
that many people who would most readily reject the label of socialism are, in fact, well on the way towards a capability for functioning in it. By the same token, socialism when it comes might be very
different in detail from what many professed socialists have in mind.
mind.

The question is the nature of the political effort to be made.
The message of the existence of statism seems to imply that socialist political action is not to be confined to opposition to capitalism in the expectation of a big-bang achievement of revolution.
On the other hand it is not to be confined to support of whatever
statist measures even a left-wing Labour government might propose
(for example some of the proposals included in the 'Alternative
Economic Strategy'). If a criticism of the revolutionary wing of
the British left is implied, there is certainly no implication that
uncritical acceptance of Labour Party policies and practice is
called for.

What seems to be indicated is first a greater understanding of
and involvement with many of the grass-roots activities which have
sprung up outside the traditional socialist movement. Unsuspected
both by their members and by the socialist movement, they may be
part of the building of socialism.

The limits of traditional trade union activity in this context
were pointed out above. If, however, the environment created by
statism induces workers to demand a greater involvement in the traditional sphere of management — what is produced, at what prices,
for what markets — then the situation is transformed. The demand
for workers' control is utopian in the absence of complementary
state action, just as state action towards industry is bureaucratic
and statist in the absence of workers' participation. But the two
might be mutually reinforcing. Demands for workers' control might
stimulate those in government who wish to make a reality of central
planning, and central planning might stimulate workers to develop an
interest in alternative product patterns.

Much of the impact made on us by statism in our daily lives is
via the activities of local authorities, and much of the impact made
by popular movements on statism must also have a local authority
sphere of responsibility as its focus.

Socialists often pay little attention to local government work
and the subject has acquired a fusty, Fabian, reformist image. We
leave it to those Labour Party members devoted enough to master its
intricacies. Many of us know more about the structure of the Common
Market than we do about the reorganisation of local government. And
local government has developed many of the more regrettable attributes of statism discussed earlier. It is often bureaucratic and
remote. Sometimes more attention is paid to the needs of its own
employees than to the quality of service provided. In any case the
service provided, not being via the market, can worsen without there
being any market signals to sound the alarm. The quality of life is
flexible — at least in the absence of grass-roots activity of a very
perceptive and persistent kind. The atmosphere is very statist in
that the questions which arise concern what we can get *them* to do
for us. And councillors often foster the willingness of the people
to leave things to them.

Yet local authority work is in fact extended in imaginative directions by many progressive councils up and down the country. Much of what they do would bring credit to any socialist regime. Many of them do attempt to encourage participation. Their work could be the forum for a vast extension of democracy. It is true that central government keeps a fairly tight watch on what they do, especially where there are financial implications. It would be too romantic a vision to conjure up a picture of socialist republics operating on a local scale in an otherwise non-socialist environment. But, as with the relationship between trade unionists' activity in their work-places and central planning, this is a two-way process in which progressive local authorities help to set the atmosphere within which central government can be changed.

Since what local authorities *can* do has vast implications for the condition of the environment, for law and order, for culture and entertainment, for the whole community framework of our lives then one could envisage a *possibility* of people becoming *willing* to pay in local taxation for an extension of the public provision which they come to recognise is better value for money than what the market provides. *That* would be a step towards the ending of capitalism and the transformation of statism into socialism.

Of course these extensions of local and work-place democracy are not capable of ending statism by themselves. A major part of the battle for socialism must clearly be through the effort to elect central governments which would themselves seek to extend statism. In fact statism at all levels will continually rear its head. But attention to the local conditions for socialism will both make more likely the voting in of a progressive parliamentary majority and will help to ensure that central government changes its character more rapidly than will happen *simply* by the election of a progressive parliamentary majority.

The socialist movement has involved itself for many years in a sterile contradiction concerning reformism. On the one hand it is regarded as a political crime, on the other hand socialists spend their political lives working for reforms. We are quite right to be suspicious of reformism when it claims to be a socialist ideology but is in fact the ideology of statism. But where political consciousness can point the way to such reforms as will entail both the encroachment of statism on capitalism and the encroachment of socialism on statism, then socialists should be fully involved, and ought not to regard it as a diversion from the main task.

NOTES

1   Helpful comments from Pat Devine, Barry Hindess, Mike Prior and David Purdy are gratefully acknowledged. To save them embarrassment, it should be mentioned that at least half of them disagreed completely with the approach of this essay.
2   Governments may be elected which try to reduce the size of the state apparatus.

Chapter 2

EUROCOMMUNISM AND THE ETHICAL IDEAL

David Fernbach

The contention put forward in this essay, that Marxist political
practice is ultimately governed by an ethical ideal, is not an attempt to reinstate any form of idealism. Indeed, it is not the
intention here to raise any philosophical questions in the strict
sense. The ethical ideal referred to is simply that defined by Marx
in his 'Introduction to the Critique of Hegel's Philosophy of
Right', as the negation of 'all conditions in which man is a de-
spised, enslaved, neglected and contemptible being'. It is easy to
object, of course, that this text predates the arrival of Marx and
Engels at the principles of historical materialism. And yet, while
the materialist conception of history can certainly explain the
emergence of an ethical principle of this kind at a particular point
in the development of human society, this is in no way to deny its
reality as a principle by which men and women, in large numbers, can
and do act. However crucial the specific struggle of the industrial
working class came to be for Marx and Engels, their commitment to
this struggle was always ultimately based on seeing it as the key
link in a general human liberation. And, indeed, when working-class
struggle has risen above the fetters of corporatism, to achieve a
genuine 'social-democratic politics' as distinct from mere 'trade-
union politics' (Lenin), has this not been dependent on working-
class militants themselves coming to take the task of general human
liberation as their governing goal?

In an age when imperialism has dug a gulf between rich and poor
countries, when humanity is torn by the associated racial divisions,
and when other social contradictions such as that between women and
men stand out with increased prominence, it would be specious indeed
to maintain that the task of human liberation is in any way reducible simply to the struggle of wage-labour against capital. Whether
this is still the key link in progress towards human liberation, as
Marx and Engels believed, is strictly a question of fact, and not
subject to any *a priori* definition. No new society, moreover, can
come into being simply out of the negative energy contained in the
contradictions of the old. It needs also a positive pole of attraction, such as Gramsci captured so well in his conception of
the 'new order', and the young Marx formulated in the phrase quoted
above.

But if it is this ethical ideal that raises Marxist political practice above the immediacy of the class struggle, to make it a practice of general human liberation, the particular role that the class struggle held in classical (revolutionary) Marxism always involved Marxists in a certain contradiction. The path ahead from capitalist society to communism had to pass through the stage of intensifying class conflict and forcible revolution. (And if it can remain open whether proletarian revolution necessarily involved 'heavy civil war', it is clear enough that it did involve a decisive defeat being inflicted by force on the old ruling class.) The task of Marxists, therefore, was destructive before it could be constructive. The ethical ideal makes its appeal to those instincts of solidarity which spontaneously bind together all rational sentient beings, and which no class society, however brutal, has managed completely to suppress. The stage of forcible revolution, however, demands that feelings of solidarity should be restricted to one's class comrades, and that towards the adversary it is the opposite sentiment of hatred that should be fostered and cultivated, the better to precipitate the revolutionary explosion. For Marxist intellectuals, this was a path that they all had to tread individually, in the footsteps of no less a person than Frederick Engels himself. Arriving in England in 1844, already a communist in his goals, Engels began at first to write for the Owenite 'New Moral World'. But within a year, after he and Marx had gone on to formulate their conception of historical materialism, he switched his allegiance to the Chartist 'Northern Star' - non-communist, but definitely an organ of class struggle.

In the social context against which revolutionary Marxist movements developed, the oppression of the working masses was so direct and brutal that the Marxist intellectuals had no need to stir up an artificial class hatred. It was in themselves, rather, that intellectuals from more privileged origins had to subordinate the original ethical impulse that brought them into the movement, and learn from the working class how to hate. In the cause of this requirement, however, the baby only too often got thrown out with the bathwater; the intellectuals came to deny the ethical impulse altogether, to classify it as 'idealist' and of no account. If the distinction could have been maintained, if the ethical ideal could have been subordinated to the class struggle, yet not forgotten, might not the anti-human crimes of Stalinism have been avoided, or at least attenuated?

What made the conflict between the ultimate goal and the means to achieve it so terribly sharp was that, of the various attempted modalities of a revolutionary Marxist strategy, the only variant that proved in any way successful was that of Lenin. For Leninism, the concrete form in which the revolutionary shift in power is envisaged is not simply a parliamentary majority for the Marxist party, nor even the setting up of a higher form of democracy against the bourgeois parliamentary state (workers' councils), but the *de facto* dictatorship of a 'Bolshevik nucleus'. This is formed and built up not just by treating the privileged class as a dehumanised enemy, but also by treating in a highly instrumental manner, as objects to be manipulated in whatever way best serves the capture of power by the nucleus, the broad mass of workers themselves.

(This leaves aside the question of similar relations within the
party itself, even within its 'leading core'.) Thus the only way
in which a proletarian dictatorship has been successfully established and maintained is one that already embodies from the start
a potential new domination over the workers.

The Leninist machine, however, was necessary, to bring at least
the first step of liberation for the toiling masses of Russia,
China, Yugoslavia, Cuba, etc. For them, the proximate goal of
forcible revolution already spelled such an advance towards freedom
that all means that promoted it could easily be justified. In so
doing, however, the ethical ideal was negated, and even its actual-
isation as the 'higher state of communism' was postponed into the
indefinite future, serving no practical purpose except, eventually,
as a myth to persuade people that the present task of 'building
socialism' was indeed preparing the ground for true liberation.

The very concept of 'socialism', in fact, as accepted in the
Leninist vocabulary, serves drastically to scale down the radicalism
of the ultimate goal. This is reinterpreted in such a way that its
essence is already achieved - the 'lower stage of communism' - when
the proletarian dictatorship has expropriated the capital of private
owners and centralised production in the hands of the state. This
ideological manoeuvre was at least originally an unconscious one -
a side-effect of the revolutionary concentration on the proximate
goal. When Stalin declared socialism as already achieved in the
Soviet Union in 1935, he might perhaps be charged with bad faith.
But essentially the same reduction of the goal was expressed by
Trotsky, in his essay 'If America Should Go Communist' (1934). Here
Trotsky argues that, spared the material backwardness to which he
ultimately ascribed all the problems that beset Soviet Russia, a
proletarian revolution in the USA would reach its communist goal
within a few months! Precisely the same reduction of human liberation to something that can be achieved by the acts of a new and
strong government. (1)

The situation that Marxists face in the advanced capitalist
countries today is fortunately very far from that in which revolutionary Marxism developed and found its Leninist embodiment. For
reasons that I believe are generally accepted by the contributors
to this volume, and which I have tried to formalise in my essay
Marxist Strategy in Britain ('Problems of Communism', no.11, summer
1978), there is no prospect of the class struggle in our part of the
world intensifying to the point of revolutionary explosion, and
being guided through this vortex to proletarian dictatorship by a
Marxist intervention. It would be misguided, indeed quite unmate-
rialist, to see it as a 'bad thing' that this perspective is thus
closed. Such a strategy is unfeasible precisely because it is undesirable, i.e. the working people in our countries do not desire it
and cannot be led to desire it. The reason for this is their own
experience of class struggle, which has shown that the political
institutions of parliamentary democracy, however imperfect, are responsive to working-class pressure, and can be got to carry through
ever new series of reforms in the working-class interest (including
reforms that democratise their own functioning). In other words,
the working people of the advanced capitalist countries have already
won, over at least a century and a half of protracted struggle, an

important element of freedom, just as real as, if very different from, that involved in the abolition of private property which revolutionary Marxism, for the reasons given above, makes into such an absolute.

The perspective that lies ahead for our societies is therefore one in which popular struggle will erode piecemeal the various structures of domination and exploitation that stand in the way of a communist society, the continuation, in fact, of a path that the popular movement has already been embarked upon for decades - in the British case, for over a century. How, indeed, could the intervention of Marxist or any other theories be so great as to displace the gradualist path of historical progress by a revolutionary one - or vice versa, for that matter? What lies within our power is, as always, to 'shorten and lessen the birthpangs' of the new society, by analysis of historical reality, by representing the overall and long-term interest against sectional and short-term interests, and by indicating the optimal course of action in any given conjuncture.

Now one fundamental feature of this gradualist path is that there is no proximate goal between the present society and the communist future, such as is provided in the revolutionary strategy by the decisive shift in power. Of course, there are always tactical aims, the next step forward. But these are precisely no more than tactical. The point is that tactics here are not guided by any proximate goal short of communism itself. The criterion by which tactics are to be judged is not their contribution to the projected seizure of power, but directly their contribution to the ultimate communist goal itself. The question is simply: how do they concretely promote certain elements of this goal?

The ethical ideal of communism can consequently intervene today as a political mobilising force in a way that was impossible for revolutionary Marxism (*is* impossible, in those large parts of the world where a revolutionary road is still indicated). It is possible to win people to communism on the basis of the ethical ideal, without having to lead them on to accept and even make a virtue of the necessities of hatred and dehumanisation that accompany violent revolution - particularly in its historical form of Leninism. Before developing this idea more fully, a few notes are needed on certain pertinent structural features of the advanced capitalist countries that distinguish these societies from those to which a revolutionary Marxist strategy is applicable.

I have already asserted that the degree of class privilege and domination over the workers is significantly less than in the original Marxist model - precisely as the product of a century and a half of struggle. There is no absolute measure for class privilege, and experience persistently shows that the advances which satisfy one generation subsequently appear as an intolerable compromise to the next. Yet somewhere along the line between the hysterical repression of the English ruling class at the time of the anti-Jacobin wars and the situation today, it became more rational for the privileged sections of society to allow the working class into the constitutional pale, providing the framework for an ongoing struggle for reform, rather than risk the development of a revolutionary movement. Once the process got under way, in the second half of the nineteenth century, it came in time to acquire a self-perpetuating

character, the 'entrenched gradualist dynamic' which I have discussed more fully in my 'Marxist Strategy in Britain'; and despite
the occasional wobble from this groove, particularly in the era of
the First World War and Russian revolution, the long-run tendency
has been for this entrenched gradualist dynamic to become ever more
firmly established. Sir Keith Joseph found a very good metaphor to
describe the advance of 'socialism', that of the ratchet. Each
round of reform may be small, but once made, it is exceedingly
difficult to reverse. And the more the privileges of the rich and
powerful are whittled away, the less possibility do they have to
attempt a forcible counter-revolution, since the working-class advance encompasses, among other things, the gradual democratisation
of the state apparatus and the breakdown of elitist ideologies.

A further relevant characteristic of the present social structure
is that, relative to the classical property contradiction, other
forms of privilege and oppression assume a proportionately greater
importance. It is no longer possible, for example, to see the
division of labour within the 'collective worker', as Marx did, as
inessential compared with the privilege accruing from capital ownership. Any class analysis of advanced capitalist society, undertaken
with a view to enabling the under-privileged and oppressed to advance their cause, must see large sections of the 'wage-earning
class' itself, whether managers, engineers, civil servants,
teachers, etc., as enjoying privileges, cultural even more than
economic, that must be redistributed. A third contradiction, moreover, and one which cuts completely across that of class, is the
sexual contradiction, and it is an everyday fact of political life
in the advanced capitalist countries today that this *will* not be
subordinated to the class contradiction. For ever more women, and
working-class women too, male privilege is a problem of equal significance to class privilege, with no excuse accepted that this can
only be dealt with 'under socialism'. A fourth contradiction is
that of race, and with links both to the situation of racial minorities and the situation of women, there is the oppression of gay
people. Yet a further social contradiction that structures a division of interests is the ecological problem, for it is no coinci-
dence that it is precisely sections of the middle class, being that
much freer from the pressure of immediate material need, who show
greater sensitivity to the need for control over the human meta-
bolism with our natural environment. As opposed, therefore, to
the model of one dominant contradiction, that defined by the property relation, to which classical Marxism oriented its strategy,
the situation we face today is one of a plurality of overlapping
contradictions, a multiplicity of forms of privilege and oppression.
At one end of the scale, there are few people indeed who combine all
the attributes of privilege - the celebrated ruling-class, hetero-
sexual, white males, to take only these variables into account. On
the other extreme, however, there are almost equally few who combine
all the variables of oppression - say the working-class black
lesbian (in Britain possibly 0.05 per cent of the population).
The great majority of our people both enjoy certain forms of privilege (e.g. either of class, of sex, of race, etc.) and suffer from
certain forms of oppression under the same set of categories. Thus
not only is this a situation in which it is doubly impossible to at-

tempt a Leninist strategy based on a very sharp and irreducible polarity between privileged and oppressed. It is impossible even to isolate one group as embodying absolute oppression and an opposed group embodying absolute privilege, such that the struggle of the one against the other would bear with it the essence of historical progress. Certainly, the advance to communism consists in the struggle of oppression against privilege. But in this struggle, or rather these struggles, the same individuals, and they form the great majority, find themselves at different times in opposite positions: sometimes on the side of progress, sometimes on the side of reaction. This is the typical situation of overlapping contradictions, in which I shall argue the direct intervention of the communist goal as an ethical ideal is particularly appropriate.

The third characteristic is the greatly increased cultural level of the working masses in the advanced capitalist countries. If a certain intellectual level is required of people before they can act on the basis of a vision of the historical process as a whole, rather than simply their own immediate interests, then this level is attained by an ever higher proportion of our population. Classical Marxism was always the doctrine of the intellectuals, shared only by a small minority of intellectualised workers while the majority were sufficiently motivated by the promise of satisfaction of their immediate interests. Today there is so great a quantity of 'surplus consciousness' as compared with the classical situation that a qualitatively different approach is possible. The 'broad masses' no longer have to be seen by the Marxists as an essentially passive object for manipulation. A sufficient section of working people have time, energy and knowledge enough that they can be won to act on the basis of the same ethical ideal that moves the initiating vanguard.

We can now define more precisely what is involved in the intervention of the ethical ideal as a mass political motivation.

I have already explained how classical revolutionary Marxism came to scale down the ultimate goal of communism to the dimensions of something called 'socialism' – the society brought into being by the monopolisation of the means of production by a proletarian dictatorship. In their political practice of working to achieve this dictatorship, the Marxist or Marxist-Leninist parties had to effect yet a further scaling down. The broadening of the revolutionary front that was needed to construct a strategic majority involved the mobilisation of support on the basis of more limited aims even than that of proletarian dictatorship/socialism – for example, the overthrow of a particular reactionary government; the satisfaction of certain immediate requirements of the working masses; resistance to fascism; national liberation; bread, peace and land. This is still the heritage of the communist parties in the advanced capitalist countries today, but it is the very reverse of what is required when the role of these parties is no longer to try and seize power, but rather to act as ideological vanguard in the protracted transition to communism.

Today, scaling down the communist goal to fit the immediate interests of certain oppressed groups offers no way out of the thicket of overlapping contradictions. For immediate interests constantly conflict, and there is no front of unity here behind

which a strategic majority can be built. When this is attempted,
and the 'enemy' accordingly reduced to the 'small handful of
monopoly capitalists', this is done precisely by importing the
greater part of existing privilege into the camp of the people
itself. For far more class privilege (even leaving aside sexual or
racial) exists diffused among the variegated sections of the vast
contemporary middle class, than is concentrated at this evanescent
summit. The only possible way to overcome the network of overlapping contradictions is to rise above it, by motivating people to
act on the basis of an ethical ideal with which they can identify as
their long-term interest, even when this goes against their immediate sectional interests. And this ethical motivation will be
strengthened not by scaling down the definition of the communist
goal, but precisely by radicalising it to embrace and integrate dimensions of social criticism that Marx and Engels passed over in
their critique of political economy. If communists in the advanced
capitalist countries today were to stand not only for an end to the
privilege of capital ownership, but also for the radical breakdown
of the division of labour, and not only for this, which is already
central to Marx's own original concept of a classless society, but
also for a society freed from the tyranny of sexual oppression and
gender stereotype, and for a society that develops its productive
forces in the context of a rational ecological policy, then this
radicalisation, far from narrowing our appeal, would precisely
broaden it by showing more and more people that there is something
here really worth striving for. In this way the role of the communist party is decisively changed, away from an organisation seeking
power for itself - even in a parliamentary sense - towards a movement that pulls society forward bit by bit by acting as ideological
vanguard of the transition to communism.

Only by such a transformation of its role, involving a radicalisation of its proclaimed goal, can the Eurocommunist tendency
escape the danger that presently faces it - that of a collapse into
social democracy. We are accustomed to associate radical goals with
violent revolution, while gradualism goes together with more limited goals. But today, when it is no longer possible to accelerate the historical movement by a seizure of power, we can and must
make up for this by putting forward our communist goal in more
radical form. The advance towards communism can only be a gradualist one. But this gradualism can be guided by a communist movement
which, even though itself a minority in relation to the mass organisations of workers, women, and so on, is constantly present to
point out the next step forward and inspire the present struggle
with its synthetic vision of the communist future. This would be
as different from the gradualism of social democracy, which sees
no further than the next round of reforms, as the revolutionary
movement guided by Lenin was from the revolutionary movement that
existed in Russia prior to any Marxist intervention.

If it is necessary to reinstate and indeed deepen the original
utopian goals of Marxism, this is in no way a utopian enterprise in
the negative sense. For partial aspects of the communist utopia are
being raised today even from sources quite disconnected with
Marxism. Two such aspects that are particularly important are the
radical goals of the ecologists and feminists. As immediately put

forward by their respective movements, these goals are often one-
sided and lack an adequate understanding of the historical process,
let alone the practical modalities of effecting social change. And
yet here, independent of the Marxist tradition, we have two radical
critiques of the existing social order that provide vital elements
for a genuine communist advance - advance towards a society in which
the productive forces unleashed by the capitalist era can at last be
consciously harnessed to the goal of a happy life for all humanity.
The relationship that Marxist organisations presently adopt towards
these new forces is the very opposite of that now needed. At
present we see an unwillingness to budge from a dogmatic reductionism that already claims to have all the answers.

To cite just one instance with which I myself have been involved,
a tremendous struggle has been necessary to get even a minimal
defence of gay rights adopted by British Marxist groups. And what
has eventually been accepted are simply the immediate demands of the
gay movement (an end to discrimination, etc.) and in no way the
radical critique of gender stereotypes that the gay liberation wing
has developed. The reasons for this difficulty are clear. The
traditional revolutionary front that such groups hope to build up
might lose more prospective supporters than it gained by seeming too
keen on homosexuality. But in the perspective of a communist movement not seeking power for itself, but seeking rather to signpost
the direction of advance from capitalism to communism in an all-
round and synthetic manner, it would be necessary for communists
actively to seek to broaden and deepen their theory by integrating
new insights such as the feminist and gay liberation movements have
produced.

I have already explained how the 'ethical strategy' that communists in the advanced capitalist countries require today avoids
the traditional bitter conflict between end and means that followed
from the proximate goal of a seizure of power. All the energy that
can be mobilised for social change by the communist ideal can thus
be channelled productively, without the great wastage that has traditionally occurred when a large proportion of theoretically committed communists find themselves unable to bend to the requirements
of revolutionary violence and Leninist organisation. This also has
its implications for relationships between people within the communist movement, and for the organisational forms that this movement
should take.

A further source of strength that the ethical strategy can tap
derives from the undoubted spiritual crisis that afflicts ever
greater sections of the population in the advanced capitalist
societies. Already in 1956, Allen Ginsberg could write: 'I saw
the best minds of my generation destroyed by madness, starving
hysterical naked/Dragging themselves through the negro streets at
dawn looking for an angry fix'. Constantly, in the Anglo-Saxon and
Nordic countries above all, where traditional Marxism is a weak pole
of attraction, the 'best minds' of successive generations drift into
phoney new religions or drug abuse for want of a sufficiently viable
ethic of communism. How can Marxism win out against the power of
heroin or hare krishna, when it is reduced to the level of further
nationalisation and a more complete welfare state? Even in societies where Marxist movements of the classical kind have changed the

world, Marxism has had to grip large numbers of people with the power of religion, a belief strong enough to dominate the lives of individuals. If we are to compete successfully with all the false gods that seek people's allegiance in the West today, then we Marxists must show that our belief, too, is worthwhile for people to devote their lives to. But this is only possible if the communist ethic is formulated in terms significantly more radical than in the past, and an organisation of communists is built up on the basis of such a radical commitment.

To conclude, I am well aware of the sketchiness of this essay, and the many questions it raises but leaves unanswered. Its aim will have been more than accomplished if it promotes further discussion. One point of which I am especially conscious, is that I have refrained from discussing the greatest contradiction of all in the world today, the biggest obstacle to communist humanity, i.e., the abyss between the rich industrial countries to which we belong and to which my discussion is oriented, and the poor and poorest countries of the Third and 'Fourth' Worlds. Yet here too, I can only see the direction I propose for communists in the West as confirmed. For on this question more than any other, it is necessary for all classes in our countries to rise above considerations of material self-interest and act in the interest of humanity as a whole.

NOTE

1 It is of course this absolutising of the abolition of private property that still serves the present Soviet regime as its ultimate justification, and is accepted as such equally by the more orthodox Trotskyists. Yet today this state monopoly in means of production is far more of a barrier to new working-class advance in the Soviet Union than a surviving 'conquest of October'. The commanding heights of the Soviet economy need no defence against private reappropriation. Even in the West today, the real appropriators are ever less individual capitalist owners, ever more the managers of state or non-state corporations. It is against the formation of forms of ownership that are closer to the workers - whether individual, co-operative, or even small-scale private enterprise which is technically 'capitalist', yet far less alienated from the direct producers - that the Soviet state stands guard on the economic front, even at a colossal cost in economic efficiency and lack of service to the consuming public.

Chapter 3

PARLIAMENTARY DEMOCRACY AND SOCIALIST POLITICS

Barry Hindess

This essay discusses some of the problems of socialist politics under conditions of parliamentary democracy. Since Marxism has provided the most significant theoretical foundations for socialist discourse in the modern period, I begin by looking briefly at what we might call the classical Marxist conception of parliamentary democracy as elaborated in the work of Lenin. (The 'classicism' of that conception is largely the product of subsequent systematisations, but that is another story.) Lenin's conception thoroughly repudiates the idea of a (parliamentary) democratic road to socialism. Nevertheless, since the emergence of Marxist socialism as a major political force in late-nineteenth-century Germany there have been proposals for a democratic road to socialism, and it is clear that parliamentary democracy has posed a persistent problem for Marxist theory. This essay shows why the 'classical' position can cannot be accepted and considers the implications of its rejection for socialist analysis of politics and the state in parliamentary democratic regimes.

Socialists are concerned to displace commodity and bureaucratic forms of production and distribution through the development of non-commodity forms subject to popular democratic control. Proposals for a democratic process of socialisation must take account of the severe obstacles to effective democratic control of state apparatuses and nationalised industries in the advanced capitalist democracies: the absence of democratic controls in sectors such as health and education that are largely non-commodity in form; the lack of democratisation within nationalised industries; the limitations on electoral or parliamentary control over the practices of the state apparatuses; the 'independence' of the judiciary and the central bank; the House of Lords; etc. Consideration of these and other obstacles shows that any significant process of socialisation must involve both parliamentary and non-parliamentary forms of struggle.

To set the scene for subsequent discussion, consider the following, by no means untypical, remarks from Lenin's 'The State and Revolution' and his speech, The State:

The petty-bourgeois democrats, those sham socialists who replaced the class struggle by dreams of class harmony, even

pictured the socialist transformation in a dreamy fashion - not
as the overthrow of the rule of the exploiting class, but as the
peaceful submission of the minority to the majority which has
become aware of its aims. This petty-bourgeois utopia, which is
inseparable from the idea of the state being above classes, led
in practice to the betrayal of the interests of the working class
('Collected Works', vol.25, p.403)

Is the state in a capitalist country, in a democratic republic -
especially one like Switzerland or the USA - in the freest democratic republics, an expression of the popular will, the sum
total of the general decision of the people, the expression of
the national will, and so forth; or is the state a machine that
enables the capitalists of those countries to maintain their
power over the working class and the peasantry. That is the
fundamental question. ... The forms of domination of the state
may vary ... but essentially the power is in the hands of capital
... - in fact, the more democratic it is the cruder and more
cynical is the rule of capitalism. ('Collected Works', vol.29,
pp.484-5)

Two features of these remarks should be noted here. First,
Lenin's hostility to the idea of a parliamentary democratic road to
socialism is in no way restricted to Russian conditions since he
specifically refers to the most democratic republics of his time.
Second, he counterposes the notion of the state as a class state to
that of the state as expression of the popular will; either you
conceive the state in one way and consequently betray the working
class or you conceive it in the other way. We shall see that this
is a false dichotomy and that rejection of the one alternative by
no means implies acceptance of the other.

Central to Lenin's position is the view that the state is essentially a machine for the suppression of one class by another.
The state is always a form of class dictatorship so that a democratic state in particular always has a definite class content.
It is always democracy for one class and against some other; 'the
form of democracy is one thing, and the class content ... is another' ('Collected Works', vol.28, pp.268-9). Notice the character
of Lenin's argument here. He starts from a general theory of politics as ultimately reflecting class interests and of the state as
representing the interests of the economically dominant class.
Parliamentary democracy then appears as a feature of some, but not
all, capitalist states. It follows that the institutional conditions of parliamentary democracy must represent a form of class
dictatorship.

According to Lenin the class character of parliamentary democracy
is manifested in several ways, the most important of which are:
First and most significant, the state machine is not neutral with
regard to the class struggle. Lenin refers again and again to
Marx's and Engels' comment on the lessons of the Commune that 'the
working class cannot simply lay hold of the ready-made state machinery, and wield it for its own purposes'. Hence, he argues, the
need to smash the state machine and to replace it by another. Of
course Lenin, following Marx and Engels, does not absolutely exclude
the possibility of revolution 'without the precondition of destroy-

ing the "ready-made state machinery"' ('Collected Works', vol.25, p.415). But he has in mind only those 'rare exceptions' in capitalist societies where the public power is weak: Britain, in 1871, 'without a militarist clique and, to a considerable degree, without a bureaucracy' and North America 'in its pre-imperialist days where the free colonist predominated' (p.390). The validity of Lenin's characterisation of Britain and the USA need not be considered here. What matters is that the sole conditions in which the machinery of the capitalist state does not need to be smashed seem to be when that machinery itself is poorly developed. No contemporary parliamentary regime could be regarded as falling in that category. Second, under capitalism the democratic rights of freedom of association, press, media, assembly, etc., in fact benefit the bourgeoisie through their ownership of the media, control over meeting places, money and other resources.
Third, the protection of the rights of minorities and of individuals in bourgeois democracies is a myth. Whatever recognition and protection of political minorities there may be is always partial and selective, favouring bourgeois parties, while on all fundamental issues the proletariat 'gets martial law or pogroms, instead of the "protection of the minority"' ('Collected Works', vol.28, p.245)

Thus to talk of a democratic and peaceful road to socialism using the procedures of bourgeois democracy in a modern state is to confuse the issue. Even the most democratic form of state is a class dictatorship – and without class dictatorship there cannot be democracy for that class. Lenin argues that the extent of the franchise does not affect the dictatorial character of the state one way or the other. Thus the withdrawal of the franchise from the ruling class and their allies after the revolution 'is not absolutely necessary for the exercise of the dictatorship, it is not an indispensable characteristic of the logical concept of "dictatorship"' (p.256).

We will return to these points below. For the moment notice that Lenin's arguments on parliamentary democracy were developed in response to what many Marxists had argued with regard to the parliamentary regimes then emerging in parts of Western Europe, and especially in Germany. Indeed, the presence of 'representative' mechanisms in the organisation of government does seem to pose a problem for the view of the state as simply a machine for the suppression of one class by another. For example, while not exactly proposing a democratic road to socialism, Engels argues, in his 1895 Introduction to Marx's 'The Class Struggles in France', that the growth of support for German social democracy shows that the bourgeoisie have more to fear from the legal than the illegal actions of the socialists:

To keep this growth going without interruption until it of itself gets beyond the control of the prevailing governmental system, not to fritter away this daily increasing shock force in vanguard skirmishes, but to keep it intact until the decisive day, that is our main task. (Marx and Engels, 'Selected Works', p.655)

Bernstein and later Kautsky, both subsequently reviled as revisionists, went further and argued explicitly for a democratic road to socialism. In 'The Dictatorship of the Proletariat' Kautsky argued not only that socialism could be achieved through democratic

means, but that it could only be achieved that way. The idea of an
insurrectionary alternative was an illusion: it would lead only to
the dictatorship of a small minority, not to a socialisation of the
economy under democratic control. More recently the 'eurocommunist'
currents in several western communist parties have argued that, at
least in societies with parliamentary-democratic forms of government, socialism can and should be achieved through peaceful and
parliamentary means. In these views, the class character of the
state apparatuses is to be transformed through a combination of
parliamentary action and extra-parliamentary popular struggle. Thus
we are presented with a scenario in which movement towards socialism
is to be achieved by means of parliamentary majorities backed by
mass popular struggles. At each stage in the national progression,
parliamentary democratic procedures will decide the issue: 'The
British Road to Socialism' (the policy statement of British Communists - hereafter 'BRS'), for example, insists that the Communists
will accept the electoral verdict even if right-wing parties are re-
turned to power.

Now, this discrepancy between the 'classical' position of Lenin
and the persistent arguments for a democratic road to socialism
poses a crucial problem for Marxism with regard to the analysis of
politics in parliamentary democratic regimes. Do we follow Lenin
in regarding parliamentary democracy as still essentially a form of
class dictatorship, and conclude that socialism cannot be achieved
without its overthrow? Or do we accept that parliamentary democracy
may provide conditions for a peaceful socialist transformation of
society, that parliamentary and electoral machinery is not essentially an instrument of class domination? I argue that the first
view cannot be accepted, but that the second is not without its own
problems.

WHY LENIN'S TREATMENT OF PARLIAMENTARY DEMOCRACY MUST BE REJECTED

It is important to be clear about the sense in which Lenin regards
parliamentary democracy as a form of class dictatorship. Returning
to his account of how its bourgeois character is manifested, it is
clear that much of that account is not disputed by advocates of a
democratic road to socialism, it is simply a matter of analysing
political practices and organisations in class terms. Certainly few
would dispute that the conditions of electoral competition, control
of the media, and so on, are far from neutral in their effects. The
same point could be made about the practices of the parliamentary
state. It is not a matter of denying these features of parliamentary-democratic politics, but rather of arguing that they can
nevertheless be overcome, thus transforming the character of the
state. The class character of the state is generally admitted by
proponents of a democratic road to socialism, for example by Kautsky
and more recently by Carrillo and the authors of the 'BRS', who
argue that it can be overcome by parliamentary majorities backed by
a sufficiently strong and determined popular support.

This brings us to the central point. What is at issue between
Lenin and Kautsky is not the class character of the state, but how
that is to be understood. Kautsky, for example, argues that the

state is indeed a form of class rule and that what Lenin calls the
real business of the state may well be conducted in the bureaucracies rather than in parliament. But he also argues that the
power of parliament within the state depends on the balance of
extra-parliamentary forces. Thus the democratic road involves both
transforming the character of the bourgeois state by increasing the
significance of parliament within it, and transforming the class
character of parliament itself. Something similar has been argued
by many other democratic road supporters, although their arguments
are by no means equivalent.

   But Lenin will have none of this, and he characterises Kautsky's
view of parliamentary democracy as liberal rather than Marxist.
Central to Lenin's argument is the view that the institutional conditions of parliamentary democracy essentially reflect the interests
of the bourgeoisie. Thus a politics that works within those conditions, whatever its intentions, must also serve the bourgeoisie.
This essentialism is brought out particularly clearly in Lenin's
'Theses and Report on Bourgeois Democracy and the Dictatorship of
the Proletariat' ('Collected Works', vol.28), where he presents
parliamentary and soviet democracy as distinct and incompatible
forms of class rule: either you have a parliamentary democracy
which serves the bourgeoisie or you have a soviet democracy which
serves the mass of the working people, but you cannot combine the
two. Lenin's counterposition of parliamentary (bourgeois) and
soviet (proletarian) democracy raises issues which cannot be considered here. What must be noted for the present argument is the
essentialism of his view that the very institutional conditions of
parliamentary democracy reflect the interests of a class.

   That essentialism is the reason why Lenin's treatment of parliamentary democracy must be rejected. The reason why the classical
Marxist theory of politics and the state does not work is that it is
economistic. What is meant here by that (much abused) term is that
the classical theory treats political institutions and practices and
political ideologies as the more-or-less direct expression of the
interests of classes and class fractions - so that the state, for
example, may be said to play a functional role in maintaining the
interests of the ruling class. I say 'more or less' here because
many of the great Marxist political leaders have effectively recognised the irreducibility of politics to classes and their interests
in their practical political analyses. But they have failed to do
so in their theoretical writings on politics. Lenin is a classic
example, combining an acute anti-reductionist analysis of concrete
political situations in many of his writings with a reductionist
theoretical position in others, in 'The State and Revolution', 'The
Proletarian Revolution and the Renegade Kautsky', and so on. It is
this discrepancy between practical political analyses and political
theory that recent Marxists have tried to cover over by means of the
concept of 'relative autonomy' and similar notions. Economism in
this sense may take many forms, depending on the precise nature of
the connection that is supposed to hold between politics and ideology on the one hand, and the structure of the economy on the other.
While they may differ in the way they impose a class reductionism on
political analysis they nevertheless share the central fact of that
reductionism. For example, Lenin and Kautsky are equally econo-

mistic in treating parties and the state as representing classes
and their interests, but they differ over the institutional conditions of parliamentary democracy: Lenin argues that they represent the interests of the bourgeoisie while Kautsky treats them as
'neutral', in the sense of allowing a fundamental transfer of state
power from the bourgeoisie to the proletariat.

The objections to this reductionism have been argued in various
publications, most recently in 'Marx's Capital and Capitalism
Today', and there is no need to go into that argument here. It is
precisely because political organisations and institutional forms
cannot be analysed as just so many manifestations of class interests
that the representative institutions of parliamentary democracy
cannot be reduced to instruments of rule by a capitalist class. But
it is important to recognise that if the critique of economism dis-
poses of Lenin's treatment of parliamentary democracy, it is equally
damaging to many of the theoretical positions in which proposals for
a democratic road to socialism are articulated. We have seen, for
example, that, for all their differences over parliamentary democracy, Kautsky's conception of politics is no less economistic than
that of Lenin. The problem with Lenin's analysis lies not so much
in his treatment of parliamentary democracy in particular but rather
in the attempted reduction, shared by many of his Marxist opponents,
of political forces and ideologies to the interests of classes and
class fractions. There is little to be gained by rejecting Lenin's
economism in favour of another, however much the latter may be the
more amenable to our political concerns.

Now, to say that politics and ideology are not reducible to
effects of the structure of the economy is not at all to say that
there are no connections between the economy and the kinds of struggle that develop in a society. But what those connections are may
be subject to considerable variation both over time and from one
capitalist society to another. It is to say that there is no one
general mechanism of connection between the economy and politics and
ideology that is characteristic of capitalist economic organisation
as such, and that there may be significant issues of political concern in no way reducible to the struggle between capitalism and its
opponents. The forms of political organisation and ideology that
develop and become dominant in a particular capitalist society are
not a reflection of its capitalist economic organisation as such,
but rather the outcome of specific conditions and struggles, of
struggles to organise around particular objectives, of victories
over competing organisations and defeats at their hands, and so on.
For example, the weakness of socialist politics in the USA is not a
simple reflection of the structure of its economy, it is the outcome
of a long series of political struggles in which socialist forces
were heavily defeated. But, if politics and ideology do not simply
reflect the structure of the economy, then neither capitalism nor
socialism should be conceived as total societies, in which the capitalist or socialist character of the economy informs every other
aspect of social life. This suggests that the notion of a road to
socialism, implying a definitive state of affairs utterly different
from capitalism, may be misleading. Socialists are concerned to develop non-commodity forms of production and distribution, subject to
popular democratic control, and that clearly involves displacing

both commodity and bureaucratic forms of organisation. The
question, then, is not so much one of a democratic road to socialism, but rather of the possibility of a process of socialisation
which respects and extends the democratic forms that have already
been developed.

But, returning to the analysis of parliamentary democracy to see
where these arguments leave us, consider the alternatives set out in
the above quotations from Lenin: either the state is a class state,
a dictatorship of the ruling class; or it is the expression of the
popular will, the instrument of the majority, and so on - which
Lenin represents as the state of liberal democratic theory and of
Bernstein and Kautsky. This is a false dichotomy: it depends on
the conception of the state as an essential unity, so that if one
organising principle of unity is rejected another must be set up in
its place. But in the absence of an essentialist reading of politics and the state it is perfectly possible to reject the first
alternative without falling into the illusions of the second.

We are concerned with relationships between and within the
following sets of elements: assemblies (or assemblies and presi-
dent) and their organisation by cabinet, sub-committees, etc.;
state apparatuses (note the plural); the electorate and organisations of electoral struggle; other organisations and institutions,
capitalist enterprises, financial institutions, media, churches,
etc. The effect of Lenin's argument is to treat· electoral struggle
as a representation, necessarily distorted, of the different class
interests. The forms of franchise, and the distribution of money
and property in the non-state sector all operate in favour of the
bourgeoisie. But, in any case, he argues, the real business of the
state does not go on in the assembly but in the state apparatuses, a
more or less unitary body operating in the interests of the ruling
class. Thus liberal-democratic theory constitutes a mystification
of the sphere of politics with reactionary political effects. None
of this means, for Lenin, that we should not make use of electoral
and parliamentary means of struggle. Quite the contrary, but we
should not expect them to be the principal instruments of socialist
transformation.

What Lenin presents as the only possible alternative is a liberal
conception of parliamentary democracy which accepts the claim of
constitutional discourse that, with some qualifications, parliament
is sovereign and that the various disjunctions between assembly and
electorate, legislature and judiciary (and executive), and sometimes
a Bill of Rights, are necessary to prevent the tyranny of the majority and to defend the rights of the individual. Now I have
argued that it is necessary to reject one central feature of Lenin's
analysis, viz., that the state and politics represent classes and
their interests. But that does not mean that we are thereby con-
demned to accept what he presents as the alternative. Leaving presidential systems aside for ease of exposition, a parliamentary
democratic form of state means:
(i)   that there are three interconnected arenas of struggle: within
the electorate, within parliament and within parties, relating to
the conduct and composition of government. There is a more-or-less
extended franchise and a variety of more-or-less qualified liberal
freedoms (of organisation, press, assembly, etc.). This specifica-

tion of arenas is by no means exhaustive and there may well be other
significant arenas of political struggle
(ii) that, in constitutional law, the assembly governs the practices of the state apparatuses by broadly regulating their activities - and even here, in advanced capitalist democracies, the
judiciary, the central bank, and possibly other state institutions,
occupy a more independent position.
But these two points do not tell us very much. They do not tell us
what other arenas of political struggle exist in the society in
question and they certainly do not tell us that the state apparatuses are simply instruments of the will of the assembly, that they,
the form of franchise and the electoral system, are effectively
neutral as between competing political positions, or that the media
and the distribution of property and other resources are similarly
politically neutral. I shall comment on two issues: first, the relations between the assembly and the state apparatuses, and second,
the implications of parliamentary democracy for forms of socialist
political struggle.

THE ASSEMBLY AND THE STATE APPARATUSES

The first point to notice is that the notion of a 'parliamentary-
democratic form of state' can be very seriously misleading, since it
takes as the crucial defining characteristics of a form of state
precisely the two features just indicated but says next to nothing
about the connections, other than in the discourse of constitutional
law, between what goes on in the assembly and what state apparatuses
do. It is well known that those connections vary considerably from
one democratic society to another and, within any one society, over
time and from one part of the state apparatuses to another. Both
liberal-democratic theory and classical Marxism treat the state
apparatuses as instruments, of the assembly (and therefore of the
people) or of the ruling class respectively. It is this conception
that leads to the treatment of the state as a unity: the apparatuses are united by the hand that wields them. But the instrumentalist
conception of the state is a grotesque misconception. It is necessary to treat the various state apparatuses as arenas of struggle in
their own right. This implies:
(i) that their actions are not determined wholly externally, by
parliamentary or cabinet decisions. On the contrary, those decisions represent one important condition of action of the state
apparatus in question but they are only one among a variety of external pressures and their effectiveness depends on a complex interaction of these external forms of pressure and internal struggles
(ii) that the state apparatuses, or elements within them, themselves act on the conditions of struggle within parliament or
cabinet and within the electorate. It is clear, for example, that
there may be significant internal debates within the Treasury or the
military, and that sections within them lobby the press, MPs and
ministers
(iii) that there is no necessary coherence or unity of action among
the different state apparatuses.
   Now, to say that state apparatuses are arenas of struggle is to

say that they constitute potential arenas of left intervention - and
to say that is to point to an area of massive ignorance and inaction
by the British left. We know remarkably little about the precise
articulation of parliamentary and cabinet discussions and the different state apparatuses, or about the terms and conditions of
debate within those apparatuses. The lack of action on the left in
these areas is obvious. There are, of course, various issue organisations, CPAG, PROP, CASE, and so on, many of whose activists are
committed socialists, which do attempt to influence the policies and
practices of particular state apparatuses. It is easy to underestimate the significance of such organisation. But they can
hardly be said to represent a concerted socialist politics of intervention in the state apparatuses as arenas of struggle: their
status as distinct and discrete issue organisations, separated from
each other and from the manifest concerns of the Labour and Communist Parties is sufficient evidence to the contrary.

PARLIAMENTARY DEMOCRACY AND THE FORMS OF SOCIALIST POLITICAL
STRUGGLE

To describe a state as parliamentary-democratic is to say little
about the political forces at work in the society or the sites of
struggle and political issues in which they are engaged. Electoral
and parliamentary politics do constitute definite arenas of struggle
but they are by no means exclusive of other arenas of struggle or of
significant non-electoral political forces, the state apparatuses
themselves, agencies of foreign powers (open and covert), and a
whole variety of non-state organisations and institutions, trade
unions, large capitalist enterprises, religious organisations, left-
or right-wing terrorists, and so on. The point about these political forces is that they do not, in general, operate primarily
through the attempt to influence the votes of the electorate, and it
is therefore absurd to assume that the electorate and elected assembly constitute the sole, or even the most, significant arenas of political struggle. It is impossible, then, to lay down general propositions concerning the forms of struggle most appropriate to parliamentary democracies, since that designation alone simply ab-
stracts from the precise character and distribution of political
forces at work in particular societies. Nevertheless, in a situation of widespread popular commitment to parliamentary-democratic
forms and the liberal freedoms with which they are associated, and
where the outcomes of parliamentary struggles are significant, but
not exclusive, determinants of state activity, it is necessary to
consider the relations between electoral and other forms of
struggle.
       The most important thing to notice here concerns the tremendous
obstacles to democratic control over the practices of the state
apparatuses in parliamentary democracies. I have already noted two
significant issues in this respect. First, whatever the situation
may be in constitutional and legal doctrine, the organisation of the
state apparatuses and their practices are not determined solely
through the decisions of parliament. The action of the military in
Chile is a sanguine reminder of that point. But that is only an
extreme case of the general phenomenon, viz., that state apparatuses

and groups within them may be important political actors in their
own right. Second, there are a variety of organisations and institutions which act on parliament and state apparatuses without being
subject to democratic control, and some of them may have a major
impact on government policy. For example, the World Bank, hardly a
representative institution, is a powerful political force in many
third world countries and the IMF has played a significant role in
shifting the balance of forces in British Cabinet and Treasury discussions of economic policy. And we can all think of numerous other
examples of the exercise of political muscle by organisations that
are in no sense representative of the general population.

   But another set of obstacles concerns the 'representative' institutions of parliamentary democracy themselves. Notice first that
parliamentary government itself depends on the presence of bureaucratic state apparatuses: a body that issues laws, decrees and instructions can govern only by means of bodies which (are supposed
to) put them into effect. In this sense parliament both presupposes
bureaucratic state apparatuses and poses the problem of their
control. The nature of this relationship between parliament and
state apparatuses imposes limits to the effectiveness of parliamentary control. It is sufficient to consider the means of control
that are or may be open to parliament, the issue of laws, decrees or
instructions, questioning of ministers and civil servants, committees of inquiry, motions of censure, and so on, to see that there
will be many corresponding opportunities for its evasion. With the
best will in the world, no parliamentary body can hope to investigate more than a small fraction of the practices of the state machinery. There are inescapable limits to the effective power of parliament within the state. It is not my intention to claim that
these limits are even remotely approached by any existing parliament. The point rather is to reinforce the earlier argument that
state apparatuses can never be considered as mere instruments of
parliament's will, that they must be considered as, actually or
potentially, significant political forces in their own right.

   When we consider the connections between parliaments and state
apparatuses the inescapable limits just noted must seem extremely
remote in relation to the severe obstacles to democratic control
that these connections represent. In most capitalist democracies
the central bank is subject only to limited governmental control.
Or again, the judiciary always has a significant degree of independence from any form of democratic control and accountability.
This has an obvious importance in Britain where common law is effectively made by judges and statute law is subject to their interpretation in ways which are far from being politically neutral. One
consequence is that forms of popular struggle not specifically prohibited by statute can still be rendered illegal by judicial decision or by the police acting with judicial connivance. As for the
constitution itself, which 'The British Road to Socialism' describes
as giving 'a left government the democratic right *and the means,*
backed by the mass struggle of the people, to carry through drastic
and necessary reforms ...' (emphasis added) - we should be so lucky.
It is clear that all parliamentary democratic constitutions have
built-in obstacles to the powers of democratic control: the separation of powers, the House of Lords, the French presidential system

(effectively based on one imposed as a result of a military coup in
1958), the constitutional forms imposed on Japan and West Germany by
military defeat (not that the forms imposed on the GDR give more
scope for democratic control), the distribution of governmental
powers in Australia that allowed an appointed official to depose the
Whitlam government, the reactionary traditions of the House of
Commons and similar bodies elsewhere, the political effects of
electoral procedures and the law as it relates to political activities, and so on.

   Incidentally, on this last point, it may be worth dwelling for a
moment on the political conditions of late-nineteenth-century
Germany discussed by Bertrand Russell in his 'German Social Democracy'. Consider, for example, the constraints on political associations in the period after the expiry of the anti-socialist law.
In Prussia, political associations could not have 'women, scholars
or apprentices' as members or allow them to attend meetings, and in
most states political associations could not enter connections with
other associations 'whether by letters, committees, central organs
or officers, or in any other way'. Russell makes clear the significance of this second constraint:

   If an association extends over more than one police district - a
   case regarded by the law as abnormal - notice of its constitution
   must be given to the police of each district. If the members of
   one district have any independent activity, even a meeting, they
   form a branch association, which has to give separate notice, and
   a connection between two such branches is interpreted as illegal,
   under the above provisions. (p.119)

As Russell also notes, these and many other restrictions were used
against the Social Democrats more systematically than against other
parties.

   This case is interesting in the light of Lenin's attacks on
Kautsky and other advocates of a democratic road. Obviously it is
precisely this kind of legal harassment that appears to confirm the
view of democratic rights as a fraud perpetrated against the left.
More recent examples of legal and extra-legal harassment of the left
in advanced capitalist democracies readily spring to mind: the
'Berufsverbodt' in West Germany; the campaigns of the FBI against
the American Communist Party and militant black organisations; and
so on. In fact, the extreme harassment of social democracy in nineteenth-century Germany is far from typical of parliamentary democracy. Where, as frequently happens, state agencies do harass particular parties and political positions, it is not because to do so
is characteristic of parliamentary democracy as such. It is always
the product of particular conditions and struggles, of political
victories and defeats both within the state apparatuses and outside
them. But what these examples clearly show is that the forms of
franchise and the law relating to political activity and its enforcement cannot be regarded as neutral in their political effects.

   Now, I have emphasised these limits and obstacles not in order to
argue that a democratic process of socialist transformation of
modern capitalist democracies is impossible. Quite the contrary.
The point rather is that parliamentary democratic regimes invariably
involve severe obstacles to further democratisation. In the event
of an attempt to shift towards greater democratisation and popular

control we must expect at least some of these obstacles to be effective in providing significant means of political action for opposing political forces. (Consider the fate of British attempts to
liberalise the Official Secrets Act, to introduce some form of
Freedom of Information legislation, or simply to derestrict certain
categories of official documentation.) What is important to notice
about these obstacles is that their effectiveness does not depend on
any right-wing coup but rather on the constitution itself, the legal
and constitutional powers of the judiciary and the state apparatuses, and the diverse extra-legal practices that are possible under
their cover.

These points may be illustrated by referring to the conditions of
popular, extra-parliamentary struggles. It is clear that any significant transformation of British politics in a socialist direction
will involve, inter alia, the development of forms of popular struggle. But existing forms of popular struggle, let alone more developed forms, may be rendered effectively illegal in a number of
ways. For example, given the devolution of significant law-making
powers to magistrates, the judiciary and the police, and the possibilities of injunctions, it is clear that on-going or planned
actions may frequently be rendered illegal. This applies to a whole
range of widely employed means of struggle, strikes, picketing,
work-ins, rent-strikes, which are not specifically prohibited by
statute. Or again, changes in the law on picketing or the law of
trespass, whether effected by parliament or by judicial initiatives,
may render illegal a variety of well-established forms of working-
class or popular struggle.

These examples illustrate the point that it is practically impossible for there to be any expansion of popular and democratic
struggles in British conditions without coming into conflict with
existing legal forms and that perfectly constitutional practices may
be deployed against them. Furthermore, the history of encroachment
by the police and judiciary on the rights to strike, the organisation of picketing and other forms of working-class struggle, and of
resistance to that encroachment, demonstrates beyond question that
the widespread popular commitment to democratic forms and the prevailing liberal freedoms does not imply any corresponding commitment
to the preservation of legality at all costs. On the contrary, the
labour movement quite correctly regards the judiciary as an obstacle
to its perfectly justifiable objectives and practices.

What the obstacles to further democratisation are and how they
may be combatted will, of course, vary from country to country and
with political changes in each country. There is, therefore, no
point in trying to lay down general models for the pattern of socialist transformation in parliamentary regimes. The problems confronted by nineteenth-century German social democracy, the left in
Italy today, or in Britain, are obviously very different and would
require different political strategies in response. But if there is
one point that can be made at a general level, it is that parliamentary and electoral struggle alone are not sufficient to achieve
significant further socialisation. To say that parliamentary democracy sets the stage for socialist politics in Britain and several
other advanced capitalist regimes is not to say that electoral and
parliamentary struggle are the only significant arenas.

Why is it so important to develop non-parliamentary forms of
political activity? One reason is that mass mobilisation provides a
means of putting pressure on parliament or government. But there is
another important reason which has to do with the limits to parliamentary means of democratic control. We have seen that parliamentary government involves an effective separation between the parliamentary body proper and its executive bureaucracy and that that
separation imposes both a problem of parliamentary control and inescapable limits to its effectiveness. It is clear that however
much it tightens up its scrutiny, the control exercised by parliament over state apparatuses must always be severely limited. And
the same applies to local authority control over its executive departments, housing, planning, education, and so on. While there
may be room for considerable improvements in its effectiveness, the
scope for democratic control operating solely through the electoral
and representative machinery is ultimately limited by the institutional forms of parliamentary government themselves: an elected
assembly debating a wide variety of issues, issuing generalised decrees and instructions, and trying to exercise some level of scrutiny over complex administrative machines by means of very limited
investigative procedures. Thus, if we take seriously the objectives
of democratisation of control over state apparatuses and over the
non-commodity forms of distribution currently organised in some of
these apparatuses (education, health, housing, etc.), then we must
also recognise the need to develop means of democratic control in
addition to the electoral apparatuses of parliament and local
government. This involves not only forms of public scrutiny operating through the press, public inquiries, and access to official
documents, but also other forms of democratic intervention. To take
a concrete example, there is no reason why control over local
authority housing should be restricted to working through councillors, why tenants' committees should not be involved in the management of particular estates.
      The absence of forms of democratic involvement has been a major
weakness in labourist strategies concerning the expansion of the
state sector in Britain, involving both the lack of democratisation
in nationalised industries and the absence of democratic controls in
sectors of state provision that are largely non-commodity or semi-
commodity in form such as health, education and much of housing.
The latter is important not only in relation to the general argument
for further democratisation but also because bureaucratic forms of
central or local government provision remain particularly vulnerable
to governmental economies, changes in policy or in the party in
power. To the extent that they also embodied forms of popular
control these state-provided non- or semi-commodity services would
be less subject to cutback as a result of political setbacks at the
level of the central or local government authority concerned. They
would provide points of popular resistance over and above that of
state employees and their unions.
      This point suggests the need to campaign for legislative pro-
vision for democratisation within the state sector. But it is also
clear that democratisation cannot simply be imposed from above. It
would also require the development of organs of popular struggle
around existing areas of state provision with a continuing basis in

organisation so that there is opportunity for popular representatives to acquire the specialised knowledge of the problems and
issues concerning the local health authority, or whatever, required
if legislation for democratisation is to have any meaning.

CONCLUDING COMMENTS

This essay has considered the severe obstacles to effective democratic control over state apparatuses and the legal system operating
solely through parliament and local government, and has argued that
we need to develop additional means of democratic control. This
would involve campaigning for a Freedom of Information Act and
against the operation of the Official Secrets Act, for thoroughgoing
reforms of the legal system, as well as for new forms of democratic
involvement in the activities of industry and of national and local
government. It is necessary, in conclusion, to comment on some of
the implications of these proposals for the development of popular
struggles in a variety of heterogeneous political arenas in conjunction with electoral and parliamentary struggles. Notice first
that the objectives and forms of struggle developed in different
arenas may well conflict with each other, and that popular struggles
as such have no necessary socialist or democratic content. If a
process of parliamentary and non-parliamentary struggles in the direction of further socialisation and democratisation is to be developed, then socialists will have to develop means of articulating
objectives for those struggles and of arguing for and deciding on
priorities. In other words, it is necessary to elaborate a socialist ideology comprehensive enough to be relevant to the problems and
political conditions of modern Britain, to issues of popular concern
and actual or potential popular struggle. This would aim to provide
a means of analysing situations and setting objectives in particular
arenas of struggle and of linking struggles which develop in different arenas both to each other and to more general socialist objectives. Such an ideology must be based on a clear analysis of the
conditions it confronts and hopes to transform, of the organisation
of health and education, social security and pensions, of the
structure of the housing market and its determinants, and the
problems these generate, as well as of the structure of industry and
the financial system. Unfortunately, although socialists themselves
may be active in a wide variety of arenas, generally available forms
of socialist ideology do not perform this role: workerist forms of
socialist ideology are unable to articulate many significant issues
of popular concern and, partly for that reason, have a sectional appearance and effect, while appeals to democratisation and a broad
democratic alliance are generally too abstract and undeveloped in
relation to the serious problems and concerns of British society.
     Second, it is clear that conflicts between popular and parlia-
mentary forms of control over the practices of the state apparatuses
are unavoidable. To the extent that organs of popular control provide points of resistance to reactionary government policy, they
provide points of resistance to government policy as such, whatever
its character. Once organs of popular democracy have developed,
there can be no guarantee that socialists will approve of their de-

cisions or that they will not conflict with decisions of a democratically elected parliament or local authority, just as the decisions of local authorities may sometimes conflict with those of
the central government. Conflicts of this kind are an inevitable
feature of a democratically organised society, and any extension
of democratisation must also extend the opportunities for them to
occur.

   Now, it is precisely at this point that the doctrine of the
'ultimate sovereignty of parliament' may be invoked as a reason for
not supporting the development of organs of popular control in the
state sector, on the grounds that they would inevitably infringe on
that 'sovereignty'. On this view, extra-parliamentary activity may
be perfectly legitimate as a means of putting pressure on government, of demonstrating the strength of popular feeling on particular
issues, and so on, or even, in some scenarios, as a weapon to be
used in case of a right-wing coup. But the ultimate decision should
always be left to parliament or the relevant local authority. The
trouble with this view is that it fails to take account of the
limits to parliamentary control over the practices of the state
apparatuses and, more generally, of the limits to effective democratic control given by the institutional forms of parliamentary
government. To argue against the extension of popular democracy in
the name of the sovereignty of parliament is to say that democratic
control should be confined within those limits. Consider what would
be required if conflicts between organs of democratic control were
to be avoided. There would have to be a single elected central
governing body, aided perhaps by other elected bodies acting only
within such powers as may be delegated to them from time to time.
Decisions by the central body would have to be effected either directly by its own bureaucracies or indirectly by the subordinate
elected bodies. To ensure that these latter do not conflict with
the central body they would have to be closely supervised by the
central government bureaucracies. Few capitalist democracies have
achieved quite that degree of centralisation but the general character of this 'democracy' will not seem too unfamiliar: it is 'democratic' in the sense of having an elected assembly with the ability
to pass laws and appoint governments, but it suffers all the limitations to effective democratic control that we have already identified in parliamentary systems of government. It does not escape
from conflicts between distinct centres of decision; it merely ensures that those conflicts are between the assembly and sections of
its bureaucracy or within the bureaucracy itself. Conflicts between
organs of democratic control cannot be avoided without drastically
reducing the level of democratic control that is possible in a
society. Conversely, the possibility of conflict between parliament
or elected local authority and organs of popular democratic control
- say, over management of a housing estate - is a sign, not of the
anti-democratic character of the latter, but rather that they represent a real extension of democracy.

   Finally, a distinct but closely related issue concerns the inevitability of conflicts between the law and forms of popular struggle
noted above. Given the effective devolution of significant law-
making powers to magistrates, judiciary and police, and the possible
uses of injunctions, it is clear that on-going or planned actions

may be rendered illegal even though they are not specifically prohibited by statute. We have to recognise the possibility of perfectly legal and constitutional interventions by the judiciary,
police and other state apparatuses to suppress popular and democratic initiatives, or even, in some circumstances, as part of a
reactionary political suppression of the left in general. The fact
that the latter may seem remote from present British conditions does
not render it unthinkable, and there are parliamentary democracies
where it is far from remote. The point to make here is that a commitment to work within the forms of parliamentary democracy, and to
work for further democratisation, is not at all a commitment to obey
the law at all costs, and it is important to recognise this distinction. In one sense there is no problem here since few parties
have been averse to supporting breaches of 'unreasonable' laws in
practice. But such slogans as 'law and order' and 'respect for the
law' are effective elements of current right-wing ideologies and
they are widely used in media campaigns against trades unionists,
tenants, students - and some left practices seem designed to
strengthen such campaigns. It is necessary to recognise that any
development of popular and non-parliamentary struggles is bound to
come up against legal harassment from time to time, and that even
current forms of struggle are not immune from police and judicial
encroachment. This issue raises complex problems of strategy and
tactics, both in relation to the transformation and democratisation
of the legal system and to potential points of legal intervention
against developing popular struggles, to which there can be no easy
answers.

REFERENCES

COMMUNIST PARTY OF GREAT BRITAIN, 'The British Road to Socialism',
1978.
CUTLER, ANTONY, HINDESS, BARRY, HIRST, PAUL and HUSSAIN, ATHAR,
'Marx's Capital and Capitalism Today', London, Routledge & Kegan
Paul, 1977 and 1978.
ENGELS, F., Introduction to Marx's 'The Class Struggles in France',
in K.Marx and F.Engels, 'Selected Works' (one vol.edn), London,
Lawrence & Wishart, 1970.
KAUTSKY, K., 'The Dictatorship of the Proletariat', University of
Michigan Press, 1964.
LENIN, V.I., The State and Revolution, 'Collected Works', vol.25,
London, Lawrence & Wishart, 1964.
LENIN, V.I., The Proletarian Revolution and the Renegade Kautsky,
'Collected Works', vol.28.
LENIN, V.I., Theses and Report on Bourgeois Democracy and the
Dictatorship of the Proletariat, 'Collected Works', vol.28.
LENIN, V.I., The State, 'Collected Works', vol.29.
RUSSELL, BERTRAND, 'German Social Democracy', London, Longmans,
1896.

Chapter 4

ON STRUGGLE IN
THE ENTERPRISE
Paul Hirst

Since the last war the British trade union movement has developed an
unprecedented position of strength in bargaining over wages and
conditions. The institutionalisation of 'industrial relations'
between the officers of national unions and management, together
with a strong, militant and capable shop steward's movement are the
two most significant features of this position. This strength is so
obvious that we tend to ignore the singularity of its conditions.
The organisation of bargaining and trade union structure are markedly different in this country from other countries which also have
high levels of unionisation and strong union bargaining positions,
for example, Sweden or the Federal Republic of Germany. In those
cases industry rather than *trade* unions and national agreements on
pay scales prevail. In Britain, plant level bargaining and the determination of earnings at the level of the shop by agreements about
piece rates, overtime, bonuses, speed of work, etc., have given the
rank and file of the trade union movement a vital measure of independence from the national organisation and its officials. It has
also led to the phenomena, much lamented by advocates of 'industrial
efficiency', of 'earnings creep' and 'wage drift', the capacity in
certain industries to bid up earnings levels by means of plant and
shop level agreements (particularly in periods of boom).

The trade union movement has learnt the lessons of its successes
in the 1950s and 1960s. Both the official 'industrial relations'
specialists and the mass movement have stressed freedom to bargain,
freedom to settle affairs at industry, plant or shop level with a
minimum of legal restraint and government intervention. This
freedom has brought real material benefits. The alternatives
appear to have little to recommend them. Workers have no reason
to trust the courts; from Taff Vale to Rookes v. Barnard to
Donaldson the bias of the judiciary and its capacity to subvert
the statutory rights of trades unions have been all too clear.
Likewise, the main forms of government intervention in wages
questions have been arbitrary in their application and often
ineffectual. Wages freezes are partial and inequitable, and state
intervention in strikes has depended on the government's estimation
of its strength (as with the 1972 Post Office workers' strike) or
the economic consequences (as with the 1966 seamen's strike) and

has had little to do with the merit of the claims. Attempts to limit this power to bargain by legislation have twice failed in recent years; 'In Place of Strife' and the 1971 Industrial Relations Act collapsed under mass trade union resistance. Many, perhaps most, realistic industrial relations experts in management would also concede that bargaining with unions and workers is a better alternative in terms of maintaining production and continuity of work than fighting them through the courts or with the police.

This commitment to and success of collective bargaining at industry and lower levels has been connected with two widely shared official and mass attitudes about the determination of wages and the place of wage bargaining in the national economy. (1)

First, it has come to be assumed that 'full-employment' is the normal state of affairs, that wages and real incomes will rise steadily and that there are no given determinants to the price of 'labour power' or the level of wages. Workers expect to be in work and to receive regular percentage increases in their wage rates from year to year. Wages are determined by a contest for shares in a growing national income: the shares workers receive depend on their capacity to bargain.

This contrasts markedly with official trade union attitudes before the last war. Neither the Labour Party nor the trades unions had an 'alternative economics'; most of the leaders and the masses in the Labour movement accepted (however ruefully or reluctantly) the prevailing capitalist economic theories about the determinants of economic activity and wages. The syndicalist movement of the early 1900s and the Great War left little in the way of economic ideas, and, like Marxism, was anathema to the largely right-wing trade union leaders. Hence the predominant expectations were pessimistic and defensive. A given rate of unemployment (about 10%) was widely accepted as normal. Wages were regarded as industry-specific and set by conditions of cost and profitability in that industry. National income was not expected to rise steadily but to fluctuate unpredictably with the cycle of boom and slump. The primary task of most unions in this period was to resist wage *cuts* and a worsening of working conditions; wage reductions were commonplace in the 1920s and early 1930s. (2)

Second, union negotiators and the rank and file have stressed take-home pay above all else; all other issues within the enterprise (organisation of work safety, what is made, investment and company strategy, etc.) have been considered as secondary or ignored. Shop-floor workers have a strong tendency to express those of these questions they do raise in terms of bargaining about monetary rewards, questions of safety serving to promote claims for danger bonuses and so on. But many potential issues of struggle in the enterprise cannot be expressed in terms of personal benefits. Short-term material gains commit the workers to little in the way of continuing struggle in the enterprise. Often only short-term material issues can be taken up by transient and organisationally divided workforces (labour turnover and union structure are significant limits on forms of struggle). With a lessening competitiveness (from 'traditional' declining industries like shipbuilding to 'new' ones like consumer electronics, motor vehicles, etc.) many workers are coming to be more concerned with the nature of the enterprise

they are in, its prospects and the future of their jobs. These
concerns cannot be settled by pay rises. Often they cannot be effectively raised as issues of struggle because of the organisational
divisions of the enterprise workforce and the different policies of
their respective unions. The resolution of differences in union
structure is not simply a 'management' issue (simplifying bargaining
and the policing of agreements). It also concerns the ability of
the working class to struggle about certain issues at a grassroots
level.

The commitment to collective bargaining and its past success,
together with the continued expectations of a steadily rising
national income have led the majority of trade union officials and
the rank and file to oppose incomes policies and also to oppose
workers' participation schemes. The 'Social Contract', like every
other incomes policy the trades unions have agreed to since the war,
in 1948, 1964 and 1966, has been conceived as a short-term emergency
measure to be followed by a return to 'normal' collective bargaining. But wage restraint of one kind or another has been an almost
permanent feature of the policy of British governments since the
1961 'pay pause'. Part of the 'price' of the Social Contract, the
Bullock Report on industrial democracy, was dismissed by the unions
(although not by the TUC) with a mixture of open hostility and un-
comprehending indifference. This essay will be concerned with the
reasons for this opposition to incomes policies and to Bullock, with
the consequences of this opposition and to argue the necessity for
alternative policies and practices in the trade union movement. To
consider these problems it is necessary to examine the changing
economic conditions under which the trade unions will have to
operate, conditions which make a continuation of collective bar-
baining practices like those of the 1950s and their results increasingly improbable. It is also necessary to examine the likely
political conditions the trade union movement will encounter if it
does attempt to continue 'free collective bargaining' under these
economic conditions. It will be argued that wages cannot be determined by a bidding for shares in a rising national income primarily because that income will *not* be rising in a way that would
allow the distributional effects of wage rises to particular groups
of workers to be ignored. It follows that the opposition of the
left and the trade union movement to all incomes policies and
workers' participation schemes per se is mistaken. Further, the
more successful an incomes policy is in organising the distribution
of national income the greater the need for effective workers' participation schemes if the industrial and, therefore, the political
strengths of the shop steward's movement are to be retained and enhanced.

It is necessary to outline the economic conditions with which
trade union policy will have to come to terms in the next few years
and possibly for much longer. These read like a reversal of the
popular expectations of the 1950s and 1960s, but there is no reason
why they should lead back to the defensiveness and pessimism of the
1930s. The conditions of union power are very different from the
1930s. Unlike the 1930s these economic circumstances, given the
right policies and practices, permit major advances in the power
of the organised workers. These conditions are as follows:

   i   That national income will continue to grow relatively slowly
(at 1 or 2 per cent p.a. at best).

   ii   That (as an overall generalisation) Britain will remain a
high-cost, low-profit producer relative to her main competitors.   In
consequence, the ability to absorb wage rises or to compensate for
them by increases in productivity will be limited.   The capacity for
increases in productivity (even given existing technique) is substantial, however.   But most organised workers will strenuously
resist changes in working methods or new techniques precisely
because they displace labour and weaken shop-floor and union control
over working methods and systems of payment.

   iii   That the rate of unemployment will tend to remain at something like the present level in the near future and well above 1950s
levels for the foreseeable future.   (However, it should be noted
that unemployment does not directly affect the wage levels of the
majority of those employed.   Union organisation prevents a worsening
of the conditions of many workers.   Also the determinants of wage
levels cannot be reduced to supply and demand on a homogeneous
'labour market';   differences of skill, location, company position,
etc., differentiate the labour markets, as they did in the 1930s.
It should also be noted that this does not imply a passive attitude
towards unemployment.   Unemployment can be reduced by specific
government action in directly creating or supporting new jobs and
enterprises.   But the scope of any general 'counter-cyclical' policy
of reflation is limited, first, because unemployment is not primarily temporary lay-offs, and second, because the traditional counter-
cyclical instruments like tax-cuts will probably work to boost
imports and saving rather than create new jobs.)

   iv   That, even given a substantial measure of wage restraint, inflation will remain well above the levels of the 1950s (5 per cent
or above).

This is to contend that there will be little change for the
better away from the present economic conditions and it involves
certain assumptions.   For example, that a major upturn in world
trade is unlikely in the next few years and, even if it does occur,
Britain is of the major industrial capitalist countries the one
least able and likely to benefit from it.   Further, it supposes that
none of the 'alternative' policies of national economic management
currently proposed by the left can be carried out or would, if
tried, lead to any rapid improvement in these conditions.   They are
generally premised on the assumption that economic reconstruction
under conditions of international capitalist competition can be
achieved without some sacrifice in respect of rising living
standards and without real increases in productivity on the part of
the mass of workers.   Reflation would be difficult even *with* effective price and wage controls, *without* them (and without real increases in productivity) it would lead to increases in the rate of
inflation.   The left, as evidenced by Holland and Ormerod's proposals ('Guardian', 12.10.1978), still has not learnt to take inflation seriously.   Its failure to recognise the deep-seated fear
of most ordinary people on this question means that the 'alternative' economic policies will continue to lack mass support.   Moreover, whatever technical economic merits these various policies may
have, there is little political chance of their implementation.

Centre-right Labour, Tory, or coalition governments - which present
patterns of voting indicate that we are likely to get - will ignore
them. This means, among other things, that the left cannot base its
overall strategy on their implementation. The Labour movement
cannot *rely* on certain policies of managing the economy to resolve
certain issues of vital and immediate interest to workers, but which
cannot be taken up by existing practices of struggle at enterprise
level. In this context union and mass struggles cannot be confined
to wages, on certain crucial economic issues workers will need to
struggle at enterprise level. National pressure through the TUC or
Labour Party organs is insufficient.

These remarks cannot amount to an economic analysis. They are
necessarily dogmatic and they certainly cannot be justified in the
compass of this essay. But inflation and balance of payments problems really do constrain public policy (independently of the objectives of governments) and also trade union practice. Most of
the 'alternative' strategies of the left hardly accept this. The
left as a whole has only recently abandoned strenuously arguing that
'wage rises do not cause inflation' and has not started to face up
to the consequences of the alternatives. The determinants of inflation are various and situational, and some of them have nothing
to do with wage rises, but to argue the irrelevance of wage-fuelled
inflation in the middle of the wage-price spiral of the 1970s was
little short of madness. An incomes policy became a necessity, and
was accepted as such by most unions and workers, precisely because
of that spiral. Wage restraint was the only effective means of
breaking the spiral relatively quickly. Price controls or controls
on incomes other than wages have, on their own, limited effectiveness in controlling inflation. Price controls might be effective
within certain conditions: (i) that there are also effective *wage*
controls, otherwise company incomes may be unduly squeezed before
the measures can have effect (economists can always argue about the
room for manoeuvre which companies have, workers have to face the
consequences of company liquidity and plainly many large firms do
not have the profit levels or reserves to cope with a squeeze of
more than a few months); (ii) that they concern those large companies which can be policed, thousands of other price setters are
beyond control; (iii) that they are related to domestic price
changes, as changes in the prices of imported goods cannot be controlled without also squeezing company income. Price controls are
not an alternative to wage restraint. Like subsidies on basic items
such as foodstuffs they are an effective adjunct and supplement,
helping to mitigate the consequences of foregoing rises in money
wages and, therefore, to strengthen willingness to accept pay restraint. Controlling personal incomes other than wages cannot
control prices as these amount to only about a third of the total
of national personal income (wages and salaries 70 per cent, self-
employment 9 per cent, rent interest and dividends 10 per cent and
social security 11 per cent - Wootton, 'Incomes Policy', p.85).
Self-employment income is notoriously difficult to regulate, whilst
control of social security would be anathema to most socialists.
Any incomes policy must mean primarily a policy of wage control and
restraint.

Inflation has made an incomes policy of some kind necessary. But

more than that it could have provided the urgent pretext for the
introduction of national income planning. The left and the trade
union movement have shunned any prospect of this, preferring to
insist on the autonomy of free collective bargaining. The reasons
for this response are not hard to find. Effective incomes planning
would make most of the present trade union practices redundant. It
would remove one of the major sources of left influence with the
organised working class, support for militant wage claims and
struggles. A national incomes policy it is argued would strengthen
the state, the TUC and a handful of union officials, and through
them the employers, against the mass of organised labour. The
spectacle of socialists opposing incomes policy and supporting
'free collective bargaining' is not as bizarre and irrational as it
might appear. 'Corporatism' and 'tripartism' are feared because it
is supposed that whatever 'influence' they give the TUC in directing
national policy and control over state apparatuses (Manpower
Services Commission, Arbitration and Conciliation Advisory Service,
etc.), an 'influence' always subject to political reversal, will be
bought at the price of demobilisation and policing of the mass movement.

The successive incomes policies of the Labour government survived
as long as they did and enjoyed some success because the mass of
workers were scared to death at the prospect of inflation running at
levels above 30 per cent. They could begin to guess at the long-run
consequences for their living standards and their jobs. Incomes
policy collapsed because that fear is now receding among groups of
organised workers most able to engage in bargaining and to benefit
from it. If no stable incomes policy can be devised then the consequences of a return to 'free collective bargaining' in current
economic conditions, whether under a Tory or Labour government,
must be considered. Let us note to start with that such a 'return'
will be partial. The Labour government as employer attempted to
keep wage rises to a norm where it could and encouraged managements
to resist excessive claims. It tried to continue to use sanctions
against firms breaching some upper limit. The Tories will probably
do this too, preferring to act through macro-economic policies or
taxation on the incomes derived from bargaining rather than by some
general restraint of bargains struck. Let us also note that, to the
extent that it is not partial, a new round of wage bids will prime
the wage-price spiral once again.

What the economic conditions outlined above effectively prevent
is a general process of 'bidding-up' of wage levels by claim and
counter-claim between different occupations, industries and regions
which characterised the 1950s and the 1960s. To attempt to continue
such a process would (whatever its other economic effects) produce
a wages-prices spiral in which only a small minority of organised
workers could keep ahead of the game. Those workers who were poorly
organised, lacked appropriate industrial bargaining power and did
not benefit from 'status' lost out in the 1950s and 1960s: most
left-union sentiments about 'low pay' are crocodile tears. The
absence of a wage-price spiral means the ending of a 'ladder' of
claims and this will sharpen the distributional consequences of
differential wage rises between different groups of workers. A
minority of workers will benefit under any implicit or explicit

incomes policy which simply exists to police wage rises. The end
of the 'ladder' of claims makes questions of the present distribution of income between groups of workers explosive. The present
wage structure is not the product of some uniformly acting general
economic laws. It is primarily the result of decades of collective
gargaining, of differential capacities to bargain, and of notions by
government, managements and unions about 'statuses', forms of
payment and the organisation of tasks. Those most able and organised to bargain, irrespective of official and popular notions about
'status', have benefited most.
    'Free collective bargaining' is under the conditions outlined
above only an effective option for workers in certain enterprises
and trades. As the conditions have become tougher, more organised
workers will find themselves in positions analogous to the 'low
paid' in the 1950s and 1960s. In conditions of semi-stagnation,
increased foreign competition in the home market and low returns
on capital, more industrial firms will tend to resist wage rises in
a way they did not do in the 'go' periods of the 1950s' and 1960s'
domestic demand. Most public employees, most organised workers, and
the bulk of the 50 per cent of the labour force which is not unionised will have few opportunities to strike favourable bargains.
Their living standards will be eroded by the general level of inflation and by the transferred wage costs of some of their favoured
brethren. Under 'free collective bargaining', whether as a consequence of a wage-price spiral or of the ending of a 'ladder' of
claims, the long-run mass political pressure will be towards some
form of incomes policy and state control of bargaining rights. This
will be primarily because of questions of distribution of income
between groups of wage-earners. Given the fundamental changes in
expectations about income since the 1930s, outlined at the beginning, differentials could become an explosive question. To see a
minority of people, like oneself in other respects, enjoying a
constant or increasing standard of living whilst one's own is declining or stagnant, simply because of the accident of the trade,
firm or place where they work, will be generally unacceptable. This
is what the ending of a 'ladder' of claims will produce. The irra-
tionalities of the wages structure, differentials, regional differences, etc., have been accepted and defended precisely *because* they
offered pretexts to bargain and the prospect of 'moving up' the
ladder. The minority who can maintain or increase their living
standards will become increasingly isolated and vulnerable to political pressure through the ballot box. Pensioners, the unemployed, housewives, and recipients of social security have votes
too. To the extent that the socialist left continues to dig-in
behind the slogan of 'free collective bargaining' that pressure will
tend to favour the centre and right. The left has drawn the conclusion from the defeats of Barbara Castle and Edward Heath that in
a showdown the unions cannot be beaten and will enjoy mass support.
In 1974 that was true primarily because the 'ladder' was not yet
broken and the potential effects of price-wage inflation were not
yet publicly feared, it could be accepted that the miners were a
'special case' and that control of wages was not an issue on which
it was worth making the country ungovernable. Now everybody considers themselves a 'special case' and knows that we all cannot be.

Effective public support for control of bargaining rights is by no means impossible.

'Free collective bargaining' has become entrenched as the ideology of the trade union movement at the very same time as it and the mass of the people have come to expect effective state action to stabilise the economy and to preserve full employment to be part of the normal state of affairs. In this 'interventionist' climate, where the prospects of effective state action are if anything over-rated in public eyes and failures to achieve policy objectives create disillusionment with politicians, wages can be considered (like the supply of credit) as one of the factors subject to government regulation and control. Virtually no one believes in an 'iron law' of wages, they are almost universally held to be a matter of public policy and bargaining. Wage control is rejected not because militants and officials adopt a free market ideology but because of the benefits an elite of organised workers expect to get from 'free collective bargaining' and because of widespread fears that wage restraint is practically and politically unworkable.

Prolonged wage restraint *is* practically and politically un-workable. Except, that is, in conditions of suspension of many basic political rights and the destruction of the political conditions of the unions and workers' capacity to bargain. Support for controls of bargaining rights, which may well result from the frustrations of differential capacities to bargain, does not mean these controls will be successful. The trade union movement has reluctantly accepted 'wage freezes' as emergency measures but only on the assumption that they are temporary. The 1966 wage freeze was effective because it was temporary – the Labour Government could discover no effective incomes policy to replace it. Its 'controls' became a laughing stock. Incomes policy has come to *mean* wage-freeze or restraint for most trades unionists. But this attitude, that incomes policy is temporary and can be forgotten about as a mere setback in earnings, is intelligible only on the assumption that sustained economic growth is the norm. It has been contended that on any other assumption this attitude becomes deeply problematic. In conditions of virtual stagnation *and* inflation 'free collective bargaining' *is also* practically and politically un-workable.

Only a policy which attempts to tackle the reliquary of our wages structure, the partially frozen result of a bargaining process, can hope to succeed and achieve a sufficient measure of consent and compliance. Such a policy *cannot* be imposed on the trade union movement by any national government, however enlightened, because the recognition and resolution of differences between groups of workers is the main stumbling block to any policy. Only a mass commitment to the objectives of such a policy could make such a process of recognition and resolution possible. Something 'as limited' as a policy of wage restraint will only work for more than a couple of years if it is something more, a policy which resolves the *obstacles* to wage restraint. In order to do this it must involve the active participation of a significant number of trade unions and masses of trade unionists.

Without national income planning, all 'incomes policies' do amount to an arbitrary and uneven 'wage freeze'. Such policies

produce both the intractable problems of those who can bargain and
break the 'freeze' and of the disturbed differentials which are the
results of the point at which the last round of 'bidding-up' was
terminated. The Labour Government's policy crumbled under these
very strains. In the 'Social Contract' all the trade union movement
did agree to was a measure of wage restraint. The norms of that
policy have been a matter of continuous dispute. But even if a
percentage limit to pay rises were agreed, this could not settle
the mass of distributional questions which remain from an entirely
different system of setting wage and earnings levels. The problems
which incomes policies have faced in Britain since the war can only
be resolved by turning them into something broader. The difficulties of wage limitation show that an incomes policy which persists
for any period of more than a year or so, requires a set of
'ideological' objectives which can secure the commitment of the mass
of workers and which can serve as criteria or bases of principle in
settling hard cases. Fear of inflation or other pragmatic economic
policy goals cannot secure this commitment in the long run, such
pragmatic commitment is weakened to the extent that economic conditions improve. Such 'ideological' objectives must necessarily
transcend immediate economic policy objectives and must involve
commitments to broad principles. Without such principles disputes
are insoluble. This is what underlies 'national income planning',
it cannot be a mere economic technique directed by civil servants.
National policy can only be secured by the elaboration of commitments and objectives at a mass level. This is only possible if the
trade union movement *itself* adopts an incomes 'policy as an objective
and actively assists in organising its application.

Such an objective could only be the planned re-organisation of
the wages structure, attainment of national minimum wage, reduction
of regional inequalities, arbitrary differentials etc. Trade union
involvement in setting and realising the objectives is the key to
the success of any non-authoritarian incomes policy. The only
progressive basis for such involvement is an egalitarian and socialist commitment towards the equalisation of the distribution of in
income and wealth. The trade union movement has argued that the
'price' of consent to temporary wage limitation is government
control of profits and high incomes. It must also be accepted,
however, and it has not hitherto been, that the main problem of
inequality confronting any incomes policy, and the main obstacle
to planning national income, has been differentials between wage
earners themselves.

The trade union movement on its own cannot effectively run such
an incomes policy. Certain actions are necessary both to secure the
conditions of long-run mass commitment and to adjust the various
components of the policy to short-run economic conditions which only
governments and state apparatuses have the capacity to undertake:

i   the control of high salaries and non-wage incomes (stringent
taxation of personal incomes from rents, interest and dividends,
control of 'fringe benefits', control of dividend levels [many
companies derive much of their income from shares], and measures
against accumulating company incomes in reserves and financial
assets rather than industrial investment), these are essential
measures to preserve working-class wage restraint that only the
state can provide.

ii   A policy which seeks to equalise earnings and introduce a national minimum wage requires that the tax and benefits systems are modified to serve these objectives. As both of these systems are in chronic need of reform, a need admitted by far from socialist tax experts like James Meade and by the Supplementary Benefits Commission, it would be difficult not to make a strong case for changes which both rationalised these systems and promoted a widely desired economic policy objective (inflation control).

iii A measure of control of prices.

iv Measures to create employment and the introduction of non-punitive levels and conditions of benefit for the long-term unemployed.

These objectives could only be attained over several years and are subject to other policy constraints (inflation, public expenditure implications, etc.). The Tory government will find it very difficult to commit itself to a programme of this kind, whatever the benefits for economic policy; Mrs Thatcher's current cabinet will find it impossible - however real the commitments offered by the unions. A centre-Labour government probably could commit itself and, given effective union commitments to their side of the bargain, could be forced to deliver. The Labour centre and right are especially weak to pressures of this kind; without effective reform programmes of their own, their sole claims to mass electoral support are fear of Tory monetarism and the possibility of a deal with the unions which controls inflation and limits mass conflicts over wages. The unions have never attempted to force the terms of such a deal. The 'Social Contract' was limited in scope and commitments precisely because of the desire not to limit the conditions of a return to 'free collective bargaining'.

Such economic policy commitments by governments *to* the trade unions do necessarily involve a price. In the short run, a fairly severe and rigid overall percentage limit to wage rises and priority to the low paid. This would require enforcement by other than voluntary means or the forms of discipline the TUC and the unions can provide. Even mass worker commitment to an incomes policy will not prevent some unions and groups of workers from opposing it and others from deciding that they are 'exceptional cases'. To cope with this an essential reserve of state power is necessary. This state power can be effective not only to the extent that it does enjoy mass support for the policies which it enforces, but also that those policies embody ideas which it is difficult for elements in the Labour movement to oppose. It would be difficult for socialists and trade unionists to justify striking against a policy which attempts to redistribute income towards the low paid and unemployed. There is, however, a real problem of the means chosen. Using overall economic policy measures, as the Tories plan to do, is impossible; this would mean unscrambling the whole incomes policy to deal with limited groups. Legal control of bargaining rights is, as we have seen, too tied in with recent bitter experiences and would involve too much of a reversal of loudly declared policy for the unions and left to swallow. Something like Barbara Wootton's 'Income Gains Tax', which enforces the norm through the taxation of personal incomes and could act directly through PAYE in the case of workers, has definite attractions in this context. First, because

(unlike the Liberal proposals for a merely punitive tax) it is
designed to act as part of an egalitarian redistributive policy.
It would involve differential gradings of tax rates on income gains
depending on the level of earnings and other factors. Second, because it acts on all earnings irrespective of the means of payment
by which they are obtained. It thereby covers non-wage earners and
so overcomes a major difficulty which has bedevilled previous
incomes policies, which have merely set a norm for settlements, that
is 'earnings creep' - the fact that in many industrial employments
as much as half of weekly earnings are derived from sources other
than hourly basic rates.

National level policies and powers can only be the starting point
for workable wage restraint, and the reserve of compulsion for an
incomes policy of the type outlined above. To resolve the chaos of
wages structure, to cut the differentials knot and to redistribute
income between classes of wage and salary earners involves a protracted programme and practice of negotiation and struggle *between*
unions and groups of workers. The most intelligent Labour-oriented
arguments for an incomes policy, left-centre in the case of Wootton
and right in the case of Clegg, both recognise the need to resolve
and rationalise differentials. Both, however, despite many acute
observations and proposals on other matters fall into the absurdi-
ties of 'job-evaluation' on this question. Differentials cannot be
resolved by calling in management trained 'experts' or by ranking
people's 'feelings' about the merits of a variety of jobs (pilot
studies cited by Wootton reveal the notorious fact that people tend
to 'over-rate' their own job in the general scale of merit). To
change differentials involves changes in the organisation of work
and in the composition of tasks. It requires *means* whereby workers
in particular industries and companies can discuss and resolve these
issues, *objectives* for them to follow in doing so and *powers* to get
managements to accept the results. This can only begin from the
bottom up within definite enterprises between the workers involved
in particular divisions of labour. The same is true of the related
question of rationalising methods of payment. On this basis *unions*
can begin to negotiate changes of rules, procedures and scales, exchanges of membership and amalgamations.

These changes are not something which can be undertaken in a
matter of a couple of years, nor are they something that workers
will do merely to support the working of an incomes policy. They
must relate to other basic objectives and practices in the enterprise itself that workers can see to be bringing them real benefits
(greater job security, more control over work, etc.). As differentials will tend to be erased *upwards,* this means of securing compliance with an incomes policy would work against one of its major
objectives and would need to be phased over some time to counter
inflationary effects. Workers will not accept re-grading, loss of
'status' and relative benefits unless other people's work is
changing too and they can see personal advantages in reorganisation.
It is for this reason that we have linked questions of incomes
policy to Bullock. Differentials can best be tackled within a
strategy of progressive increase in workers' control.

If such a 'socialist-egalitarian' incomes policy were to be
adopted and implemented by the trade unions and the state this

would necessarily weaken the role of local wage bargaining. Many
left militants argue that this must involve a massive strengthening
of the TUC and the state and a reduction in the power of the shop
stewards' movement. But the conditions of *general* shop-stewards'
power in wage bargaining are conditions of economic growth and
relatively full employment. Wage bargaining has tended to mono-
polise trade union struggle and virtually exclude all other issues
from a permanent place. Closures, investment policy, what is produced, health and safety, the organisation of work and the level of
employment, are all factors which *can* be struggled over at enterprise level. The idea that there are inherent limits to the content
of trade union politics rests on an essentialist notion of organisations and their location ('economic' level, 'political' level),
as I shall argue later. It is true that the powers which workers
have within enterprises originated through wage bargaining, but
capacity to control the enterprise now depends on the strength of
the workers' organisation itself. This strength can be extended if
the scope of collective bargaining were widened and workers sought
the power to determine enterprise policy on these other issues.
They have been neglected in the past but will, given the present
economic conditions, become far more important to the fortunes of
workers in the future.

   There is no reason why the powers of shop-stewards need be
weakened by a successful incomes policy. What is needed is the development of new objectives and new forms of struggle at enterprise
level. The scope of bargaining must be extended from questions of
immediate personal benefits to questions of enterprise policy and
operation. This change in the issues which are involved in bargaining means radical changes in the information and skills required in the struggle for those objectives and the forums through
which the struggles can be conducted. It requires forms of co-
operation between unions and commitments to managements of a scope
and timescale hitherto rare in collective bargaining. Many union
leaders are now arguing the need for 'extended collective bargaining' as an addition to the wages struggle, both in order to
cope with questions of redundancies and levels of investment, and
to offer some alternative to Bullock or other participation schemes.
Most trade unionists have rightly welcomed the Employment Protection
Act 1975 precisely because it does provide them with certain of the
means to engage in 'extended collective bargaining'. The hostility
to Bullock in the Labour movement from left and right is intelligible and has the same sources of opposition as to income policies.
It is the fear that 'traditional' trade union forms and issues of
struggle will be confused, displaced and subverted by formal participation in management. If an incomes policy becomes necessary
then something far stronger and more radical than experiments in
'extended collective bargaining' is needed to preserve workers'
capacities to defend themselves and to extend their capacities for
control in their enterprises. The opposition by organised Labour to
Bullock was an untimely error; it will be infinitely more difficult
to get as close to legislative proposals satisfactory to trade union
interests in the near future.

   Bullock was defeated by default. Organised management and the
right mounted an unprecedented campaign against the Report. Thereby

manifesting, in *their* fears and hostility, that they did not expect
its effects, if put into operation, to be a whitewash job or legitimation exercise in the service of management. The Minority
Report indicated very clearly why a scheme of single channel representation through trade unions on a unitary management board was unacceptable to representatives of management, it gives 'sectional
interests' direct access to policy formation in companies. The
scheme would extend the information and capacities to bargain of
the trade unions whilst preserving their existing structures and
capacities of struggle. As John Elliot demonstrates in 'Conflict
or Cooperation', Bullock became possible because elements of the
leadership and officials of the TUC, notably Jack Jones and David
Lea, were able to exercise a disproportionate influence in formu-
lating the overall policy of the movement and then after the 1974
election pursue it at the highest level with the Labour government.
Management, civil servants and the right were kicking an open door
in their opposition as Jones, and a few other TUC leaders, were
isolated with an advanced policy which was only nominally that of
the movement and lacked any kind of mass support. The question of
how 'feasible' the Bullock proposals would have been as legislation
is therefore open, they were never fought for.

In this context, before discussing how the Bullock proposals
would complement an incomes policy, it is necessary to consider in
detail the grounds of the opposition to them in the Labour movement.
A common theme, uniting right and left, is that board representation
would conflict with the traditional structures and forms of accountability to the membership of collective bargaining. Thus the
EETPU argued in its submission to Bullock:

> First, there is the institutional impossibility of separating the
> boardroom consultation from the potential negotiating implica-
> tions behind the issues under discussion. Second, there is the
> irreconcilable split loyalties of the worker directors them-
> selves. They will find it immensely difficult to separate their
> boardroom responsibilities dictated by business priorities from
> their representative functions derived from their relationship
> with the workforce. The pursuit of trade union objectives will
> not then be helped by the disunity created in such an atmosphere.
> And this ignores the crude disagreements that must occur on
> occasion with worker directors, in possession of all the in-
> formation, being party to a decision or a policy that is opposed
> by the collective bargainers. Far better in the interests of
> those affected by a managerial decision that the responsibility
> for that decision is firmly laid at the management's door; then
> the collective bargaining machinery can oppose and moderate the
> impact of the decision when necessary. (Bullock, pp.39-40)

A rightist like Frank Chapple clearly will want trade union
struggles and organisation to be limited to questions of personal
and material benefit to the members. To take up other issues forces
the introduction of 'politics', because it involves proposing alternative policies and forms of organisation for enterprises, and
this requires higher levels of discussion and political knowledge
among members than do questions of take-home pay. It is not easy
to see where such a process might go; it might not stop with
issues, forms of member organisation and skills which traditional

trade union officials would feel comfortable to live with. The
trade union right has a clear and very limited conception of the
scope of union issues and action. Others take a broader view of
the issues capable of being taken up in collective bargaining, for
example, the Communist Party of Great Britain argued in its submission to Bullock that:

> The proposals we are making are for extending industrial demo-
> cracy within the framework of capitalist society today. We
> believe that full workers' control can only be developed in a
> socialist society. There has been an extension of industrial
> democracy over the past 100 years in that the questions subject
> to some form of negotiation between the two sides of industry,
> management and labour, have been increased ... Bit by bit
> collective bargaining has been able to encroach on new areas,
> bringing what was hitherto regarded as managerial right under
> some form of control. We therefore see the major advance in
> industrial democracy coming through the further development of
> collective bargaining, with all major decisions being the subject
> of mutuality. This would cover negotiation on such matters as
> investment, location or expansion of the industry of enterprise,
> forward manpower planning, training, etc. (Elliot, p.75)

Chapple, given the position he takes, is quite right to oppose
Bullock. For traditional collective bargaining on wages and shop-
floor conditions it adds nothing and is a diversion of effort. The
proponents of 'extended collective bargaining' have a rougher time.
Consider the EETPU's arguments against Bullock:

1 that bargaining issues and general company policy cannot be
easily separated;
2 that the existence of two channels of representation, worker
directors and shop stewards, creates a conflict of loyalties which
must make the directors' position impossible in any conflict of
interests.

Both these points take on special sharpness if wages are determined at enterprise level and if representatives are not following any strategy agreed with their union colleagues in the enterprise. These objections have much less force under an incomes
policy. Wages cannot be the primary question in TU struggle at
enterprise level in this case, and it is wage bargaining that has
provided the pertinent examples of a conflict of interests in the
opposition case. Under the incomes policy discussed here, on the
other hand, bargaining and general company policy would indeed be
difficult to separate, the unions in an enterprise would require a
company strategy, and they would need to use access to management
discussions as a means of its pursuit. In any clash with the rest
of the Board the union members could vote against, report back and
expect their position to be reinforced by industrial action.

'Extended collective bargaining' is possible, but it is not
something different in nature from workers' representation on the
Board. First, in order to work it requires new levels of disclosure
of company information. Whilst the Employment Protection Act does
make this possible, the information gleaned tends to be about past
performance rather than future policy, and the provisions in the Act

are sufficiently general to be evaded (how unions will fare seeking enforcement in the courts remains to be seen). Where other detailed information is given on the plans or position of the company this will be given to negotiating officials and senior shop stewards at the discretion of the management and in confidence. The membership are as much dependent on officials reporting and recommending policies on the basis of confidential information as they are with worker directors. Further, the information given is what the Board has decided to make available, conflicting views on policy and so on will not be communicated (whereas a worker director will be aware of these in reporting back and advising on policy). In respect of the problems of coping with information and monitoring performance, shop stewards under 'extended collective bargaining' and worker directors will face common problems.

Second, 'extended collective bargaining' is *bargaining,* it involves commitments on both sides. Complex bargaining on *wage questions,* like the Fawley Productivity agreements, commits workers to long-term policies on issues like the right to strike and work organisation. It involves co-operation with the enterprise and a restriction of the scope of struggle (certain issues become subject to agreed procedures). If bargaining is extended to questions of company policy the commitments demanded in return for guarantees on employment, investment, etc. will be no less extensive or binding. 'Extended bargaining', by the nature of the issues at stake and the 'bargains' struck, must limit the scope of trade union struggle and involve co-operation with the management. In itself it does not extend the forms of or the means of struggle; 'bargains' will limit the right to strike, involve reorganisation of jobs, etc., otherwise managements will not agree to them. This has been a recognised part of wage bargaining for many years. In this sense bargaining has never been 'free' but constrained by past agreements. Bullock offered an extension of the means of struggle which parallels the commitments of 'extended collective bargaining'; it was not some form of co-option to which 'extended collective bargaining' is an alternative. Extending the *scope* of issues for negotiation and agreement must commit the organised workers to the enterprise in a way that limited wage negotiations never did. To limit struggle to wage questions (and to eschew productivity agreements, etc.) is to limit what needs to be fought over and what can be won. 'Extended collective bargaining' is a sign that the unions recognise that changed economic conditions and their own strength necessitate and make possible an extension of the scope of bargaining. It is a pity that they have not recognised the possibility of new forms and methods of struggle.

Bullock did offer a new forum of struggle to the union movement, one whose potential benefits offset the risks of confusion of representation and co-option. The same cannot be said for the White Paper of the Callaghan government. Bullock, it should be remembered, incorporated the thinking of advanced socialist trade unionists. Jones, Lea, Wedderburn and Jenkins formed the core of the majority group and had a decisive influence on the proposals. It reveals a clear understanding of the need to adapt the proposals to the complexities of British industrial relations and to tailor them to the strengths of the trade union movement. We will consider the

advanced and distinctive elements in the Bullock Report in relation
to the question of how they could further trade union struggle
within the enterprise:
1   Central in this respect is a single channel of representation
based on the trade unions.   This makes possible the harmonisation
of representation with the shop stewards' movement, it draws representatives from organised workers experienced in dealing with
management and it connects them with their colleagues through the
Joint Representation Committee and 'reporting back'.   It means that
struggles, strategy and information can be co-ordinated.   It also
means that representatives have access to national union structures
for information about policies in other companies, advice and so on.
It contrasts clearly with the German system of drawing representatives from a constituency of individual members of the firm, acting
as 'representatives' of labour by reason of being workers themselves.
2   The Joint Representation Committee brings the various unions in
one enterprise together in order to determine the pattern of representation.   This makes possible both the solution to differences in
organisation that has prevented more than a limited range of issues
being taken up in the past, providing a forum for thrashing out a
common strategy discussing demarcation questions and so on, and it
provides a means whereby the more advanced unions and personnel can
attempt to lead the others.
3   The Unitary board adopted in Bullock represents an important
advance over the representation on the supervisory part of the two-
tier board in the TUC's 1974 document on 'Industrial Democracy'.
Doubtless this was proposed to minimise the possible conflict of
roles involved in being directly responsible for decision-making
and policy formulation.   A unitary board has the advantage over a
supervisory board that it formulates policy;   given a substantial
presence and sufficient ability it would be difficult to prevent
union members from sitting on board committees with management.   In
this way differences and policy discussions would become more apparent than when policies or reports on performance are presented to
a supervisory board for approval.   As members of a unitary board,
worker representatives would be responsible for its decisions,
equally however they would have some capacity to influence them and
to fight for alternative policies.   The advantages and disadvantages
are similar to those of left Labour ministers in the cabinet.
    There are a number of evident weaknesses in the Bullock proposals
which must also be recognised:
1   $2x + y$ is a formula which is probably the maximum that could be
got through legislation;   it is clearly not sufficient for control
but probably enough for significant influence, particularly if the
y component were sufficiently broadly based.
2   The limitation to firms with 2,000 employees is clearly unsatisfactory, many smaller firms are also highly unionised and in them
workers often have a better chance of understanding the firm's
workings, controlling the whole process of production and suggesting
policy alternatives than larger companies.
3   The proposals for groups of companies and subsidiaries are de-
fective in many ways, making too many concessions to group management - which is the level most difficult for workers to intervene
in.

Bullock would complement an incomes policy of the type suggested above in three main ways. First, it would provide for the first time in many companies a forum (the JRC) where union members could get together to discuss policy and resolve differences at enterprise level. This is an essential precondition for considering methods of payment, differentials, demarcation, work organisation, etc. It has the advantage of being able to press proposals developed in this forum as company policy through board representation. Second, it provides a means of monitoring management commitments on investment, employment levels, etc. and potentially, of the formation of union personnel at enterprise level with the knowledge and skills to press for alternatives to those proposed by management. Third, it would force at least some unions, through contacts at the base between members and demands for information and guidance, to consider in some depth the economic policies their members should pursue in definite companies and industries. Hopefully this would lead to changes in the nature of political/policy discussions in the unions concerned. Unions also might start placing less reliance on merely pressing governments to remedy unemployment, under-investment and so on by changes in economic management - pressures government can all too easily evade.

Legislation would have served as a catalyst to the unions to enter into this process and as a means of compelling managements to accept union representation. As we have seen, workers' representation does not contradict with 'extended collective bargaining', it is one of the means by which it can be made effective. It will be infinitely more difficult for unions to group together to bargain without Bullock and the scope of the issues entering into bargaining without such co-operation will be severely restricted (one union's commitments cannot bind another). It will be much more difficult to get managements to concede what Bullock would have compelled them to do.

Upper Clyde Shipbuilders, Meriden and the other co-operatives, the Lucas Aerospace workers' struggle for alternative policies and products all show that workers in this country are capable of taking control of their enterprises or taking an active and continuing concern in what they produce and how. Bullock did not fly in the face of all trade union practice, it attempted to build on and extend the most advanced forms of trade union struggle.

A key element in the failure of the Bullock Report and the left TUC thinking behind it to have any real impact in the mass movement is the lack of a theoretical/ideological basis on which to present and justify these proposals. What is required is an alternative conception of the scope and methods of trade union struggle. If unions are to limit themselves to collective bargaining about wages and conditions, no such rationale is necessary, but equally unnecessary is workers' representation. 'Industrial democracy' can only make sense as a means towards definite political objectives. Having shown considerable intelligence in devising the institutions of Bullock the TUC left had nothing to say in their defence. They seem to have left that to Lord Bullock himself. He drew the analogy with political democracy, arguing a historian's parallel with the 1832 and 1867 Reform Act, 'industrial democracy' is part of the gradual process of extension of rights - a recognition of the realities of

an increasingly democratic and egalitarian society. Enfranchisement
will harness the giant, it will channel the real but often destructive power of the workers into a positive direction. Lord
Bullock also probably provided the rationale, the provision of 'a
new legitimacy for the exercise of the management function'
(Bullock, p.28) will reduce conflict and promote industrial efficiency.

'Industrial democracy' is as such a completely incoherent notion.
Management opponents of Bullock seized on this incoherence and challenged the 'democratic' character of proposals based on the trade
unions rather than all employees. 'Democracy' conceived as the realisation of rights must lend to this conclusion. The EEC Green
Paper contends: 'those who will be substantially affected by decisions made by social and political institutions must be involved
in the making of those decisions' (Commission, p.9). But G.D.H.Cole
provided the Labour movement with the means to counter this over
fifty years ago in his 'Social Theory' and other works. Representation is a specific political mechanism, not the realisation of an
individual 'right'. *What* is 'represented' when individual persons
vote and elect a representative to some body? Their wishes or per-
sonalities, which must be diverse? Representation is a method of
providing the personnel of certain bodies, a method with the added
advantage of claiming the legitimacy of endorsement by the electorate (even in local government elections - by a majority of the 20
per cent or so of the electorate who voted). Whilst universal
suffrage is important in certain contexts it cannot serve as an un-
problematic justification for 'industrial' democracy. Here the
question of *what* is to be represented is crucial. The means of representation are designed to serve certain political objectives. As
clearly intended by Jones et al. these objectives are the extension
of the power of the trade unions and the shop stewards. The mechanism of provision of 'representative' personnel must therefore be
based on the specific constituency which is to be represented. This
'constituency', organised workers and shop stewards, has definite
means of producing personnel for the bodies in question who are capable of representing the policies agreed on by the unions at
company level. The 'electorate', through organised bodies of shop
stewards and the JRC, stand in a definite relation to these representatives. 'Industrial democracy' cannot be even handed, it either
extends the unions' powers or it confers a 'new legitimacy' on the
management as it does in the Federal Republic of Germany. In
failing to recognise this and insisting that there is no one form of
democracy, that it is always a means of political organisation adjusted to certain objectives, the architects of the Bullock Report
left themselves open to the charge of being 'undemocratic'.

Further, whilst the TUC document and Bullock do present
'industrial democracy' as part of a growing process of trade union
involvement in planning and administration, of co-operation with the
state and the CBI, they can only justify the proposals for representation on company boards by reference to a 'gap' at this point
in the network of means of influence and consultation (Bullock,
p.24). In part this absence of objectives is reasonable because the
policies to be pursued in this new form of struggle cannot be given
in advance and will depend on what conditions unions encounter and

the policies they adopt. But it can hardly appease the left or
rouse the masses. I have attempted to argue that only by seeing
Bullock in the context of an incomes policy and in relation to the
problems of extended collective bargaining can its political importance to the left be appreciated. It is a means of allowing the
shop stewards' movement to adapt to the necessities of incomes
policies without being wholly or partly demobilised. It is a means
to extend the economic and political scope of trade union struggle
at enterprise level. It offers, therefore, the prospect of a mass
movement less committed to immediate and defensive struggles and
able to exert new kinds of policy pressures on the national union
organisations and the Labour Party.

The argument so far presented will no doubt appear to be a
curious one for a Marxist to adopt. There has always been a strong
body of opinion in Marxism which has argued that trade union
struggles are necessarily limited in scope and that workers can
only wrest control from the capitalists by means of a socialist
revolution. The majority of Marxists have always been strongly
anti-syndicalist. These positions are based on three main arguments
which I will deal with in reverse order of validity:
1 the thesis of the 'despotism of capital';
2 Kautsky and Lenin's critique of 'trade union consciousness;
3 that enterprise level decisions cannot secure effects at the
level of the economy.

The notion of the 'despotism of capital' is widely used among
modern Marxists. It means that capitalists and management enjoy the
right to dispose of the means of production as they wish because
they are private property in their possession. Further, that on the
basis of this property capitalists can compel workers (who lack
possession of the means of production) to submit to their direction,
to accept the forms and conditions of work the owners and their representatives consider necessary. These powers are limited only by
the resistance of the organised working class. A clear expression
of this view is given by some German theorists of the state: in the
factory 'Labour power counts no longer as the fine free legal
subject but rather as a factor of production which the property
owner can do as he wishes' (Blanke et al., p.128). Similarly, Nicos
Poulantzas in a widely read text, 'Classes in Contemporary
Capitalism', refers to the 'despotism of the factory', that is, the
authoritarian direction of the working class by capital in the place
of production 'is the form taken by political relations in the extended production of social classes, actually on the site where the
relations of production and exploitation are constructed' (p.229).
The organisation of work in the factory is a necessary part of
capitalist class relations, and Poulantzas considers engineers,
technicians and foremen as petty bourgeois servants of bourgeois
power, maintaining the social division of labour necessary to
capital.

Such positions, if correct, severely restrict the scope of trade
union struggle. The problem with such positions, particularly the
former, is that it considers property *rights* to be given in form,
as an expression of the real economic relations of possession in
the capitalist mode of production. But forms of property and the
rights attaching to them are constituted in law. The rights of

property can be changed by legislation and that change enforced,
given the political and organisational means to do so. For example,
the Town and Country Planning Acts, severely restrict the freedom of
a land owner to 'do as he wishes'. The legal capacity of the
factory owner to 'do as he wishes' has been restricted since the
introduction of the Factory Acts in the nineteenth century and has
been increasingly restricted in different ways for different reasons
ever since. Legislation to limit shareholders' rights and give
workers' representatives on company boards is neither inherently
impossible nor is it necessarily ineffective.

To treat rights as the recognition of the realities of possession
supposes that there *are* settled realities of possession. But the
capacity of a management to enforce *any* decision is not given. It
is possible to cite well-known cases in British industry of proposed
changes in plant organisation and methods of working, from the
installation of a new process to the removal of the tea lady, which
became impossible to implement and have had to be abandoned or
revised. The thesis of 'despotism' is in the context of British
industry an absurdity. To take what might appear to be a strong
counter-example, an authoritarian boss able to beat down workers'
demands for union recognition with the aid of police and courts,
solicitous to enforce his rights to enjoy his property. George Ward
was able to survive unprecedented Labour movement opposition at
Grunwick, partly by outside financial aid, partly by police support,
but mainly because a substantial part of the original work force was
willing (for whatever reason) to continue and to face the picket
lines. Grunwick demonstrates neither the despotic rights of property nor the inherent realities of despotic capitalist possession,
it shows that rights and capacities depend on the outcomes of
struggles and those struggles depend on the forces in play.

There is no necessary 'despotism of capital'; existing capitalist property relations and forms of work organisation can be and are
being modified by legislation, state enforcement and trade union
practice. Good current examples are the Employment Protection Act
and the Health and Safety Act. But to do so, to extend control by
the work-force from the capacity to thwart or modify management decisions to the capacity to direct the enterprise towards certain
positive objectives, requires that the workers increasingly come to
take responsibility for the continuance of the enterprise. Taking
over functions hitherto exercised by specialist managers involves a
commitment to running the enterprise, it also involves some practice
of co-operation and bargaining with management over the way it is
run. This changes radically the nature of the bargaining process
and the objectives of trade union practice.

It may be argued, however, that the trade unions as organisations
are incapable of giving rise to such practices. Trade union
practice and consciousness are necessarily limited to the struggle
for wages and conditions. Karl Kautsky argued that socialist
consciousness was something 'introduced into the proletarian class
struggle from without'. By means of their own experience alone the
workers were capable of producing no more than trade union
consciousness, a form of *bourgeois* ideology. Socialism is the
product of theoretical work and scientific comprehension of modern
society on the part of a radical section of the bourgeois intelli-

gentsia. Trade union consciousness is merely concerened to bargain
for a better price for labour power within existing conditions. It
is a form of bourgeois ideology which makes possible an improvement
in the terms of sale of a commodity, labour power. Kautsky was
thereby opposing Bernstein's revisionism; Bernstein having argued
that the non-revolutionary character of the English labour organisations demonstrated that the workers did not become more revolutionary as capitalism became more advanced. Trade unions for
Kautsky could *never* be a revolutionary force. But even the most
casual re-reading of this ideological conflict at the turn of the
century should remove any question of its pertinence to current
debates.

Rehashing the critique of 'economism' cannot serve to criticise
the type of demands and practices being proposed here, precisely
because what is proposed is a shift *away* from bargaining about wages
towards struggling for a measure of control of enterprise policies.
'Economism' as Lenin argued in 'What is to be Done?' is a politics
within the trade union movement and not the necessary form of enter-
prise-level politics. Unlike Kautsky, who does seem to have considered trade union struggles to be necessarily limited, Lenin
thought it necessary that the workers' movement at enterprise level
go beyond limited economic demands, 'economism' limited the spontaneous efforts of the workers themselves.

The trade unions as workers' organisations are not limited to
'economic' (wages and conditions) demands or to 'political' demands
which merely concern their freedom to bargain. Demands to determine
enterprise policy and to control the organisation of work are not
'economic' merely because they concern organisations which produce
commodities; such demands would lead to a·wide-ranging change in
the conditions of political power and in the capabilities of the
workers' movement. Struggles are not 'economistic' because their
site or point of reference is the enterprise. Trade unions and the
shop stewards' movement have no given character as political organisations and forces. Trade unions are political organisations which
involve ordinary working people because they concern issues which
directly affect their lives. Wages and working conditions have, for
that reason, always been a central part of their demands. They
differ from other political organisations in that they draw their
members on the basis of occupation and generally organise them on
the basis of the enterprise in which they work. Trade unions, like
certain 'issue' organisations, tenants groups, etc., but on a much
larger scale and with a more systematic organisation, are vital to
socialist politics because they continue to draw in and train ordinary workers in political skills and objectives. The Labour Party
has virtually ceased to do this, and mass apathy towards national
political parties has steadily grown since 1945. The Labour Party
organisation is substantially staffed by people who entered the
Labour movement as trade unionists. Trade unionists and the shop
stewards' movement are important because they are capable of as-
similating new issues and forms of struggle, reinvigorating the mass
movement and putting definite pressures on the Labour Party. This
is one basis on which the composition of politics and practice of
that party might be changed. The current need is to build on the
advanced forms of thinking and practice produced by the trade union

movement itself, the IWC, Bullock, Lucas Aerospace, Meriden, UCS, etc., for the left to support these forms of practical leadership and draw out their implications. On the contrary, the mass of the Marxist left has chosen to sneer.

It should be clear that I am not advocating a form of syndicalism. Trade unions are *national* organisations, and the campaigns considered here (incomes policy, workers' representation) require the co-operation of governments and legislation. The Marxist critique of syndicalism is quite correct in that struggles at enterprise level cannot of themselves resolve questions that need to be settled at the level of the state (this applies equally well to conditions of the dominance of parliamentary democracy as it does to a revolutionary situation: strikes are not legislation, occupations are not election victories, etc.). Likewise, even if workers' representatives were to gain control of most large enterprises or if they were converted into co-operatives, then decisions which favoured the workers in each of those enterprises (increasing investment, preserving jobs, etc.) would not necessarily produce economically viable results or results which benefited the working people as a whole. The economy is not simply the sum of its enterprises, and enterprises, as independent centres of decision in specific conditions, are not automatically constrained to make decisions and act in ways which are compatible one with another. Securing the jobs of workers in employment in existing enterprises does nothing for the unemployed; improving the market position of Chrysler does nothing to resolve the problems of British Leyland, and so on. This criticism of the economics of syndicalism-co-operativism is quite correct. National economic policies are required, including protection of the public *from* the actions of worker-managed enterprises (employees are not repositories of all that is wise and good). Unionised employees in firms with more than 500 workers are neither a majority of the Labour force nor of the population: millions of people who are not wage workers - pensioners, housewives, the unemployed, the sick, small traders and craftsmen - need economic policies too. But strengthening the bargaining position of workers on a wider range of issues is not intended by the advanced elements in the trade unions or any other serious advocate as an overall economic programme. Workers' representation provides a forum of struggle and a means to articulate issues which can find no expression in wage bargaining. In conjunction with an incomes policy it provides a mechanism whereby the unions and the workers' movement can both make a real contribution to the position of the low paid and those not in employment, struggle for demands which improve the conditions of workers in enterprises and pursue, as a consequence of struggles at enterprise level, national policies of a socialist character. The tragedy is that the Marxist left has actively worked with the forces opposing these advanced demands emerging from the workers' movement.

POSTSCRIPT - THE ORGANISATIONAL LIMITATIONS OF BRITISH TRADE UNIONS

In the main body of the paper essentialistic arguments within Marxism as to the necessary limitations of trade union struggle have

been challenged. Arguments of the kind advanced by Kautsky assume
that the unions are assigned a particular function by the capitalist
mode of production (bargaining over wages) and a horizon of consciousness set by that function. This was countered by contending
that there is no general 'logic' to capitalist production which
assigns the trade unions and enterprise struggle a particular set
of objectives, mode of organisation or form of action. Union
structure, practice and ideology is a specific level, it differs
between national capitalisms and even industries within them, and
it affects the form of political action and effectiveness of unions
as organisations. The object of this challenge is not to promote a
rival essentialism, syndicalism or workerist spontanism, which privileges the enterprise level and mass action as the only revolutionary path.

Strategies, such as those advanced by the Labour left or the
Communist Party, which accord an important place to workers' representation or extended collective bargaining and 'industrial regeneration' as an element or condition of socialist advance all involve a
change in both the scope of the objectives and the arenas of trade
union struggle in this country. This change is not a peculiarity of
the position advanced in the essay, which stresses the role of
workers' representation, it is also the case with positions like the
CPGB's which, whilst hostile to Bullock, stress the extension of the
issues over which bargaining takes place. Long-run negotiation with
companies, employers' federations, state agencies and other unions
are implied in these strategies. Such objectives and forms of
struggle will stretch the existing organisational capacity of trade
unions and workers' organisation at enterprise level, it will bring
policy up against the organisational limits of British trade unions
in their current form. For to insist that there are no *essential*
limits to the form and content of trade union struggle is not to say
that in any definite case there are *no limits*. Struggle is not
limited by some inherent logic of capitalism but by the *specific
forms in which that struggle has been organised,* by unions of a
particular type, shop stewards' committees, etc. The way unions
are organised, the economic and industrial conditions in which they
operate, and so on, constrain and create real difficulties for a
policy which tries to advance beyond short-term bargaining for wages
and personal benefits. Analysis of these limits is necessary in
order to see the ways in which they might be overcome and the least
constraining directions of advance.

There are four main limitations imposed by present trade union
structure, practice and ideology to the changes towards the new objectives and forms of struggle we have considered in the main essay.
1 The primary ideology* which serves to formulate objectives and
the conduct of the struggle for their realisation - 'bargaining' -
limits (to the extent that its terms are adhered to) what can be
fought over and won at enterprise level.

To begin with it is necessary to insist that 'bargaining' is not
a coherent and monolithic ideology, its terms are in consequence
difficult to define although it does have definite and marked

---

*   Ideology is conceived here à la Althusser as inscribed in a
    practice, as a discourse/practice.

effects in its organisation of practice. 'Bargaining' is a conception of the practice of trade unions as sanctioned negotiation
to achieve an agreed relationship between hours and conditions of
work and the benefits obtained. That practice is conceived on the
analogy of a commercial contract or a treaty between two independent
powers, central to it is a specifiable quid pro quo. It should be
noted that this has little in common with the Marxist concept of
commodity exchange, rather 'bargaining' stresses the diplomacy of
'industrial relations' skills and the extra-economic sanctioning of
the terms of agreement by force. 'Bargaining' cannot be regarded as
a commodity ideology reflecting the form of value, but a complex and
incoherent articulation of the realities of trade union practice.
Labour power is not regarded as a commodity with a definite 'value',
wages are regarded as a function of bargaining strength and skill.

Personal benefits of members can easily be accommodated in the
notion of 'bargaining'. It is less easy to 'bargain' for long-run
changes in the policy or the working practice of an enterprise, for
legislation or government action. Such broader objectives tend to
merge the form and means of enterprise and trade union struggle with
other forms of political campaigning and of seeking to determine
policy within organisations. They involve a move from a conception
of negotiation between two independent parties, each with its powers
and prerogatives, capable of making or breaking an agreement, to
that of different 'sides' within an organisation struggling to
determine the direction of its policy, whether that organisation
be the state or a company. The consequences of that policy cannot
be specified or traded over in the way a wage deal or a manning
agreement can. Policy cannot be viewed as a succession of separate
'deals', but as a continuing commitment. Such broader objectives
involve *sustained* action and mobilisation, and the articulation of
a defensible policy in the form of an industry or company strategy
or a political programme.

'Bargaining' has seldom involved this kind of defensible
rationale. The 'case' for a particular round of negotiations is
often little more than a pretext composed of ad hoc arguments
suitable for a claim, and it may differ radically from the case advanced in previous or subsequent claims. However, it should be
recognised that forms of pursuing wage claims are not for ever given
and depend on the political and economic conditions in which they
are settled. For example, the Heath Government's incomes policy had
the interesting effect of making wage claims much more of a matter
of winning national political conviction for special treatment
against the government's policy; thus the case made out for special
treatment for the miners in 1973-4 was much better presented than
are most bargaining positions.

'Bargaining' has depended on the calculation of the short-term
balance of forces, rather than on considerations of the viability
of a policy proposal or whether a campaign for it can be sustained.
This calculation of advantage suited traditional wage negotiations
well enough. It cannot operate very effectively in questions of
national economic policy or company strategy. Union officials and
workers are ill-equipped by reason of the forms of calculation involved in the practice of 'bargaining' to handle broader questions
of policy. Union research staffs and the training of members in

techniques of management calculation have been neglected areas. For
example, the miners' case was ably prepared with substantial help
from Ruskin College, but clearly neither that institution nor the
TUC has the capacity to function as a trade union 'general staff'.
Workers start out from a position of inferiority if they cease to
rely exclusively on the notion of negotiation between two 'independent' parties, on the calculation of advantage and the trial of
strength characteristic of 'bargaining', and instead seek to negotiate on long-term issues of policy or seek to participate in
management to determine those issues. Indeed, the dominance of
'bargaining' calculation will lead most active trade unionists to
be hostile to such extensions of the issues and forums of struggle
precisely because they cannot specify their advantage in terms of
an immediate quid pro quo.
2 The primary *means* of struggle - strikes, disruption, non-co-
operation - are effective as immediate sanctions to secure material
gains or in defensive struggles to block unacceptable innovation.
They are sanctions because they render impossible an adequate level
of performance of the activity subject to dispute: be it production, distribution, services, management, etc. But as such they
do not provide sufficient means of struggle for *transforming* the
administration or decision-making in enterprises, they leave these
powers in other hands and merely seek to act on those hands externally. This limitation to these *means* of struggle is evident
in cases of the winding-up of enterprises; workers opposing redundancy have been forced to adopt different means - occupations,
work-ins and extended political lobbying - either, to replace the
management themselves, and/or, to secure a political intervention
which does so. Extended collective bargaining, securing appropriate
contents in planning agreements, etc., cannot rely on the sanction
of strikes alone, but needs to attempt to acquire managerial
functions and to enter directly into political campaigning with
alternative company policies. Lucas Aerospace is a case in point,
workers accepting the need to make management decisions in a different way and fight for their implementation.
    The more struggles concern the co-operation of workers in de-
cision-making about enterprise policy the less effective do strikes
become: decisions about the future are conditional and are implemented over time, strikes rely for their sanctioning power on being
damaging in the short run. Strikes are a weapon which may *supplement* other modes of securing these objectives at certain crucial
junctures. Strikes can be effective in deciding issues like wage
claims because their disruptive results are direct and immediate.
It is essential in a continuing enterprise that they be of limited
duration and not too frequent periodicity. It is impossible to
direct the policy of an enterprise by the external sanction on its
makers of a semi-permanent strike.
3 It is a truism that British unions are organised around trades
and workers are employed by enterprises, but these 'obvious' circumstances have important consequences. (i) In the absence of industry
unions it follows that the particular organisations representing the
workers in any given enterprise depend for their presence on the
occupations relevant to that activity and on the agreements made
between the management and particular unions. The unions, as

workers' organisations, have at best a limited capacity to determine
the form of their representation of the work-force: which unions
are present in an enterprise and what proportion of its work-force
they act for. (ii) Despite wage negotiations at national level,
agreements between unions and employers' federations, and so on,
workers have a contract of employment with a particular enterprise
and are largely dependent on their continuing to have a job in that
enterprise to be represented by a trade union.

Unions are organisations of a specific type, representative of
workers in respect of certain objectives in a particular way. This
specifity is no invariant product of capitalism, equally it has
effects and these cannot be transformed without appropriate
practices.

The pattern of representation of workers is affected by the
occupational structure and the distribution of different categories
of workers to firms. Agreements between unions, mergers and 'general' unions modify this proposition to some extent but do not erase
its general significance. Organisational formation and change on
the part of unions has been mainly in reaction to changing patterns
of occupation and changes in the character of enterprises (growth,
merger, etc.). It is only relatively recently (say, since the last
war) that the unions have on any large scale been able to successfully fight management-directed changes in technique, manning levels
and employment patterns. Far from rationalising the structure of
representation this new power has served to rigidify it, preserving
within enterprises organisations of work and grounds for union
presence which would otherwise have disappeared.

Unions as organs of workers' representation have grown up in an
unplanned way, often competing with one another, and each exclusively concentrating on the fortunes of its particularly defined cohort
of members. This means that the structure of the trade union movement, reflecting more or less adequately the successive phases of
the organisation of work since the nineteenth century, often representing the existing divisions of workers in enterprises in inadequate ways which bear little relation to the realities of the production process, is ill placed to serve as the vehicle for the
radical *transformation* of the organisation of work. It represents
a real obstacle to any policy or practice of extending workers'
control to forms of technique and division of labour, unless that
control were merely preservative of certain existing patterns. The
existing patterns of occupations and their employment by enterprises
will be defended by union organisations not least because *as organisations* they have a vested interest in the existing system which
provides the basis on which they represent their members. Change
the occupational structure away from differentiation of grades and
skills and certain unions are faced with the extinction of their
basis of representation.

This way in which representation is patterned means that union
organisations exist to defend both their members' current occupations and their employment in them in a particular enterprise.
Certain unions (particularly craft and technical unions) would undoubtedly resist proposals for changes in the working methods of
enterprises even if the proposals were supported by the majority
of workers and their own members in that enterprise. Further, they

may have effective sanctions they can impose on their members, expulsion and consequent inability to move to another enterprise with which their union has a closed-shop agreement or the ability to exclude workers it opposes by informal means. Also in the enterprise, its members may perform a vital function which it is not immediately possible to devolve onto others and be therefore able to paralyse a plant or organisation. The danger of 'managerial' unions pursuing the latter sanction is a very real one.

Trade union structure, therefore, tends to limit the flexibility of these organs of representation to respond to new strategic objectives that might be actively supported by many of their members, given the right leadership and conditions. 'General' unions are not necessarily a way out of this difficulty. To the extent that they are federations of particular occupations they can be stubborn defenders of existing organisations of work, or they can be caught in the contradictions between the different interests of sections of their members, for example, when the dockers attempting to preserve employment in traditional methods of goods handling picketed the Midland Cold Storage depot (had they been successful other members of the same union would have been made redundant).

4   The problems raised by trade union organisational structure are reinforced by the relative weakness of inter-union institutions which might serve as vehicles for co-operation over policy, propaganda for change, and a means for reconciling differences.

Shop stewards' committees are a valuable and vital form of inter-union co-operation at enterprise level. But they are by no means universal, and are often feared and opposed by union officials. They are particularly difficult to develop and to sustain coordinated policies at group level in multi-location, multi-product firms organised in subsidiaries. This type of organisation has become increasingly important as a result of the merger boom, no respecter of organisational or industrial logic. Group level decisions are crucial for questions like investment and its location, product lines and manning policy. Such questions require coordinated union policy and action in order for workers' objectives to be pursued. Moreover, even when a policy is agreed on by the immediate representatives of the workers in an enterprise it may not receive the backing of some of the unions involved, and the policy may be challenged within the union by members in other enterprises who are or feel threatened by the policy.

Trades councils have never served and were never intended to serve as organs of comprehensive representation of the unions in a locality or as inter-union decision-making bodies. The basis on which members are appointed is inadequately representative for them to have either the knowledge or the legitimacy to make decisions resolving disputes between unions or their members in local firms.

The TUC is representative of union *organisations* not of workers in particular enterprises. The TUC has restricted itself to a very limited role in mediating between member unions in dispute. It could hardly attempt to arbitrate in a dispute between an affiliated union and some of its members. Nevertheless, the TUC has been an important vehicle for promotion of policies transcending wage bargaining as its support for a number of key measures like the Employment Protection Act illustrates. The TUC leadership is no

simple reflector of majority attitudes among union organisational
leaderships or the rank and file, as its recent advocacy of Bullock
and its support for the Social Contract bear witness. Its line is
very dependent on the kind of leaders who emerge in the major
unions.

But, in addition, its policy is influenced by the arenas in which
it acts as the collective voice of the trade unions. It has become
drawn into a process of consultation on state and industrial policy
often referred to as 'tripartism'. As part of this process it has
become a distinct organ of policy and articulation of interests in
its own right. Its role is increasingly to push for overall
economic and social policies in national level negotiations with
the CBI and state agencies. It enjoys the advantage of direct consultative links with members of the NEC and Labour cabinet. It directly participates in state sponsored forums like NEDDY and in
state agencies like MSC and ACAS. This range of connections and
representative role forces its leaders and officials to concern
themselves with issues the leaderships of particular unions can
often ignore. It also exposes them to the need to present a credible political/economic argument rather than merely rely on 'bargaining'. The move away from a mere 'shopping list' in return for concessions on wages levels, etc., has been slow to emerge. It requires a policy capable of being agreed on and forced through at
national level. The close collaboration between the TUC leaders
and the NEC in the period 1973-4 produced a definite economic strategy, whatever its defects. The TUC remains committed to national
policy agreements (including questions of wages), it will continue
to attempt to obtain them and is constrained by the degree to which
it can guarantee the compliance of member unions.

However, although the TUC has been forced into a calculation of
national economic policy the form of that calculation has been to
concentrate on general macro-economic measures which appear to
benefit all workers and unions like increased public spending, reduction in unemployment, agreements by the CBI to increased investment, etc. When it has proposed measures for particular industries
or enterprises these have been of a defensive or conservative kind,
preserving existing jobs and firms through subsidies or other support, or the taking of the enterprises in question into public
ownership. If radical workers' participation schemes and/or a
strategy of 'industrial regeneration', which instead of working
through some inducement to increase aggregate investment tried to
deal with particular problem industries, were to become a reality,
then this policy stance of the TUC would have to change. It would
have to decide whether or not to back policies for particular enterprises. Policies which in reorganising firms in pursuit of greater
industrial efficiency and exports might damage certain groups of
workers' interests. Calculations of this kind and decisions of this
kind are needed to counter Britain's industrial malaise. It is
possible that the TUC might serve as the vehicle for promoting their
acceptance among unions and their members.

This discussion of limitations has been necessarily negative.
What it does point to, however, is that the sources of change in the
objectives and methods of struggle at enterprise level must be
sought largely outside trade union organisations. These organisa-

tions as they stand are not the best representative framework
through which to advance the types of change in forms of struggle
advocated in the main essay. They are not the only possible framework, three others seem more fruitful.

1   The extension of shop stewards committees and the scope of the
issues they raise. The major innovations in forms and issues of
struggle in recent years have come from such inter-union enterprise-
based organisations: occupations and work-ins, co-operatives,
alternative company plans, and so on. Workers organised in this way
have had and will have to appeal both to their unions and also to
wider political forces for the forms of support necessary to further
their action.

2   Legislation. The implementation of Bullock, as we have seen,
would have acted as a spur to the development of enterprise-based
inter-union policies. Struggle at enterprise level on issues which
are wider than wages and conditions can be extended and fostered
most effectively by appropriate legislation and administrative back-
up, something which can only come through parliament. Supporting
the development of certain kinds of struggle at enterprise level
does not mean fighting for them at that level alone. It also involves winning the battle of ideas and policies inside the Labour
Party once again, revitalising and revising the policies of 1973-4
which were forfeited by default.

3   The TUC is often portrayed on the left as a major source of
right-wing pressure to hobble mass militancy and as an arm of the
state in the workers' movement. The TUC is neither unitary in the
policies it fosters nor invariably successful in securing their
implementation. There is no intention here to suggest that the TUC
is an inherently 'left' institution. However, much of the
'evidence' cited to demonstrate that it is inherently reactionary
rests on the assumption that unrestrained militancy on wage issues
is progressive. Its co-operation with the state in trying to limit
unofficial strikes and its acceptance of incomes policies are the
main basis for this assessment. TUC attitudes towards rank and file
action have not been merely restrictive, it has supported actions by
shop stewards' committees against redundancies and closures, for
example, at UCS. Its opposition to some of the more negative and
short-sighted aspects of rank and file action can only be considered
rightist and wrong if one considers a revolutionary breakdown of
capitalist relations is possible in the near future. The ultra-
left, unlike the TUC, refuse to consider deficiencies in industrial
discipline and restrictive work practices as something which must be
changed. Restrictive attitudes towards work organisation, reinforced by strong plant-level organisation are a major stumbling
block to any strategy of 'industrial regeneration'. We are faced
with the paradox of an obstacle to a widely supported left strategy
being created by the practices of workers' movement itself and reinforced by the left's support for these practices. The TUC element
on the Bullock Committee clearly thought that workers' representation would be progressive in forcing workers themselves to face this
problem and to co-operate with management in resolving it. The
question of productivity and restrictive practices is a nettle that
any 'alternative' economic strategy will have to grasp. Recognition
of these difficulties and a willingness to raise these unpopular
questions is not reactionary.

TUC policy tended in a leftward direction in the Jones era. But the TUC remains very much a law unto itself. The ways in which its leadership and line are determined are neither obvious nor readily open to popular pressure. In this respect it is probably no less difficult to influence than the policy of the Labour cabinet.

NOTES

1 This essay presupposes no *general* theory of the determinants of wages. It does not argue that wages are determined by the cost of reproduction of labour power nor does it argue that they are determined by the marginal productivity of the factor labour. It rejects both of these general economic theories of the determination of wages. The wage structure of any given country is not an effect, however imperfect, of the workings of general economic laws but a 'synthesis of many determinations', some of the most important of which are not 'economic' at all. Barbara Wootton's 'Social Foundations of Wages Policy' demonstrates the complexity and economic arbitrariness of the British wage structure. This is not to say wages are undetermined, merely that these factors are variable and situational. Space prohibits the expansion and demonstration of this point.
2 Following the big boom in membership up to about 1920, trade union numbers were falling in the late 1920s and 1930s. Only in the 1950s and 1960s did they rise sharply again. Obviously the direction of membership trends affects the capacity to bargain and the attitudes of leaderships. This is particularly true where unions have to bid for members against other unions; they will tend both to be more responsive to members' demands and constrained to equal or better a 'norm' of gains for their members. This has clearly been important in staff unions with the Association of Scientific, Technical and Managerial Staff leading the way, and in the motor industry where the engineering and transport unions have been locked in conflict to become the dominant union.

REFERENCES

BLANKE, JURGENS and KASTENDIEK, H., On the Current Discussion of the Analysis of the Form and Function of the Bourgeois State, in 'State and Capital', ed. J.Holloway and S.Picciotto, Arnold, London, 1978.
BULLOCK, LORD, 'Report of the Committee of Inquiry on Industrial Democracy', HMSO, London, 1977, Cmnd 6706.
CLEGG, HUGH, 'How to Run an Incomes Policy', Heinemann, London, 1971.
COLE, G.D.H., 'Social Theory', Methuen, London, 1923.
DONOVAN, LORD, 'Report of the Royal Commission on Trade Unions and Employers Associations', HMSO, London, 1968, Cmnd 3623.
ELLIOT, JOHN, 'Conflict or Cooperation', Kogan Page, London, 1978.
GRIFFITH, J.A.G., 'The Politics of the Judiciary', Fontana, London, 1977.
HOLLAND, STUART and ORMEROD, PAUL, The 5 per cent non-solution, 'Guardian', 12 October 1978.

LENIN, V.J., 'What is to be Done?' (1905), 'Collected Works', vol.5, Foreign Languages Publishing House, Moscow.
LUCAS AEROSPACE COMBINE SHOP STEWARDS COMMITTEE, 'Lucas an Alternative Plan', IWC pamphlet no.54, Nottingham.
POULANTZAS, NICOS, 'Classes in Contemporary Capitalism', New Left Books, London, 1975.
TRADES UNION CONGRESS, 'Industrial Democracy', TUC, London, 1974.
'White Paper on Industrial Democracy', HMSO, London, 1978, Cmnd 7231.
WOOTTON, BARBARA, 'The Social Foundations of Wages Policy', Allen & Unwin, London, 1955, second edn, 1962.
WOOTTON, BARBARA, 'Incomes Policy', Davis-Poynter, London, 1974.

Chapter 5

THE SOCIAL CONTRACT AND SOCIALIST POLICY
David Purdy

1 THE INEVITABILITY OF INCOMES POLICIES

(i) The rise of the working class

Underlying the immediate economic and political pressures which have
driven successive post-war British governments to introduce incomes
policies of one sort or another has been the growth in the power of
the working class. Since the outbreak of the Second World War the
working class has exercised a power within the British political
system far more commensurate with its numbers than in the previous
history of capitalism. It was during the war years that the
'entrenched gradualist dynamic' which David Fernbach (1) has argued
is characteristic of the course of the class struggle in the advanced capitalist democracies, can be said finally to have dug
itself in.

The years 1918-26 had witnessed a temporary deviation from the
pattern of active reform (or, if you prefer, passive revolution)
laid down by Lloyd George before the First World War, whilst during
the Depression state policy stagnated as capital underwent its own
spontaneous restructuring. But from the formation of the war
coalition in May 1940 down to 1947-8, the reforming tide ran more
strongly than ever before or since. The reforms of this period we
were, it is true, backed by a broad social and political alliance,
cutting across class boundaries and political parties, obviously
weighted towards the left, but with at least the passive approval
of the right. Nevertheless, the central effect of the people's war
was to inscribe popular aspirations (which at that time overwhelm-
ingly meant *working-class* aspirations - the equation is significant)
deep into the functioning of Britain's economy and system of government.

For practical purposes the trade unions accepted the logic of
their defeat in the 1926 General Strike. They abandoned revolutionary dreams of overthrowing capitalism, or even of extracting concessions from a position of defiant social isolation. Instead they
secured an influence on the main directions and emphases of state
policy whatever party was in power. At its weakest union influence
has since been restricted to a mere negative ability to constrain

state policy, to fix the parameters of what is politically possible. The more active union-government collaboration possible under a Labour government has opened up a more positive field for union influence. But the essential point is that the qualitative shift in the class balances which occurred during the war has proved to be lasting.

From a long-term perspective the working class's wartime advance can be seen as a natural, if much delayed, consequence of the successive extensions of the franchise and the associated achievement of basic trade union freedoms during the nineteenth and early twentieth centuries. But it is significant that the decisive step forward in working-class influence on industrial, social and economic policy came during the Second World War. For the precipitating factor was not so much votes as the simple fact that the working class controlled the instrumentalities of victory in a war where success depended on the total mobilisation and co-ordination of *both* military *and* civilian effort. In this odd sense the old syndicalist view of the road to power was vindicated. The Labour Party's landslide victory at the polls in 1945 was an ex-post tribute to the impossibility of winning the war without the active co-operation of the workers and their organisations: 1940 rather than 1945 was the moment of transition.   This dependent position of the state vis-à-vis the working class in an advanced capitalist democracy has repeatedly made itself felt during Britain's post-war history: most recently and dramatically in the miners' strike and the 'Who governs Britain?' election in February 1974.

It is this shift in class relations which sets up pressure on governments to formulate a policy for the development of pay in the economy as a whole.   Whether they deal with the unions at arms' length or in close consultation, government have to take account of their views and anticipate their reactions.   What is not possible is to ignore them.   Given this it is inevitable that a considerable part of any government's efforts will be devoted to working out a modus vivendi with the unions.   The confrontations of the 1970s merely confirm negatively the fact which the entire pattern of government and administration since 1940 has been designed to accommodate: that no government can rule without preserving an irreducible minimum of union consent.   This is not just a matter of fear of defeat under the parliamentary rules of the game.   Indeed, at times there may be considerable short-term political advantages for a government which is seen to be standing up to union power.   It should not be forgotten that the Conservatives came within an ace of winning the February 1974 election;   and in the early months of 1979 contrived to call the shots from the Opposition benches as the Labour government vacillated between helpless inaction, reluctant concession and dark threats in the face of the upsurge of wage militancy.   The point is simply that the state's dependence on union consent determines the imperatives of effective government.   A consistent policy of rejecting the unions as even junior partners in the business of government would release the unions from any social obligation.   It would ensure that sooner or later their organised sectional power would be used, crudely or subtly, openly or below the surface, to block and frustrate attempts to cope with the economy's problems.

As long as governments keep open their lines of communication
with the unions over the general course of economic and social
policy, the agenda of discussion is bound to include pay issues.
Discussions are not similarly bound to culminate in agreement, let
alone an explicit, formal pay policy. But the mere exchange of
views and intentions constitutes a preliminary form of negotiation
in which each side moves closer to defining its economic targets and
the methods it proposes to use to achieve them. Failure to agree on
a policy for pay simply means that the government side will endeavour to achieve its targets, including a target or preferred
range for the general level of pay settlements, by other indirect
means – principally by monetary and fiscal policy and behind-the-
scenes pressures on negotiators, particularly in the public sector.

In this sense monetarism is not an alternative to a policy for
pay, but, to paraphrase Clausewitz, the continuation of pay policy
by other means. The danger with an outright repudiation of pay
policy and the espousal of monetarist policies as a superior option,
rather than a regrettable second best, is, as the modernising wing
of the Conservative Party recognises, that primary reliance on this
method of influencing the movement of pay, would in effect make not
only pay, but also all the other main aspects of economic policy
non-negotiable. It would bypass the informal or semi-formal
machinery of union-government collaboration which has grown up since
the war. The risk of such a step is precisely that it would symbolise the breakdown of that consent without which, we have argued,
effective government within a democratic framework becomes impossible. This is true even when, as in 1978, the declared policy of the
unions is also opposed to formal limits on voluntary collective
bargaining over pay. In practice support for such a position never
entails endorsement of the monetarist alternative.

Thus the problem which has faced British governments in their
attempts to manage and preserve the existing social order has been
defined by the necessity in a democratic system not to forfeit union
consent. In a very general, epochal sense which is independent of
local variations in union power from one country to another, this
problem has confronted all the advanced capitalist states in the
post-war period. But elsewhere, because of comparative national
historical factors affecting the continuity, membership, organisational strength, freedoms and rights, internal unity, social status,
ideological formation and political weight of each country's trade
union movement, governments have been less constrained in their
ability (and willingness) to deal with the problem. (For a brief
international comparative analysis of these factors see D.Purdy
(2)).

Superficially this problem is compounded by the difficulty of
persuading a movement which was built up to meet defensive needs,
to assume co-responsibility for economic management. The tensions
and hesitations generated by the conflict within the workers' movement between a sectional-defensive and a governmental outlook are
reflected in the alternating on-off experience of British incomes
policies. But at a deeper level this difficulty makes it easier to
contain working-class power. For it ensures that the responsibility
and power of initiative for coping with the consequences of unconstrained sectionalism rest securely with the state. And in the long

run it is likely that the characteristic British cycle of tough pay
limits followed by friction, relaxation and relapse into 'free'
collective bargaining, will be weakened by a social learning mechanism. Conversely, this same difficulty is only superficially ad-
vantageous to those who wish to transform advanced capitalism by
strengthening the communist and democratic tendencies within it.
Purely sectional-defensive struggle can only create problems for
capital and the state: it supplies no means of resolving those
problems. It ultimately benefits neither capitalism nor communism,
but boosts the growth of the state's responsibility and power. The
state appears to a grateful people as the only social force capable
of preventing society from tearing itself apart.

(ii)   Secondary pressures for the adoption of incomes policies

The generalised shift in class balances which has been characteristic of the post-war epoch has brought about certain structural
changes in the state and the economy which reinforce the pressure
for the adoption of more or less explicit policies for pay broadly
conceived.
    First there is the historically evolved weight of the state
sector. The statistical proportions of state economic activity are
well known. The public sector as a whole now employs approximately
30 per cent of the labour force. In the period 1959-74 whilst the
total labour force rose by 6 per cent, the number of public sector
employees rose by 15 per cent, the bulk of this being concentrated
in local authorities with the public corporations showing an actual
fall. Total state expenditure in 1975 accounted for 57.9 per cent
of GNP measured at factor cost, total revenue 46.6 per cent, the
difference being the borrowing requirement. (The corresponding
figures for 1937 were 25.7 per cent and 23.8 per cent.) It is true
that the state claims a smaller proportion of real resources because
of the large transfer element in state spending. Total resource
expenditure in 1975 absorbed 29.6 per cent of GNP at factor cost;
transfers and subsidies 15.4 per cent; debt interest 4.2 per cent;
and other expenditure - capital grants, net lending and public corporations investment - 8.7 per cent. The corresponding figures for
1937 were 16.0 per cent, 6.1 per cent, 4.1 per cent and 0.4 per
cent. The real resource figures indicate the extent to which the
state acts directly as an employer of labour or purchaser of goods
and services from the private sector. But the state has to finance
all its expenditure somehow or other, and in considering the interrelations between its fiscal-monetary stance and the general movement of pay, it will have regard to all the income and expenditure
flows which pass through its channels.
    The weight of the state sector means that even a self-styled
monetarist policy, discretionary or not (and outside the fiction of
the steady state equilibrium beloved by neo-classical economists
there is no such thing as a non-discretionary policy), has to be
complemented by at least a minimal policy for pay. There is clearly
room for manoeuvre around each of the links between the growth of
the public sector wage bill and the growth of the supply of money
and credit. Nevertheless, success in containing monetary growth

within official ceilings must constrain the feasible set of public
sector wage settlements. Given the well-developed lines of compa-
rability between public and private sector pay scales, public sector
pay levels cannot be held down too much for too long below those in
the private sector without producing tensions. There is no reason
to suppose that government by confrontation with public sector
unions would be any more successful in defence of monetary targets
than it has been in defence of pay limits. It is true that monetary
curbs can discipline the private sector too; but with nothing like
the speed and certainty of effect needed to cope with the kinds of
discrepancies which are likely to arise for any government seeking
to administer such a shadow pay policy.

The option of allowing *rates* of pay in the public sector to move
broadly in line with private pay whilst nevertheless managing to
contain the growth of the total pay *bill* by reducing the number of
public sector jobs, is similarly constrained in the short run. Attempts to impose sudden large-scale redundancies would disrupt departments and services and provoke fierce union resistance. Over
the long run the growth of public sector employment could be cut
back gradually. This process would be assisted to the extent that
ways can be found to overcome the blockages to raising productivity
which surround the public sector economy. These blockages arise
partly from the nature of public services themselves; partly from
the lack of direct pressure to raise productivity in activities
which lie partially outside the market nexus; and partly because
state officials may have vested interests which conflict with manpower saving. But, in general, reductions in employment growth will
be at the expense of the level and standard of service provided.
This is particularly true for those categories of state activity in
which expenditure has to rise simply to keep pace with the growth
of social need within the present social order - for example, the
social services and the police. Any sharp deterioration in the
quality of life/level of public order would simply set up renewed
pressure for increased state intervention and expenditure, though
not necessarily for progressive purposes.

In these circumstances it will be virtually impossible to confine
the pay targets implicit in a particular monetary stance to the
shadows. But as soon as pay emerges from the obscurity of Treasury
memoranda into the murky daylight of political gossip, commentary
and debate, incipient negotiations over pay and allied policy issues
will be under way.

The only way in which pay policy could be made to die *and* lie
down would be for the activities of central and local government and
the nationalised industries to be squeezed back inside their pre-war
frontiers. There may be scope for this at the margins - through the
sale of council houses, the denial of funds to politically vulnerable Quangos like the Equal Opportunities Commission, cuts in the Job
Creation Programme, de facto shifts of certain items of collective
provision such as spending on school books back into the area of
private responsibility, and so on. But the prospect must remain a
reactionary utopia on any scale large enough to make a difference
to the underlying economic structure - though considerable short-
term damage may be done to the interests which lie within the
margins at risk. No doubt the Conservative government, bent on

reducing both direct taxation and the borrowing requirement, may halt or slow down the rise in state expenditure and activity. But in practice no one save the high priests of neo-classical economics and conservative libertarian opponents of 'state tyranny', seriously advocates the wholesale dismantling of state structures created in the past to remedy market failure or preserve political equilibrium. And these structures have by now acquired their own accretions of vested interest to defend them from attack.

Thus what is often presented as the main alternative to incomes policy is subject to strong pressures which tend to convert its implied policy for pay into an overt, formal policy. There are, in addition, various reasons why governments will rarely place exclusive reliance on monetary control. The first is indicated by the findings of the monetarist economists themselves. Their own empirical evidence suggests that the several links in the inflationary chain interpose a lengthy and variable lag (two to two and a half years) between changes in the rate of growth of the money supply and allegedly induced changes in the rate of inflation. A lag of this order of magnitude is usually longer than the time horizons of the average government confronted with the pressing problem of how to mediate between contradictory claims on available resources, and keeping a weather eye on future electoral prospects. The purely political advantage of an incomes policy is that it offers a readily intelligible way of being seen to act against inflation in the short run, irrespective of its long-run effectiveness.

Experience suggests that a process as complex as modern inflation can only be regulated by a *package* of measures. However, a package in which incomes policy figures prominently has the advantage of immediacy and intuitive popular appeal. These are lacking in the arcane mysteries of high finance. Admittedly even now, over forty years since the Keynesian revolution, politicians and demagogues can still drum up a certain resonance by contrasting the arcadian image of the state as a latter-day profligate prince irresponsibly debasing the coinage for its own nefarious ends, with the virtuous mirror-image of the thrifty yeoman who keeps his house and bank account in good order.

But even a government whose anti-inflation package leans heavily on monetary policy and renounces formal pay limits, has nevertheless to concern itself with the practical statecraft of short-term management and political survival. If it refrains from making a stand around an explicit pay norm, then it will have to strike up a position somewhere along the slope that descends from the safe and respectable - down to the more disreputable political options. It can endeavour to reach an informal 'understanding' over pay with the unions. Or it can counter maverick pay claims and disputes with diatribes against union privileges and monopoly power and seek to whip up crude anti-union sentiment. In the last analysis it can use coercion and emergency powers. Post-war British governments, both Labour and Conservative have in their time passed through most of the possible positions on this slope, tracing out a trajectory in rough conformity with the incomes policy cycle noted earlier. There is no rigid law of political economy compelling governments which are initially hostile to incomes policies later to reverse their stand. But what is not possible is to set the monetary controls, retire from the arena and let events take their course.

It is interesting that the monetarist explanation of the underlying social roots of post-war inflation lies in the contradiction
between the consequences of a system of government which must, on
average, respond to popular pressure, and the requirements of economic discipline and an orderly system of markets. This is how the
shift in class balances characteristic of the post-war epoch appears from the opposite side of the political spectrum. It explains
the attachment of the doctrinaire monetarists to the idea that monetary policy should be non-discretionary. A policy of expanding the
money supply by a fixed percentage each year is intended to insulate
the state against pressure from below: it would function as a kind
of de facto constitutional amendment which would curb popular pre-
tensions, corral the ambitions of politicians and state officials,
and stiffen the resolve of the authorities.

A second reason for caution in the degree of emphasis which
governments place on monetary policy is that it is generally
believed that monetary policy is asymmetrical in its effectiveness:
it works better in a contractionary than in an expansionary direction. (All this is on the assumption that the state can in fact
control the movement of the main monetary aggregates within reasonable margins of tolerance. Chiefly because of international short-
term money flows, national control over the monetary system within
a context of managed exchange rates can be highly imperfect.) It is
usually possible to curb an expansion of demand by a restrictive
monetary stance. But unless there are strong underlying forces
operating to maintain a high rate of fixed investment, it is difficult or impossible to stimulate the economy out of a slump, or, more
generally, to increase its underlying rate of growth, by the reverse
policy of monetary ease. The lesson demonstrated by the inter-war
Depression - that it is relatively easy for a capitalist economy to
sink into a slump, but difficult, once a slump is under way, to get
out of it - continues to exercise an influence on state policy.

The force of this lesson is naturally sharper in a country with
a powerful labour movement. Here three factors are at work to
reduce the likelihood of a purely monetarist anti-inflation policy.
First, as was argued above, the policy is likely to provoke resistance against wage curbs or redundancies or both, particularly
among public sector workers. Second, assuming the government felt
able and willing to ride out these confrontations, the degree of
monetary stringency needed to bring about any given degree of money
wage de-escalation is likely to be greater where the labour movement
is strong. This is particularly true if the resort to a monetary
offensive against pay is taken to symbolise the breakdown of any
possibility of a negotiated economic order and hence to release the
unions from even a minimal feeling of responsibility for the fate of
the economy. In these conditions there will be a greater danger
that a monetarist policy would have to be applied so hard for so
long that it would push the economy beyond the point of no return.
A government-induced anti-inflationary slump could so depress
business expectations that the state would have lost the ability
to stimulate even a modest later recovery by conventional macro-
economic measures.

Third, in a country where the state has long grown accustomed to
taking account of the mood of the labour movement, the more far-

sighted political leaders are more likely to be alert to the long-
term political risks of a protracted monetary offensive, over and
above the risks of short-term confrontation. For even assuming that
a monetary contraction could be sustained which succeeded eventually
in beating down the rate of increase in money wages and prices to
acceptable levels, such a policy would serve to store up trouble for
the future. It would force grievances and disappointed expectations
to accumulate without redress. At some stage, unless the workers'
movement were to be physically destroyed by a degree of repression
which certainly lies outside the experience of British workers, this
reservoir of alienation would overflow. It might find its way
through various outlets - support for political parties promising
job security at any price, conventional trade union action or even
more intractable unorganised forms of conflict such as systematic
sabotage, absenteeism, poor workmanship and so on. But whatever
the form of the reaction, the attempt to rule by monetary discipline
alone would compound the problem of government by consent.

A final structural change inclining all governments towards the
adoption of policies for pay is that the very experience of anti-
inflation policies over the past decade has caused important adapta-
tions in the behaviour of unions and the government and in the relations between them. At its weakest, what has happened is that
awareness of the interactions among the various components of the
macro-economy has been enhanced. This in itself causes adjustments
in the patterns of economic response. Consider the simplest example
which the monetarists have emphasised: since some time in the mid-
1960s it appears that workers and unions have sought to anticipate
the *future* movement of the cost of living in their current behaviour
rather than seek retrospective compensation for previous increases
in living costs. Similar changes have been brought about by the
increased proportion of average earnings taken by the state through
income tax and national insurance contributions, together with the
much greater frequency of budgetary changes during the 1970s. The
greater salience of fiscal policy has the effect of directing union
attention towards the movement of real take-home pay. Only one of
the elements of this - gross money wages - lies within their capacity to influence directly through normal collective bargaining.
By the same token, the government has acquired greater leverage over
real take-home pay through its ability to adjust tax thresholds and
rates. The same applies to the government's control over indirect
taxes and the pricing policies of the nationalised industries,
though its impact on real, after-tax wages is less transparent and
substantial. The general point is that even the narrow circle of
learned anticipations, reactions and anticipated reactions, linking
wages, prices and taxes, constitutes an embryonic, de facto form of
macro-economic negotiation. The concentration of this sequence into
explicit union-government discussions does no more than draw out and
refine the logic of events. Moreover, at a level above the immediate horizons of individual union members and negotiators are variables whose interdependence with wage movements has become clearer
and more direct over the past decade. An obvious example is the
exchange rate. Since the passing of the era of fixed exchange
rates this, like most other things that matter, has come to be politically determined, and hence, within limits, subject to negotiation.

Once the right of consultation/negotiation has been conceded, it tends to acquire the encrustation of custom and practice so familiar in enterprise industrial relations. This makes it difficult, though not impossible, subsequently to withdraw. It should, however, be noted that although evolution from interdependence to mutual antici- pation to consultation to negotiation tends to have a ratchet-like character, movement from one notch of the ratchet to the next one upwards is unlikely to be smooth. The stage of evolution reached at any particular time, and the scope and effectiveness of union influence on policy at that stage, will be the result of an equi- librium of political and ideological forces. What is at stake is the distribution of social power. Advance from one stage of economic socialisation to the next will require a certain political and ideological maturity on the union side and is certain to en- counter political and ideological resistance.

2   THE EVOLUTION OF INCOMES POLICIES IN BRITAIN

(i)   The Second World War

The argument of section 1 can be briefly illustrated from Britain's experience of union-government relations. The earliest and in many ways the most dramatic, social contract between unions and govern- ment occurred during the Second World War. There were no formal wage controls. The limits on voluntary collective bargaining took the form of Statutory Order 1305, banning strikes and lock-outs and providing compulsory arbitration for unresolved disputes. In the event, S.O.1305 was only sparingly used as a backstop power, and not always effectively at that. In reality, from 1941 wages policy rested, in the words of the official history of the war economy, on 'a combination of faith and works - faith in the moderating in- fluence of the trade unions, and action to control the cost of living'.

But the terms of the wartime social contract ranged far more broadly than this. As was argued earlier, labour rapidly became the critical factor for the entire war effort. This was symbolised by the entry of Bevin, 'an unskilled labourer' as his enemies called him, first into the coalition government as Minister of Labour, and shortly after into the war cabinet, of which he remained a member from the end of 1940 until May 1945. Bevin's giant role both as architect of wartime manpower and social policy and as a national political leader, contrasted sharply with the lowly position occu- pied by Barnes, who had been the token workers' representative in Lloyd George's war government 1916-18. An equally telling sign was that once the basic framework of wartime financial and budgetary policy had been laid down in 1941, manpower budgeting replaced financial management as the pivot of the entire war planning system.

The more particular conditions of the wartime social contract centred on two parallel measures. The first was the Essential Works Order, which allowed the Minister to schedule undertakings engaged on 'national' work. No leavings or dismissals were allowed in such undertakings without the prior permission of the Ministry of Labour's local National Service Office. This Order, devised by

Bevin in opposition to the Treasury and expert opinion, which
demanded a system of outright industrial conscription, was a way
of keeping the compulsory direction of labour to a minimum. Bevin
argued that the working class could not be expected to defend
freedom and democracy if they had to work under arrangements which
totally negated the traditional principle of 'voluntarism'. The
counterpart of the limited restrictions which the Order placed on
labour mobility was its use as a lever for improving wages, working
conditions and training and for extending union recognition. The
introduction of a guaranteed weekly wage was a major reform in the
building industry, the docks and the merchant marine. The administration of the Factory Acts was transferred from the Home Office to
the Ministry of Labour. In the Ministry's hands it became an
instrument for improving industrial medical facilities and enlarging
the whole concept of industrial health. In the course of the war,
the Ministry pushed through hundreds of detailed reforms ranging
from the introduction of factory canteens to Bevin's instruction to
the staff of the labour exchanges to say 'Good morning' to all
members of the public who came for interview or advice. The system
of Joint Industry Councils, initially set up in 1918-21 following
the recommendations of the Whitley Committee, was greatly extended.
By the end of the war these or equivalent collective bargaining
bodies, together with the Statutory Wages Boards, settled the basic
rates of pay of approximately 80 per cent of the labour force, extending the percentage of workers who enjoyed union rates well
beyond the percentage who were actually union members.

S.O.1305 complemented the Essential Works Order and in this case
the quid pro quo was price control, a points system of rationing
together with subsidies for food and clothing, an excess profits
tax and the absorption of excess private purchasing power by high
rates of taxation and a combination of forced and voluntary saving.
After 1941, inflation, though not entirely subdued, was kept on
leash. Thanks to flat rate pay increases, the structure of pay
became more egalitarian with a narrowing of all differentials; and
there was a general redistribution of income away from the proper-
tied classes.

More generally, the government began to establish for the first
time a regular practice of calling in the unions for consultation on
industrial and general economic policy. And beyond the day-to-day
conduct of economic and social policy during the war, the influence
of the workers' movement determined the broad shape of the plans for
post-war reconstruction. It is true that the details were drafted
by the army of enlightened non-party technocrats who had been mobilised to assemble and operate the new machinery of economic management and social welfare; and this in the long run was to prove a
weakness. Nevertheless, it remains true that the impetus and direction of reform sprang from the working class. The Labour Party
emerged from the defeat, confusion and divisions which had beset it
in the 1930s as the major political spearhead and beneficiary of
the reforming movement. Britain's largest ever conscript army and
a civilian population experiencing major social upheaval provided
fertile ground for the diffusion of a general vision of a new social
order. By some, the post-war order was anticipated with joy as a
victory to be won; by others with sorrow as an inevitable sacrifice

to be yielded up. What was important was the feeling that in
contrast to the empty promises of a land fit for heroes issued
after the First World War, this time the future lay within measura-
ble reach because its foundations were already visible in the
present. Though as always there were setbacks and moments of de-
spair, the prevailing sense of inexorable progress helped to nourish
the cohesion, vitality and moral force of the workers' movement.

The war emergency was unique. It would be futile to wait upon
the recurrence of a similar opportunity for social advance in the
future. Also, with hindsight, it is possible to appreciate the essentially *statist* nature of this advance. What is meant by this is
that the war and post-war social settlement incorporated working-
class pressure for shifts in the allocation of resources, and hemmed
in the social power of private capital; yet at the same time policy
formation and detailed decision-making and control within the new
state structures were largely removed from any possibility of
popular participation and accountability beyond the limited means
of access, scrutiny and pressure afforded by the parliamentary
system and established democratic freedoms. This was its decisive
weakness from a socialist standpoint.

The point of dwelling at such length on this earliest form of
social contract is partly that the period has been badly neglected
by the left. But what is more important is the general lesson it
conveys about the conditions for the success of any future union-
government agreement on an economic and social programme capable of
resolving the central problems of British society. Such a programme
must be one in which large masses of people can actively participate, and with which they can, as individuals, identify: its
success must depend not simply on the negative action of sacrifice
on their part, or even on assurances that the burden of sacrifice is
being equitably shared, but on positive actions directed towards a
tangible purpose. The Second World War clearly provided this participation and sense of identity and purpose for very large sections
of the British people; and that, for the most part, without the
ugly national chauvinism that marked out the First World War.

There is probably no attainable peace-time equivalent of such
widespread commitment, and it would be naïve to suppose that even
if an approximation to it were created it could be sustained indefinitely. But equally, it is hard not to recognise that the Labour
Government's social contract of the mid-1970s was almost totally
devoid of imagination, idealism and moral purpose. These are ab-
sences for which no amount of tough logic and economic sophistication can compensate.

(ii) The 1940s and 1950s

The wartime pattern of union-government relations was preserved and
consolidated after the war. But it became less and less an active
force directing and responding to wider social changes, and more a
set of tacit understandings about the limits of government policy
and the exercise of union power. It was accepted that the government of the day, Labour or Conservative, would maintain a working
relationship with the unions, preserve the basic structure of the

welfare state and make full employment its first priority - except
when from time to time the state of the balance of payments and/or
a sterling crisis forced it temporarily into second place. In
return, the unions would show reasonable restraint over pay, it
being understood that very rapid increases in the cost of living,
such as happened after the 1949 devaluation and the outbreak of the
Korean War, could more or less legitimately be compensated by
pushing up money wages.

Such an arrangement operated explicitly only during the 1948-50
period when the TUC voluntarily accepted a generalised responsibility to secure pay restraint. But it also persisted on an unspoken
basis through the period of Conservative arm's length government in
the 1950s. The arrangement's success depended on two conditions:
first, that the contradictions among the objectives of macro-
economic policy, especially that between full employment and balance
of payments equilibrium, should not become severe; second, that
union leaders were in fact able to restrain the growth of money
wages.

It was apparent by the end of the 1950s that both these conditions were becoming considerably more difficult to fulfil. On the
one hand the cumulative failures of Britain's growth and trade performance compared with her major rivals were gradually tightening
the external constraints on domestic policy. On the other hand
twenty years of tight labour markets had created a platform for the
rise of the shop stewards' movement and the associated development
of workplace-based pay and conditions bargaining. This meant that
national negotiations over basic rates of pay were becoming steadily
less important as a determinant of total pay increases, at least in
those sectors generally regarded as pace setters for pay. It also
meant that power and authority within the trade union movement were
being displaced downwards and dispersed.

(iii) The 1960s: planned growth and wage restraint

Recognition of these two problems forced union-government relations
into a new phase at the beginning of the 1960s. The action of the
Conservatives in setting up the NEDC (National Economic Development
Council) and the NIC (National Incomes Commission) signified a more
interventionist style of economic management and the emergence of a
planning mood. Both institutions were a halfway house towards the
more purposeful and full-blooded policies inaugurated by the Labour
government after the October 1964 election.

The new union-government relationship centred on the basic objective of raising the economy's long-term rate of growth. Faster
growth in turn was merely the economic symbol and end-product of a
wider set of purposes concerned with overhauling and modernising the
basic institutions of British society - the structure of central
government, the civil service, the education system, the collective
bargaining system, and so on. Accordingly, incomes policy in this
phase was defined in dynamic, growth-oriented terms. Its purpose
was not to squeeze real wages or replace voluntary collective bargaining, but to ensure a planned growth of incomes. The movement
of money wages was to be harmonised with the new indicative targets

for growth in order that nothing should jeopardise their achievement. The principal threat was seen not in terms of the destabilising effects of an inflationary spiral, initiated or exacerbated by excessive money wage settlements, but rather as arising from the balance of payments. Excessive pay increases would in the short term boost private consumption. Given the economy's slow underlying growth of capacity, which could only be improved gradually, and given the cumulative competitive weakness in manufactures, a consumer boom would lead to an upsurge in imports. As the current account slid into deficit, sterling would come under pressure. Sooner or later the drain on the foreign exchange reserves would force the adoption of a deflationary package which would kill off any chance of faster growth.

To emphasise the link between pay and growth, the norm for increases in money wages was set equal to the calculated trend rate of growth of productivity in the economy as a whole. And because the policy was not seen as an emergency measure, but as part of an overall medium-term programme for revamping national economic performance, it was to be operated flexibly. A quasi-state agency in the form of the Prices and Incomes Board was set up to implement and monitor the norm in an essentially political manner, allowing for exceptions which met specified criteria.

The new administrative machinery was scarcely installed and operating before the fears of external destabilisation materialised. The deflationary package adopted in the summer of 1966 and the implicit abandonment of the whole indicative planning exercise threw incomes policy into a repressive phase. This caused a steady deterioration in union-government relations. Incomes policy acquired a negative image in the eyes of union activists which it has never since lived down.

The policy's purpose was now defined in negative terms - to hold back increases in money wages, rather than to ensure orderly growth. Given the build up of shop-floor power the policy became preoccupied with ways of curbing wage drift. This was seen as requiring that shop stewards be brought within the pale of a more orderly framework of plant and company bargaining. Stewards, in turn, viewed with suspicion moves which threatened their independent negotiating role and power base.

The policy also became identified with crisis, and hence came to be thought of as an abnormal, emergency expedient not needed in normal times. This militated against the development of incomes policy on a long-term basis and the social consensus which would have been needed to sustain it. Finally, as the quest for faster growth faded from view, government policy was left devoid of any central purpose and was increasingly driven back on short-term expedients. As Harold Wilson remarked in an apt comment on his own administration and guiding political philosophy: 'A week is a long time in politics.' This in turn meant that incomes policy was forced to bear the major burden of the government's economic policy. It was during this period that the now familiar pattern was established whereby the success of the government's general economic policy came to be judged almost exclusively by the outcome of successive, more or less tense and damaging frontal collisions between unions and government over pay.

Incomes policy was forced into this repressive, crisis-bound and pivotal role at precisely the same time as a threshold was passed in the development of the shop stewards' movement. Stewards had not only grown in number and enlarged their role within the workplace. In the mid-1960s they emerged for the first time since the brief upsurge on Clydeside and other engineering centres in 1916-18, as a force with national significance. This does not imply that they presented a cohesive and unified front: simply that they were always present as a force to be reckoned with in their own right within the general network of union-government relations.

Caught between these pressures - the weight they were forced to bear on the one hand and the obstacles they confronted on the other - unilateral, formal pay limits could not survive. Despite the increasing sophistication of pay policy and the zeal, political shrewdness and the attention to detail of the PIB, discontent gradually mounted. The 1960s closed with the confrontation over the penal clauses of the White Paper 'In Place of Strife' in 1969. The first double-figure wage settlements were reached in the autumn of that year.

(iv) The 1970s and the Social Contract

The experience of a growing divergence between the unions and a Labour government was the origin of the Social Contract as a qualitatively new phase in union-government relations. Labour's narrow defeat in the 1970 election and the trials of economic strength with the Conservatives that followed only reinforced the determination of the Labour and trade union leaderships to revive their traditional alliance on a new basis.

Once again as before the 1964-6 phase it was a Conservative government which hesitantly paved the way. After the Wilberforce Inquiry into the miners' dispute in the spring of 1972 it was apparent that the attempt to force down pay settlements by confrontation in the public sector had totally failed. Similarly the use of the Industrial Relations Act to combine appeasement of anti-union sentiment with reform of collective bargaining suffered decisive rebuffs. In the autumn, with the rate of inflation approaching 10 per cent on an annual basis, a rate widely regarded as a critical threshold, the government opened negotiations over a new pay policy.

The negotiations eventually broke down and were followed by the imposition of a compulsory wage and price standstill. But this matters less than the fact that the Heath government was openly revealing its willingness in principle to engage in economy-wide bargaining. For this carried the corollary that union consent to pay limits depended on the offer by the government of an acceptable quid pro quo. The Conservatives showed themselves prepared to go a long way along this route. They stuck doggedly to their commitment to expansion, undertaken in successive budgets in 1971 and 1972, despite numerous warning signals which began to point towards the need for greater caution. Tony Benn described their industrial policy as 'the most comprehensive armoury of government control that has ever been assembled for use over private industry ... exceeding all the powers thought to be necessary by the last Labour govern-

ment. ... Heath has performed a very important historical role in
preparing for the fundamental and irreversible transfer in the
balance of power.' The provisions of the Price Code, introduced in
April 1973, could only be described as stringent. And no British
government, before or since, has been prepared to lock itself into
automatic pay escalation by offering even the limited degree of inflation proofing incorporated into Phase 3 of the Conservative
counter-inflation policy in the form of threshold payments.* If the
Conservatives ultimately failed to reach an accommodation with the
unions it was not for want of trying.

Under the Labour government which took office in 1974, the accord
which had eluded the Conservatives took shape as the Social
Contract. This was not just another variant of pay and price
policy. Indeed it is now generally forgotten that until July 1975
the Social Contract was a purely informal agreement between unions
and government. It contained no strict pay limits - merely an
understanding that the interval between successive pay settlements
should not be less than twelve months, and that negotiators should
in general aim to do no more than preserve existing levels of real
income. (In the event this latter provision was almost universally
disregarded.)

The Social Contract grew out of the meetings of the Labour Party-
TUC Liaison Committee whilst Labour was in opposition. This Committee, which met for the first time in January 1972, brought together six members of the shadow cabinet, six from the Labour Party
NEC and six from the TUC General Council. Within six months it had
formulated the broad outline of an industrial relations policy - the
repeal of the Industrial Relations Act, the creation of ACAS and
extensions of the rights enjoyed by individual workers and unions.
This programme was mostly enshrined in the new labour laws of
1974-6. Thereafter the Committee extended its scope to the area of
general economic policy. In February 1973 it issued a policy statement setting out a detailed shopping list of proposals for the next
Labour government, most of which were implemented by the minority
administration from March to October 1974. The statement declared
that 'the first task of a new Labour government would be to conclude
with the TUC a wide ranging agreement on the policies to be pursued
in all these aspects of our economic life, and to discuss with them
the order of priorities for their fulfilment'. When Labour took
office, the crucial decision was taken to keep the Liaison Committee
in existence. It was to meet monthly with the Prime Minister and
other senior ministers in attendance.

The significantly new feature of the Social Contract was that
commitments and concessions on the government side were being explicitly and directly linked with agreement on guidelines for pay.
In this sense the Social Contract marked the elevation of collective
bargaining to a higher order of collectivity stretching across the
economy as a whole. This implied a recognition that unions and the
workers they represent could not be expected to assume responsibili-

---

* Threshold payments were subsequently castigated by the incoming
  Wilson government for leaving its hands tied in the inflationary
  aftermath of the sharp rise in the prices of imported food and
  raw materials and the depreciation of the exchange rate.

ty for the fate and functioning of the economy unless they acquired the means of exercising an influence on economic policy. The problems involved in realising the principle of no responsibility without power are discussed in the next section.

3 PROBLEMS OF A SOCIAL CONTRACT FOR SOCIALIST POLICY

Introduction: some general issues

The British left has become hardened in its opposition to any kind of incomes policy on this side of the great divide which is thought to separate capitalism from socialism. Most socialists are prepared to admit the need for some form of overall pay agreement between unions and government in the context of a *socialist* society. Indeed, without such an arrangement there can be very little substance to any idea of planning the broad allocation of resources between public and private consumption, investment and foreign trade; or to the notion that the personal distribution of income should not be allowed to depend on inherited endowments, the fortunes of the market or brute bargaining strength. But it is felt that in the land of capitalism, where the distribution of rewards and life chances is governed by privilege, luck and force, to surrender the principle that each group of workers should be free to use the resources and opportunities at its disposal to the maximum advantage, is at best to leave class domination unchallenged, and at worst to strengthen its security of tenure. In addition many socialists believe that continual trials of strength over jobs, pay and conditions still remain the royal road to the development of 'class consciousness'.

To take issue with this orthodox position is to enter a minefield of dogma, prejudice, anxiety and genuine contradictions of perplexing depth. Accustomed to fighting on clear-cut issues and steeped in the lore and history of the trade union movement, many on the left will go to extraordinary lengths to evade or rebut any suggestion that the contemporary practices of money wage bargaining are flawed by desperate deficiencies from any socialist standpoint. These shortcomings may be summarised as follows:

(i) The desire to 'preserve' free collective bargaining ignores the permanent presence of the state as a mediator in the process of wage and price formation, which actively uses its considerable ability to adjust the macro-economic environment within which wage bargaining is conducted.

(ii) The emphasis on the private wage packet ignores the degree to which even the monetary component of living standards is nowadays determined by state policies on taxes, subsidies and welfare payments, not to mention the non-money elements of the social wage and the myriad ways in which public policy affects the quality of life on matters ranging from smoke control to the availability of abortion and contraception.

(iii) Free collective bargaining is ill-adapted to the economic conditions confronting most employees of central and local government and some of those employed in nationalised industries as well, where taxes and rates, not prices and profits, take the strain of cost-raising pay increases.

(iv) Wage bargaining is organised and conducted on a piecemeal, sectional basis: it contains no inbuilt mechanisms, beyond links of purely personal sympathy and moral solidarity, which might work to bind the struggles of different sections together.

(v) Consequently it fails to challenge, and often simply entrenches the time-honoured, and therefore conservative, conventions which govern pay relativities among different occupations, grades and job categories. The lines of least resistance are those laid down by these conventions; in following them free collective bargaining helps to reproduce all the privileges associated with the division of labour by craft, sex, race, age and intellectual status.

(vi) Free collective bargaining is inherently defensive and re-active. Once elementary negotiating rights have been recognised and the apparatus of bargaining established, and once the material basis has been won for an existence which rises above the daily struggle for survival, wage bargaining comes to embody the demands of a subordinate social group for a share in the capitalist spoils, not the aspirations of a rising class for social innovation and re-construction.

This last point is the most fundamental of all. For contemporary wage bargaining is a social practice in which militancy is continu-ally mobilised and simultaneously contained; the struggle over money wages both irritates and lubricates the functioning of an economy in which money is the universal equivalent. It structures our lives in a way which encourages us to think in terms of 'com-pensation' for the various personal costs, risks, deprivations and powerlessness which are characteristic of wage labour. Because wage issues are the one area on which it is possible and legitimate for workers' organisations to bring direct, collective influence to bear, there is a standing temptation to translate these real, spe-cific costs into the lingua franca of exchange values. Even the objectives of reducing the proportion of the average lifetime de-voted to paid employment and of accommodating work to life outside work rather than the other way round, fight a losing battle against the 'common sense' of the pay-chase in an epoch of unending in-flation.

Moreover, success in the pay-chase depends in general on the use of industrial muscle. Hence those with less power to keep abreast of prices come to regard the more powerful workers' organisations as the beneficiaries of inflation in an unholy alliance with big business and the state, each of which has its own means of pro-tecting its revenues against erosion. And once the wage-price treadmill is in motion it becomes impossible to step off it to re-assure the small proprietors, single parents, housewives, long-term unemployed and workers in non-union firms, that the unions really hold their interests dear. There is neither the time nor the incli-nation to give more than half an ear to the aspirations of the women's movement or the perspectives and warnings of the environ-mentalists. In these circumstances the defence of free collective bargaining stunts the growth of the workers' movement and obstructs the formation of that broad social alliance which alone can provide the impetus and dynamic of social transformation in a country so strangulated by its own past.

Yet the attachment to free collective bargaining and the re-

jection of incomes policy persist within the trade union movement
at large, despite the desire of the Labour Party and TUC leadership
for a 'better way'. This stubborn feature of our history cannot be
wished away and it is futile simply to condemn it in the manner of
the liberal and social democratic advocates of incomes policies.
The political centre has consistently rebuked the workers' movement
for its short-sighted, conservative and cussed approach to an issue
on which the rational and progressive solution is thought to be so
glaringly obvious. Yet what is equally obvious is that twenty years
of lessons in the arithmetic of macro-economics and homilies on the
ethics of the pig trough are just as much a testimony of failure.

The moralistic appeal on behalf of incomes policies presupposes
that there exists a moral community to which all can and should
defer. This assumed community is seen as the basis for introducing
the rule of law into an area of human life currently marked by destructive anarchy. Once this premise has been granted everything
else becomes a matter of finding the most politically acceptable and
technically appropriate form of pay restraint on the one side,
balanced by suitable macro-economic and welfare policies on the
other. The essence of all the ingenious schemes devised over the
years is that the unions commit their members to an agreement not
to take action on wages which would destabilise the price level and
otherwise exacerbate the economy's problems, whilst the state, for
its part, agrees to forego any action (or inaction) which would take
the economy too far for too long out of the zone of tolerably full
employment, and agrees to other subsidiary measures directly affecting prices, profit margins, dividends, taxes and welfare benefits.

There are numerous technical and political problems involved in
any such economy-wide wage bargain. These are discussed more fully
in the sections which follow. But the central problem in the
present context is one which, though common to all forms of collective bargaining, is ignored in the standard social democratic
case for incomes policy. Collective bargaining undoubtedly represents an advance for the individual worker over individual bargaining against a vastly superior adversary. By evening up the balance
between employer and worker with regard both to wage issues and the
operation of the labour process, it offers greater security, status,
dignity and, within certain narrow limits, better pay and conditions
of work. But these genuine advances are achieved against a background in which the decisive, formative decisions, whether of corporations or the state, remain beyond the reach of workers' organisations. On issues such as technological change, the volume, composition, timing and location of investment, the reorganisation of the
labour process, the choice of products and the nature of the service
provided to consumers, together with all the manpower, financial and
other issues which derive from these, the power of unions under all
forms of collective bargaining is at best the power to check, modify
or delay. Unions can, if they are functioning properly, shield the
particular section of the labour force which they happen to organise
from the worst consequences of market anarchy and employer and state
policies. But they cannot direct the course of events which makes
this shielding function necessary in the first place.

This structural limit on trade union power is inevitably experienced by rank and file workers as an imposition, imbalance or bias, which they may regard as unalterable, but the existence of which cannot at any rate be gainsaid, even when they are satisfied that their union is representing their interests adequately. Repeated perception of their subordinate and inferior position militates against any strong and enthusiastic commitment to the enterprise which employs them or the rules by which they are governed. Whilst this attitude is perfectly compatible with a fatalistic acceptance of the existing social order (and may co-exist in any individual with the most authoritarian and repressive views about women, the family, sexuality, law and order, etc.), it is also liable on occasion to give rise to actions of defiance and revolt, however partial and temporary in character. Such actions are likely to be all the more bitter and determined if it is felt that the workers' own representatives have departed from their 'proper' function of sectional defence and protection.

Thus all forms of collective bargaining are inherently precarious as a focus of loyalty and a source of moral obligation for rank and file workers. If this is true at the shop-floor and office level, the problem of constituting a moral community at the level of the national economy is enormously magnified as long as the distribution of social power is so unequal. Hitherto the only social contract which even began to satisfy the conditions for a moral community was the implicit agreement between unions and government during the war. Then, as we have seen, the overriding objective of national survival and the defence of democracy provided all classes and social groups with an external moral imperative for both wage moderation and social advance.

Short of any comparable external emergency and in the absence of any internally unified bloc of social forces whose progress could attract moral commitment and inspire vision and sacrifice, a social contract is certain to degenerate. This is true no matter how refined are the rules of the pay policy and how wisely they are administered, and no matter how generous the realised level of real wages may appear when compared with the margins available to satisfy all the other claims on existing resources. And a social contract can only sustain the social cohesion on which, in turn, it depends if its thrust is directed against the lack of democratic control and participation in industrial and state decision-making, which in the long run nurtures and is felt to legitimise resistance to pay restraint.

The Marxist left, for its part, has been accustomed by long years of conditioning to assume not only (1) that the correction of the power imbalance characteristic of the capital-labour relationship can only begin under socialism, but also (2) that socialism lies wholly outside capitalism, separated from it by a more or less abrupt discontinuity on all dimensions of social life. This supposed discontinuity is then taken to mean that there is no necessary connection between the policy and conduct needed to overcome capitalism and those needed to build socialism. Hence it becomes perfectly consistent to support unrestrained collective bargaining in the full knowledge that this will serve to deepen a crisis which is deemed to be of capitalism's making, whilst simultaneously holding out the prospect that a completely different set of policies will be

pursued under socialism. Apart from the difficulty that no one who
does not already share this faith will be inclined to believe such
claims, the view of the world which underlies it has two decisive
flaws. First it ignores the entrenched gradualist dynamic which was
referred to earlier. Short of some catastrophe which cannot be
foreseen, and which cannot, therefore, form the basis for any
rational socialist strategy, a movement which aims to change the
form of the British state has no realistic alternative but to flow
along the channels and at more or less the pace determined by the
entire previous development of British society. Independently of
anyone's will, these objective conditions of political life create
an overlap between overcoming capitalism and building socialism, not
only in time but also in policies, methods and mores.

Second, it is wholly antimaterialist to deny that the character
of a socialist society is determined by its historical antecedents.
This point has a particular corollary. A socialist incomes policy
could not be expected to succeed in resolving the various social
conflicts which in one way or another manifest themselves in chronic
inflation, and still remain within a framework of democracy and
autonomy for non-state organisations, unless the ground had been
cleared and cultivated long beforehand by a socialist movement committed to building the growing points of socialism within capitalism.

Thus a socialist approach to incomes policy and macro-economic
negotiation must both avoid the moralising and blinkered realism of
social democracy, and reject the dogmatism and blinkered unrealism
of orthodox Marxism. The problem, as Gramsci more pithily put it,
is: 'How can the present be welded to the future so that while
satisfying the urgent necessities of the one we may work effectively
to create and anticipate the other?' (3)

Whether there always exists a set of policies which will achieve
both these ends is an open issue. It may be that the forces at work
in a particular situation make it impossible to bridge the gulf between practical politics and a vision of the future. In that case,
a choice in favour of immediate political effectiveness will involve
a scaling down of long-term aims to vanishing point. British experience since 1974 shows how in their different ways both the
Labour government and its left opposition made precisely such a
choice. The government clung grimly to a pay policy whose progressive potential as an instrument of social advance was either
not perceived or was allowed to atrophy. The left, equally blindly
or wilfully, hitched its fortunes to the waning star of free collective bargaining in the delusion that whatever short-term wage
conflict ensued would somehow shift the political balance in its
favour.

In the heat of battle it is useless, perhaps even dangerous, to
point out that the war is being fought with the wrong weapons on the
wrong front. But, away from the war zone, strategy can and must be
reviewed. The present discussion should be understood as a contribution to such a review.

Moreover, it is only by attaining a certain distance from day-to-
day operations that a crucial distinction can be appreciated. To
reject a strategy based on free collective bargaining at all points,
up to some undefined moment of transition to socialism, does not

entail automatic acceptance of all forms of macro-economic social
contract in which an agreement on pay restraint is exchanged for an
undertaking by the government to pursue certain policies and priorities. By the same token to register 'failure to agree' on any particular set of terms in the continual process of union-government
negotiations, does not entail a reversion to unconditional wage
bargaining. Indeed, it is precisely when there has been such a
failure to agree that the labour movement should be most vigorous
in publicising its preferred terms for agreement. This it can only
do if (1) it is committed to the *principle* of a social contract on
some terms, and (2) it has a clear idea of what the terms ought to
be.

There is, in other words, an intermediate stage between accepting
the desirability of a social contract in general, and entering into
an explicit agreement establishing a more-or-less tight distribution
of responsibilities and obligations between government and unions.
This intermediate stage is concerned with working out what an acceptable agreement would look like if it were reached. The process
of developing such a hypothetical social contract should begin from
the most fundamental principles which define the kind of future that
actions in the present are intended to 'create and anticipate'. For
'socialism' has nowadays become no more than a generic term covering
a multiplicity of long-term objectives which have over the past
century come to overlay and modify the apparently straightforward
and one-dimensional aim of the social ownership of the means of production. (Recall that until comparatively recently the mainstream
of the socialist movement was lukewarm, indifferent or hostile to
the objective of workers' control over the labour process. It was
certainly not considered central to any long-term political programme.)

The process of policy development should then continue by degrees
to assimilate all the constraints, assumptions and judgments which
approximate to the situation as it actually is until a programme is
created which can 'weld the present to the future'. Most of what
follows in the next four sections focuses on the problems and issues
which arise at this intermediate stage in the development of a
social contract, and which are both logically and politically prior
to the more contingent questions surrounding any particular context
of negotiation.

Two further points should be borne in mind. First, it goes
without saying that in practice policy-formation will occur in a
rough and ready way, and not according to any ideal-rational scheme.
Second, it has been left unspecified *whose* policies are being worked
out: those of the trade union movement and TUC, or those of a political party, and, if the latter, which one(s)? This omission is
quite deliberate. It is in fact more natural to think of policy
programmes being drawn up by a political party, and in particular
by the Labour Party, rather than the trade union movement, at least
in the first instance. Parties are not tied to the sectional-
defensive role which circumscribes the unions' freedom of action.
But the important point is that whoever takes the initiative in
policy development, policies must gain widespread understanding and
commitment if they are to form the basis for a viable social contract. Their development must therefore be accompanied by an active

process of dissemination across the boundaries which have traditionally divided the 'industrial' and 'political' wings of the British
labour movement.

In an underdeveloped and characteristically elitist way this
point was accepted by the leaders and the Labour Party and the TUC
when they formed the TUC-Labour Party Liaison Committee to co-ordinate policy in 1972. This limited breach of the labour movement's
traditional division of labour was the statist version of the mass
networks of political argument, persuasion and mobilisation which
must become built into all socialist action.

The difficulty is that the Labour Party's electoral base is in
long-term decline, and the Party itself, tied as it has been to the
historic mission of creating the welfare state, has never had any
adequate conception of political practice outside the framework of
elections. The other parties on the left have achieved a certain
presence within the unions. But it has always been a moot point who
benefited more: the revolutionaries from their position as union
activists and officials, or the unions from the dedication and competence of the revolutionaries. And the parties of the far left
have always been marginal to the political system.

The problem of fashioning a party political instrument for the
policies advocated here has become a central part of the general
crisis of the British labour movement. The existence of such a
profound problem necessarily lends a rather speculative and idealist
cast to the discussion of a socialist social contract. It should
not, however, be thought that the issues raised are thereby rendered
less urgent, or should be postponed until such time as a political
party with all the usual desiderata has somehow been created,
whether inside or outside the Labour Party. For the weaknesses of
British socialism at the party political level are part of the same
crisis which has beset its encounters with incomes policies.

Once it has been accepted that the issue for socialist policy is
not *whether* to enter the process of macro-economic negotiation, but
how and on what terms, a number of problems arise. These can be
classified for convenience under four separate headings: (1) the
problem of economism; (2) the problem of representation; (3) the
problem of corporatism; and (4) the problem of the quid pro quo.
In reality these are all aspects of the general problem of how to
amplify and develop the growth points of communism within the framework of advanced capitalism.

(1) The problem of economism

The mere fact of achieving a system of economy-wide collective bargaining does not in itself guarantee that the ingrained economism of
the trade union movement will be overcome. It is true that the
issues under discussion at this level concern the policy of the
state, and not, as in collective bargaining at lower levels, the
policies and rules followed by individual employers or employer
organisations. But there is nothing *inherent* in this to ensure that
both the process of negotiation and the terms which may eventually
be agreed will advance the kinds of objectives which socialists are
likely to want and press for.

Consider, for example, import controls. It is conceivable that
import controls could form part of a socialist programme - though
simply because they extend state control over foreign trade they
are not automatically socialist; if people equate such measures
with socialism that is due to the force of habit. But import controls can also function as a straightforward measure of market and
job protection in sectors heavily exposed to international competition. In this respect they are no different in principle from
output or employment subsidies, and necessarily impose a cost on
the rest of society, including workers in other industries.

Doubtless the experience of top-level negotiation exposes union
leaders more thoroughly to the exigencies of politics and of the
governmental process. This may train them in the arts of
Realpolitik. But however desirable such competence may be, it is
not sufficient to invest a social contract with a socialist dynamic.
Moreover, whatever the subjective aims of the union leadership they
are ultimately accountable to their constituents, the rank and file
union members. The ties which bind them to their members are
notoriously loose; but in the long run they cannot override the
views of their members as to their proper functions. Any attempt
to smuggle a socialist programme on to the negotiating platform
taken up by a leadership sympathetic to socialist aims, would almost
certainly provoke conflict within the trade union movement if the
programme was not broadly in line with the aspirations of the
majority of trade unionists. Blatant instances of *ultra vires* would
also be seized on by the right. But more important than these political consequences is the fact that surreptitious 'revolution from
above' is incompatible with the ideal of popular self-emancipation
which has now become integral to contemporary Western socialism.

Yet the difficulty remains that without a wider transformation in
the sectional-defensive outlook of the trade union movement,
economy-wide collective bargaining can at most succeed in extending
the *scope* of this outlook. It can widen the relevant interest-group
horizontally beyond the work group, grade, department, plant, enterprise or industry to embrace the class of wage employees as a whole
(or, less optimistically, the sub-class of wage employees who belong
to trade unions). But this would still fall short of the *vertical*
extension which is needed to transcend sectionalism altogether.

Possibly a horizontal extension of the coverage of collective
bargaining may be a necessary intermediate stage in any evolution
beyond a purely corporate outlook. But the experience of the Social
Contract 1974-8 suggests that even this degree of internal unification of the trade union movement will be a precarious gain unless
the potential for vertical growth is built into the mechanism of
economy-wide bargaining. It is difficult to maintain the unity of
the union side around a common purpose, and to hold off the multiple
pressures for the abandonment of inevitably rigid centralised limits
on sectional pay bargaining, unless a sense of success in tackling
problems and of forward movement can be generated and sustained.
But this in turn would require imagination, political vision and a
capacity for gauging popular feeling and mobilising support. These
are qualities which no section of the British labour movement can
claim to have developed, or even recognised as missing from their
political practice.

It is instructive to examine the pattern of success and failure
in the TUC's influence on government policy during the period
1974-8. The TUC's greatest success lay in the area of labour legislation - precisely the area closest the corporate-institutional
interests of the unions. Even in this area there were significant
weaknesses on issues of major public controversy. The Health and
Safety at Work Act caused little stir outside those professionally
affected. The same could not be said of the unions' failure to win
a satisfactory definition of the procedures for picketing and the
rights of pickets; or the shortcomings of the machinery for winning
union recognition against the opposition of recalcitrant employers;
or the lack of safeguards against the prosecution of trade unionists
acting in industrial disputes under the charges of criminal conspi-
racy embodied in the Criminal Law Amendment Act 1977.

There was some success in alleviating some of the effects of the
slump (though not in overcoming the slump itself). The level of unemployment was lower than it would otherwise have been because of
the job creation programme for young people, the temporary employment subsidy, work experience, job release and other measures to
improve industrial training, and the generally activist role played
by the Manpower Services Commission.

Halfway between success and failure stood the continuing deadlock
over industrial democracy. Here the unions' traditional defensive
posture proved to be an obstacle to progress. If the unions had
been seriously considering the question of industrial democracy in
the past and if they had been seriously prepared to take up the
issues traditionally reserved for managerial prerogative, they could
almost certainly have driven the employers on to the defensive and
obtained a much better legislative sequel to the Bullock Report than
that which was promised, with little assurance of eventual delivery,
in the 1978 White Paper. (This mainly proposed a legal enabling
framework for voluntary arrangements between employers and unions.
even where workers insisted on claiming their statutory rights to
representatives on the Board of Directors, they were to be no more
than one-third of the total number.) Again, significantly in the
present context, the whole issue of union control over the apparatus
of workers' participation remains unresolved.

The most obvious negotiating failure was the unions' lack of
impact on the government's central economic strategy for tackling
the inflationary slump and on the detailed industrial strategy which
was derived from this. In the sphere of trade policy despite the
sharp rise in imports in many sectors, the government steadfastly
refused the unions' demands for import controls on manufactures and
semi-manufactures. Similarly, the TUC consistently advocated
domestic economic expansion at almost any cost. Apart from the
brief period between March and October 1974, the government just as
consistently ignored its promptings and took the deflationary road.
And as time wore on it became apparent that the unions were, in
practice, prepared to tolerate much higher levels of unemployment
than in the past. Union officials were closely involved in the 39
sectoral working parties charged with developing the industrial
strategy. But the main union demands for a wider interventionist
role for the National Enterprise Board (NEB) and for planning agreements which would extend union participation to investment, loca-

tion, product development and manpower decisions, made no headway. As the 1977 TUC Economic Review observed: 'No planning agreements have yet been concluded even with the nationalised industries or with companies heavily dependent on state financial support; this does not indicate that the government have given planning agreements any priority.'

The unions' failure to make any significant impact on government economic strategy was bound to make the deal appear one-sided. And union members could be forgiven for noting during the dark months of 1976 and the first half of 1977 when real wages were falling and unemployment rising, the huge imbalance between the reality of present sacrifice and the remoteness and uncertainty of future reward. In these circumstances it is hardly surprising that official union support for the pay restraint side of the Social Contract was steadily eroded.

There are other possible explanations for the position in which the unions found themselves: the ineluctable bias of capitalism; the poor bargaining skills of the TUC negotiators; the sheer impossibility of following any economic strategy other than the one which was actually followed. There is certainly room for legitimate debate about the balance of causes which led to the degeneration of the Social Contract 1974-8. The range of factors is broad. In the background, among all sections of society, were the fear, insecurity and sense of disillusion induced by the ending of advanced capitalism's long post-war boom, by the unprecedentedly intractable combination of problems which burst upon Britain in 1973-4, and by the dizzy acceleration of inflation in 1975. There was the entrenched power of British finance capital to keep any government from straying too far from the path of financial orthodoxy. There was diffuse pressure from conservative forces in the EEC, together with more precise pressure for political and financial rectitude from the International Monetary Fund (IMF). The list could be extended indefinitely.

Yet whatever the final assessment, the particular pattern of success and failure noted above must be accounted for. It suggests that in seeking to explain why the progressive potential lodged within the principle of a social contract lay largely unrealised, we should pay less attention to external obstacles and more to the inherited economism of the British labour movement. For at a time of deep social crisis, when the British capitalist sector proper had virtually seized up, and was certainly incapable of recovery without large-scale state support, the British labour movement clung to its traditional sectional-defensive outlook, fighting against capitalism when the need was to build socialism.

(2)   The problem of representation

If economy-wide bargaining is conducted as a simple extension of traditional collective bargaining this is not only likely to generate discontent on the union side: it also exposes the unions to attack from the right. The right will, in any case, always make use of the charge that in directly participating in the formation of economic and social policy the unions are exceeding their proper

place and authority. Such charges will always be received sympa-
thetically by traditionalist union members and leaders. As a general political position, the accusation of ultra vires is no more
than a Canute-like desire to reverse the post-war shift in class
balances. But what can give such charges particular effect is an
even partly plausible claim that the country is being ruled by a
government-union alliance in the sectional interest of the unions.
The union leadership then becomes politically vulnerable. A gulf
will open up between the politician-negotiators of the TUC and the
rank and file, and the right will seize the opportunity to inveigh
against 'the new establishment'.

The right's objective is to amputate the level of economy-wide
bargaining altogether in the name of preventing the growth of state
tyranny, defending the free market from further distortion and up-
holding the individual freedom of choice which is said (not without
justification) to rest on free market foundations. The facts that
union-government negotiations in one form or another are inescapable
in a democratic society, and that the free market is already considerably deformed, may be useful debating points, but they evade
the real problem to which the right is pointing. They also miss the
obvious remedy. Logically, the right's arguments could equally well
be taken to justify an extension of the framework of economy-wide
bargaining to allow the representation of other sectional interests
besides the trade unions - for example, senior management, the self-
employed, small working proprietors, the long-term unemployed, old
age pensioners, house-workers and so on.

One objection to such an extension might be that the major third
party which has been excluded from union-government negotiations -
the employers - hardly needs to acquire additional channels of influence. Private (and public) corporations already enjoy considerable leverage on government deliberations and policy. Moreover, in
a capitalist economy large corporations necessarily possess de facto
social power through their command of resources and exclusive
control over key economic decisions. By contrast, union power is
primarily reactive and defensive. The traditional argument for the
establishment of collective bargaining and the related freedom to
resort to industrial sanctions has always been that capital and
labour do not start from a position of equality. The institution
of collective bargaining helps to redress the balance of power. By
an extension of this argument, bilateral economy-wide bargaining,
excluding the employers, goes even further in this direction.

There are three problems with this position. First, it is a
purely moral-rational argument. It will not necessarily answer the
political problem of countering the appeal of the right. The
right's case is bound to have a *prima facie* plausibility as long as
the bargaining framework remains bilateral. It will gain added
weight if the unions carry their traditional sectional-defensive
stance into economy-wide bargaining.

Second, there are other significant groups excluded from bilateral bargaining besides the large corporations, which do not necessarily enjoy the latter's accumulated social power. Some groups -
house-workers or the long-term unemployed, for example, have no
effective organised presence within the political process in their
capacity as socio-economic groups with coherent sectional interests.

Others, such as senior management and the self-employed, do constitute organised interest-groups which have become increasingly conscious of their corporate identity and increasingly vociferous in demanding a voice in policy formation. Then there are groups at an intermediate stage of organisational growth such as old age pensioners, students and the various special categories of welfare claimants. There is also the thorny problem of the representation of those wage employees not organised by trade unions affiliated to the TUC. Some of these are completely unorganised and work in the most exploited areas of the labour market with low wages, poor conditions, little job security and authoritarian styles of management and supervision. Others, like the doctors, have built up powerful organisations outside the TUC to protect their sectional interests.

There are, in addition, those distinctive sets of interests which cut across the simple socio-economic classification of the population considered so far. The most obvious are the interests of women as women, irrespective of their socio-economic position, the interests of ethnic minorities and the interests of national/ regional populations. There are also minority groups with specific handicaps and problems such as the disabled and prisoners. And finally, beyond all these are the plethora of voluntary bodies which represent no specific socio-economic group, nor correspond to other dimensions of social stratification - groups concerned with the environment, culture, sport and so on.

Some of the groups just mentioned can be, and occasionally have been, taken on board by the trade union movement - for example, the old age pensioners. In a country like Britain the sheer historic weight and relative internal cohesion of the trade union movement tends to make all popular sectional interests gravitate towards it. But even on a charitable view of the scope and effectiveness of the unions as an umbrella for non-union lobbies and interest groups, there would still remain groups which could not adequately be represented in this way.

The problem of organising an extended system of representation within the framework of economy-wide bargaining appears intractable. It is nevertheless a problem which must be faced. Exactly analogous problems would arise at lower levels of multilateral negotiation - for example, in the process of working out planning agreements with particular companies. The point at issue here is that if there is no convincing case for confining bargaining to a bilateral framework, then either the framework must somehow become multilateral, or the argument of the right must be accepted that the only capacity in which people can and ought to be politically represented is that of *citizens,* and this mode of representation is already catered for through parliament.

The third objection to bilateral bargaining is an extension of the argument developed in section 1. There it was maintained that the practical alternative to formal, economy-wide bargaining was not no dealings between government and unions at all, but bargaining on an informal, de facto basis. In the present context, the argument is that in the absence of a formal multilateral bargaining framework, the government's relationship with all the various pressure groups and sectional interests competing for resources would not disappear, but would persist on a piecemeal and fragmented basis.

In this setting sectionalism would simply become entrenched on all
sides. In particular the unions would encounter no obligation or
pressure to extend their horizons and all the weaknesses of an
economistic approach to policy would be reproduced.

(3)   The problem of corporatism

Any satisfactory solution to the problem discussed in the previous
section would, in effect, create a dual system of political representation. All citizens would continue to be represented in their
capacity as citizens via the existing parliamentary system based on
geographical-residential constituencies. Alongside this would
emerge a parallel system of representation based primarily on
economic interest-groups, but with provision for the representation
of other interests which cut across socio-economic categories.
   There are two classic objections to such a structure. One is
that any system of dual power is inherently unstable. A constant
tug of war over authority, power and prestige would occur between
the citizen representative body and its economic interest-group
counterpart.
   There is almost certainly some truth in this objection, despite
the fact that norminally parliament might remain sovereign in the
sense that the government would still require parliamentary approval
for legislation and its actions would still be subject to parliamentary scrutiny. The question is whether this kind of inbuilt
conflict is avoidable, and whether it matters anyway. In some sense
the conflict already exists. The system of parliamentary democracy
has already advanced so far beyond the confines of parliament proper
that it would be totally anachronistic to re-assert the doctrine of
parliamentary sovereignty, once a weapon in the struggle to establish a bourgeois democratic system of government against the
power of the monarchy and landed aristocracy. The penumbra of
pressure groups and lobbies which has grown up around parliament
has established direct piecemeal bargaining with the state, and
between different sections of the state apparatus, as a way of life.
Moreover, the expansion of state activity makes it virtually impossible that parliament's control over the executive should ever be
more than that of a vigilant critic. Both these developments are
quite independent of the various practices by which the government
and the various state agencies manage to protect themselves against
full accountability - secrecy and information control, the use of
patronage and so on.
   Concern about the diffusion of power away from parliament both
vertically upwards to the permanent state apparatus, and horizontally outwards to other bodies which seek either to check or make use
of state power, would be better directed at the second of the two
objections to a system of dual power.
   This is that any such system would sooner or later evolve into a
type of corporate state. Modern corporatism might be more benign
than Mussolini's version, but it would belong recognisably to the
same species. A corporatist regime would combine private ownership
with centralised state control over most economic activities. In
order to satisfy the various sectional demands made on it, the state

would be forced to extend its control over the private sector including both workers and the owners and managers of capital.   In
return for these sectional gains the representatives of the private
sector would agree to collaborate with state officials in preserving
social order and attaining national economic success (however
defined).   Out of this process a ruling alliance of state officials
and leaders of the main interest groups would emerge. Within the
ruling bloc there would be perpetual negotiation over plans and
revisions to plans in much the same way as happens in any large
corporate bureaucracy, though screened from public knowledge and
access.   The bloc could extend some way down the social hierarchy
without altering the essential point that the system would be
bureaucratic, hierarchical and elitist.   The capacity of most people
to run their own lives would be heavily circumscribed by the top-
down character of decision-making and control.

Some such vision, often with nightmarish overtones based on the
experience of Eastern Europe and the USSR, lies at the root of much
contemporary discontent. But it would be wrong to suggest that
Britain 1979 is already a corporate state. For one thing, the very
autonomy and economism of the trade unions which is such a stumbling
block to both capitalist recovery and socialist advance, also embodies built in resistance to corporatist trends. Nevertheless, there
are such trends in our society, and any attempt to develop a socialist social contract must confront them. Not the least of the
reasons for these trends has been the working out of the logic of
incomes policies. One element in labour movement resistance to
incomes policies has always been the fear that the unions would be
expropriated as workers' defence organisations and by degrees converted into social policemen attached to the state.

Exactly the same logic applies on the side of capital. It has
always been recognised that pay limits would be inequitable, and
hence unenforceable, without matching controls over prices and dividends. But a consistent policy of dividend control disturbs the
functioning of the equity market. It is the first step along a road
which, if followed, leads to transmuting dividends into fixed interest returns, limits on capital appreciation and, eventually, the
extinction of the private and institutional investor. Similarly,
price controls carry with them the threat that private corporations
above a certain scale will be forced to submit to public efficiency
audits and to have their investment decisions 'politicised'. More
generally, any kind of state control over pay and prices is bound to
spawn further controls to counter evasion, to allow for and monitor
legitimate exceptions, or simply to issue guidelines to firms and
unions with genuine problems of interpretation. As time goes by,
those charged with applying the controls develop a zeal for their
work and a vested interest in its perpetuation.

The general theme of a social contract which does not accelerate
the growth of a corporate state can be simply stated: activities,
pressure and bargaining must be articulated both from the top down
and from the bottom up. The realisation of this principle in any
practical form is likely to prove immensely difficult. Some
suggestions as to what can be done are made in the next subsection.

(4)   The problem of the quid pro quo

The problem of the terms of any social contract needs to be approached in two stages. First it is necessary to define the asking
price of pay restraint, the terms which it is thought ought to be
pressed for in any set of union-government negotiations. (A subsidiary issue is to define the most appropriate *form* of pay restraint in any given context. This is necessarily rather contingent. Partly for this reason and partly in order to reverse the
disproportionate attention it has received, the issue is ignored
here.) Second, it is necessary to investigate the factors which
constrain the terms agreed and determine the actual outcome of any
social contract.

(a)   The terms demanded

We have already considered the asking-price problem in general terms
in the previous discussion of economism. The central difficulty, it
was argued, was that all the traditions and experience of the trade
union movement incline it towards a 'shopping list' conception of
the quid pro quo. The problem of economy-wide bargaining tends at
best to be conceived as one of striking the best practicable bargain
given the array and quantities of 'goods' available. The way of
life which underlies or is defined and reinforced by these 'goods'
is simply taken for granted. Within this perspective bargaining
becomes a straightforward zero sum process: more for one claim
means less for another. The boundaries of the agenda of issues open
for negotiation; and, with respect to any particular issue which *is*
included on the agenda, the limits of what is available to be shared
out, are taken as given. The only question to be decided is the
apportionment of these givens among conflicting aims and claimants.
     Perhaps a general definition of what is involved in arriving at a
socialist negotiating position is that it would seek to go beyond
zero sum bargaining. This does not mean, as many professed revolutionary groups seem to believe, multiplying the quantitative demands
of oppressed sectional groups by a factor which ensures that to
concede them would absorb more than the entire current or foreseeable resources of society. This kind of bidding up does not escape
from the logic of the zero sum game: it is simply irrational. Nor
does it suffice to press for an indiscriminate expansion of output
within its existing composition. Rather the objective is to extend
the range of social choice and negotiation to issues which within
the prevailing distribution of social power are non-negotiable. The
outcome of such issues is either decided nowhere and by no one, but
left to the anarchy of production; or is decided by the superior
force of established privilege.
     There is a vast range of issues which are the subject of open or
latent social concern, but which find no outlet or purchase on any
decision-making process. The aim of socialist policy should be to
bring such issues within a comprehensive framework of social choice
and negotiation. The issues are defined on all the main dimensions
of privilege and oppression within advanced capitalism. These include alongside or intersecting the class divisions which socialists

have traditionally, and sometimes exclusively, emphasised, the
various oppressions and injustices which are based on sex, sexual
persuasion, race, age, geographical location, the technical division
of labour and national relations with the countries of the Third
World; together with still other issues which are not easily reducible to any of these privilege-oppression relationships, but
around which clusters of vested interest cohere - issues concerned
with the environment, energy sources and uses, modes of trans-
portation and communication, and so on.

At any given time, of course, priorities will have to be fixed,
and some objectives will have to be subordinated to others or
rendered more precise if this general approach is to crystallise
into a realisable programme. The general point being made here is
that the negotiating process surrounding a social contract offers
a forum within which it is possible to bring reason and pressure to
bear for the elimination of all these sources of privilege/
oppression. To put the same point in a different idiom: economy-
wide bargaining provides a site from which state-sponsored initiatives can be launched or lower-level initiatives consolidated which
aim at the gradual construction of an economy based on the principle
of production for use.

Three other features of this general approach should be noted.
First, some objectives are by their very nature long-term and difficult to interpret and implement. An example is the ending of division between mental and manual labour, around which industrial
societies, both capitalist and socialist, have erected oppressive
systems of authority and subordination. More generally, the progress which is possible at any given juncture will be limited not
only by other claims on resources, but also by the prevailing
balance of social, political and ideological forces, and by what
might be called technical/institutional constraints. For example,
all previous revolutions have had their progress thwarted or in some
way distorted by the limited availability of reliable cadres and
experts able and willing to aid rather than hinder socialist objectives. Similarly progress towards any set of objectives will
depend on the prior development of at least the beginnings of appropriate institutional means for their realisation.

Consider a set of policies which depends on the conclusion of
planning agreements with leading private and public companies, negotiated on a multilateral basis and involving representatives of
the company work-force, local communities and wider interest groups,
as well as senior management, union officials and representatives of
the government and civil service. Clearly such policies would be
irrelevant or doomed to failure unless certain technical/insti-
tutional preconditions were satisfied. For their presence to amount
to more than tokenism, the popular representatives would need to
possess, or at least have access to, say, a certain proficiency in
company accounting, knowledge of the relevant aspects of science and
technology, and familiarity with basic economic concepts and processes of government, besides negotiating skills and political
vision.

The second point is a corollary of the first. It clearly is possible for the terms of a social contract negotiated at national
level to galvanise and inspire appropriate action at lower levels

where none existed before, or to have a certain educative or propagandistic effect. Nevertheless, centrally agreed objectives are
likely to be more effective if they reinforce or accelerate initiatives which are already under way at enterprise or community levels.
In this context, the importance of struggles such as those conducted
by the Lucas Aerospace Combine Shop Stewards' Committee, is not only
that they can prepare the ground for subsequent advance at national
level, but that when such advance occurs it will find ready-made
institutional vehicles and moral and political support at lower
levels.

Third, we have argued that the terms demanded in exchange for pay
restraint should be widened beyond concern with job security,
private real wages and the purely quantitative aspects of the social
wage, to encompass the quality of life and work and the entire
pattern of production, its purposes and results. To the extent that
this happens, awareness will inevitably spread of the multidimensional character of living standards. The standard of living has
never depended solely on straightforward economic variables - the
probability of obtaining and retaining a job; hours, conditions and
the intensity of work; wages, tax and insurance deductions and the
cost of living; the number of earners and dependants in the household; the level of accumulated savings and personal wealth; and
the various components of the social wage. Though in an obvious
sense fundamental, these factors have never been the sole determinants of living standards. The less tangible, but real, factors
subsumed under the heading of the 'quality of life' have always
mattered: the character of the natural and built environment; the
level and nature of provision for maintaining law and order; pride
in work and release from drudgery; the degree to which people feel
a sense of relative deprivation whatever their absolute level of
affluence; the quality of relations with family, friends, neighbours, workmates, supervisors, employers and the authorities. Moreover, it goes without saying that the composition of final output
and the pattern of inputs required to produce it, are hardly neutral
with respect to people's way of life and sense of well-being.

The composition of output and the quality of life have become
more important in an economy which has demonstrated its capacity to
provide the majority of citizens with private prosperity, even
though significant minorities continue to live in poverty. These
issues acquire particular urgency in the context of the much slower
growth rates in prospect for the capitalist world. Not the least of
the reasons for this is the socially destructive inflation which is
always liable to erupt from the conflict between the acquisitiveness
and heightened material expectations engendered by our society, and
its diminished ability to keep on providing satisfaction even in its
own terms. It is reasonable to expect that as awareness of the
multidimensional character of living standards develops, and, what
is even more important, as power over other issues, besides wages,
is won, the grip of money and commodity fetishism will begin to
loosen. Private money wages, which now function as a compensation
for alienation and powerlessness, will begin to recede in importance
as a component of living standards as economic and social life
becomes democratised and as social power is progressively expanded
and redistributed.

(b)   The terms obtained

Whatever success is achieved in developing a wider vision of the
objectives which *might* become embodied in the terms of any social
contract, there still remains the problem of detrmining the *actual*
terms of the quid pro quo. Any government, whatever its intentions
to deliver on commitments undertaken, is heavily constrained by the
prevailing balance between public and private economic power.   Three
related aspects of this problem can be illustrated from the experience of the Social Contract 1974-8.

First, uncertainty as to the speed and impact of any given set of
government measures tends to create lack of clarity and an under-
standable desire on the government's part to fudge the precise range
and nature of its commitments.   In some cases - for example, tax
concessions and welfare benefits - commitments have been well defined and publicly announced.   But on the central targets of economic policy - the rate of growth, the level of unemployment and the
rate of inflation - there has been a cloud of haziness over the
quantitative objectives of government policy, and the time-scale for
their achievement.   This obscurity inevitably reduces the value of
successive agreements from the unions' standpoint.   The government
appears to them to be unwilling or unable to guarantee adequate
rewards for sacrifices made on pay.

Second, any state which operates within an integrated international economy and devotes a quarter of its resources to overseas
trade, is bound to be to some degree vulnerable to external events
substantially beyond its control.   Both the Heath and the Callaghan
governments had their cherished targets and time-scales for reducing
the rate of inflation beaten off course by unforeseen events - the
commodity price explosion of 1973-4, and the precipitate slide in
the sterling exchange rate in the spring and autumn of 1976.

Third, no government in a mixed economy can simply will its
chosen economic strategy into effect: it is dependent on the active
collaboration, or at least the tacit consent of private industrial
and finance capital.   The outcome of this dependent relationship is
not automatically predetermined in favour of private capital.
Nevertheless, it does set limits both on what any government can
promise and on the extent to which it can deliver on its promises.
The most obvious examples of these constraints affect the rate of
investment and the level of public expenditure.

Investment was crucial to the Labour Government's strategy for
two main reasons. First, various aspects of investment - its overall volume, composition by sector and its productivity or efficiency
- have been singled out as sources of long-term national economic
weakness.   This weakness has been chiefly reflected in Britain's low
rate of growth of output and productivity by comparison with other
similar advanced capitalist states, and in Britain's persistently
poor overseas trade performance.   Second, whatever the truth of this
first set of arguments, it is evident that given the continuing restraint on both private and public consumption envisaged in the
government's strategy, and given the sluggish growth of world trade
and the time needed to correct Britain's competitive weaknesses, an
upturn in investment is a necessary condition for any sustained expansion of demand.   This, in turn, is a necessary condition for any

substantial reduction in unemployment, though it also has to be recognised that current and future unemployment levels contain
structural and technological components which will not yield before
any simple policy of demand expansion.

But there is no way in which private capitalist enterprises can
be forced to invest against their better judgment. Governments can
persuade, cajole, create a favourable climate, provide incentives
and exert pressure. But they cannot compel unless they acquire the
legal right of disposition over privately owned assets; that is,
requisition or nationalise them. There may well be other pressing
reasons for such action of the sort which have in practice governed
the course of nationalisation under advanced capitalism – the bank-
ruptcy of major firms; the need to overcome technical backwardness
or to amalgamate and reorganise fragmented production units; the
need to reduce capacity and employment in a particular sector with
minimum social disruption; the strategic importance of a firm or
industry to the national economy – for example, to avoid total
national dependence on imported supplies; the public regulation
of monopoly power. But in the absence of such reasons it will
always seem preferable even to a radical government to stop short
of this ultimate step and to work out some modus vivendi with the
private sector.

In a similar way the private financial sector continually
monitors the government's fiscal and monetary policies, and can
exert strong veto power over activities of which it disapproves via
the operation of the gilt-edged security market and the foreign exchange market. There is no need to invoke any conspiratorial explanations for such phenomena: they are a normal part of capitalist
reality. Private corporations are naturally reluctant to invest in
fixed capital when they are already working well below full capacity, when their future growth and sales prospects are more than
usually uncertain, when they are dubious about the government's
ability to hold the line on pay and inflation, and when, finally,
there may be profitable outlets for capital investment in those
Third World countries which are rapidly industrialising. Similarly
private investors and institutional financial managers will be reluctant to endorse either what they themselves believe to be a
fundamentally unsound fiscal-monetary stance, or what they believe
to be so regarded by most other investors.

The standard left response to these difficulties is to advocate
some version of what has come to be known as the alternative economic strategy. Essentially this envisages a radical and comparatively rapid shift in the underlying balance between public and
private economic power. This would encompass an extension of the
scope and powers of the NEB, a system of compulsory planning agreements, increased state control over the private banking and financial sector, extended restrictions on international flows of both
long-term and short-term capital, and so on. This strategy is often
advocated alongside calls for the restoration of free collective
bargaining. But it is clearly inconsistent to demand that everything be centrally planned and controlled except wages. Thus the
more logical role of the alternative strategy is as a radical quid
pro quo for the acceptance of voluntary pay restraint, a way of
evening up the balance between the two sides of the bargain.

This is not the place to carry out a comprehensive evaluation of the left's alternative economic strategy. It is evident, however, that this approach to defining and realising the terms of a social contract is essentially statist in its objectives and methods. As such it does not offer a novel principle of social organisation, but rather extrapolates and seeks to accelerate the state collectivist trends which, particularly since the Second World War, have overlaid the regulatory mechanisms of free enterprise capitalism. Specific elements of economic centralisation under state auspices are undoubtedly needed to countervail the still powerful elements of market anarchy which, we have argued, stand in the way of a satisfactory quid pro quo. But what needs to be recognised is that a *socialist* policy, as distinct from a policy which happens to be put forward by socialists, can no longer simply equate socialisation with statification.

This equation presents an unedifying image of socialism. It is not only vulnerable to attack from the right; it is also genuinely repugnant to many people whose hostility to nationalisation and cognate forms of state control is neither baseless nor transient, but has grown out of long experience of the forms of state activity adopted under advanced capitalism. The point is not that socialist policy should be trimmed to conform to the popular mood, but that the alternative economic strategy does not address itself except in a purely propagandistic way to the limits which deep rooted popular attitudes place upon greater state intervention, and contains no inbuilt mechanisms for overcoming them. These limits can only be pushed back to the extent that people's experience of state control changes, and this in turn requires forms of state activity which complement and assist the development of popular accountability and democratisation in economic decision-making and promote comprehensively *social* standards of economic appraisal and budgeting.

The degree to which the traditional socialist aspiration that individuals should be able to control their own destinies, can be reconciled with the equally traditional socialist idea that the economy should be operated as one large enterprise, is an open and urgent question, which cannot be properly pursued here. But three relevant general points can be invoked. First, it may be a mistake to assume, as progressive opinion for the past two centuries has tended to, that all 'good things' are compatible: a choice may have to be made. Second, if there is no such thing as a 'correct' balance between centralised and decentralised decision-making, then the balance which should be sought can only be judged in relation to the needs and problems which have the greatest salience at any given time. Third, it seems improbable that the conditions for which on historical experience extreme forms of economic centralisation under state control are well adapted, coincide with the conditions, problems and needs of contemporary Britain.

SUMMARY

The argument of this essay can be summarised as follows:
(i) Economy-wide bargaining must be considered a permanent social institution which has evolved from the dynamics of class relations

in Britain since 1940. A social contract is not an unpleasant expedient designed to cope with a short-term inflationary crisis, but
represents a stage in the socialisation of the advanced capitalist
economy.
(ii) The purpose of a social contract is primarily social and political rather than narrowly economic. In intention it provides a
framework within which the claims of diverse and conflicting sectional interests can be mediated. Provided the trade union movement
can look beyond its own sectional interest and develop the capacity
to initiate and direct, the framework of a social contract can be
used to enlarge the range of interests and issues which are brought
to bear on economic decision-making and the process of government,
and correspondingly to enlarge the scope and effectiveness of social
responsibility and control.
(iii) Socialisation does not in itself entail democratisation. If
corporatist trends are to be subordinated, there is a need for
policies and procedures which can capture the imagination and
enthusiasm of large numbers of people, and harness their creative
powers. Accordingly, the traditional socialist emphasis on the
centralisation of the economy under state control should be reversed in favour of measures which sustain or require popular participation. Economic democratisation is also the most appropriate
form of economic mechanism for tackling the central problems of the
British economy.
(iv) In view of the essentially long-term nature of the distinc-
tively socialist aims which it would be desirable to incorporate
into the terms of a social contract, and in view of the various constraints which limit the pace and scale of progress at any given
juncture, it would be unwise to look for quick results. It is far
more important to embed long-term objectives solidly into the
functioning of the economic and social system. This requires a
patient and skilful 'war of position' articulated across all levels
of society.
(v) The trade unions and other progressive forces need to broaden
and deepen their conception of the quid pro quo so as to bring all
the sources of oppression, injustice, and social irresponsibility
within the framework of public debate, choice and action. The development of the productive forces under capitalism and the working
of political democracy have enlarged the range of issues subject to
socio-political determination, and restricted the range determined
anarchically by the market or by the unequal distribution of social
power. It is now time to build on these foundations a society which
can regulate and contain internal conflicts without violence or oppression, and which deliberately and habitually adjusts the patterns
of its economic activities to meet the needs of all its members.

NOTES

1 David Fernbach, Marxist Strategy in Britain, 'Problems of
   Communism No.11', Summer 1978, British and Irish Communist
   Organisation.
2 David Purdy, British Capitalism Since the War - Part One -
   Origins of the Crisis, 'Marxism Today', September 1976.

3 Antonio Gramsci, 'Selections from the Political Writings
   1910-1920', Lawrence & Wishart, 1977, p. 65.

Chapter 6

ON THE POLITICAL PRECONDITIONS OF THE ALTERNATIVE ECONOMIC STRATEGY

Geoff Hodgson

The Alternative Economic Strategy owes its genesis to the period of
debate and critical self-examination within the Labour Party following the defeat of the Wilson Government in 1970. It consists of
a series of proposals which could form the outlines of an economic
strategy under a left Labour government of the future. It is the
object of this essay to place this strategy in a political context.
This includes giving reasons why it is necessary for the left to
give the strategy its political support, albeit in a critical
fashion, and locating the place of the strategy in a general offensive for socialist change. This is particularly important in the
present situation when Labour is preparing its strategy to regain
popular support and win the next election.
      What is the Alternative Economic Strategy? First it locates the
central problem of the British economy (one that will still be there
even if a left socialist party is in power) in the poor quantity and
quality of investment. Most advocates of the Strategy, particularly
Holland, (1) have emphasised the low quantity of investment in
British manufacturing industry. Some other writers, such as Purdy,
(2) have emphasised the qualitative aspect and the connection of investment with social relations at the point of production. Singh,
in an excellent article, (3) has shown that the most prominent
effect of 'de-industrialisation' has been a loss of employment in
the manufacturing sector. The Strategy attempts to deal with this
by a programme of industrial regeneration, including a virile and
well-funded National Enterprise Board, compulsory Planning Agreements, and the like. Needless to say, the post-1974 Labour Government adopted these proposals in name but not in essence and spirit.
      The architects of the Alternative Economic Strategy also high-
lighted the problem of multinational penetration into the British
economy. Whilst some, such as Holland, have made the exaggerated
and unsubstantiated claim that these multinational companies are
the main cause of Britain's economic crisis, there is little doubt
that their activities do pose a serious problem and the proposals
within the Alternative Economic Strategy do begin to deal with it.
The problem is further discussed in a pamphlet by the Cambridge
Political Economy Group. (4)
      Another part of the Strategy is import controls. The lack of

113

clarity within the Strategy itself has led to some confusion on
this. One version of the Alternative Economic Strategy sees import
controls as the centrepiece, making it appear as simply old-style
protectionism in socialist disguise. Not surprisingly, both the
right and the far left have reacted to this with hostility, both
giving support to the old-style slogan of free trade, the former
in explicit, and the latter in implicit, terms. However, the slogan
of import controls should not be conceived as simply protectionist.
It should be regarded as a demand for *state control of trade,* and
state negotiation of trade with other countries on progressive
terms. Ideally, this state control would be part of a democratical-
ly-determined national plan. But in any case, advocacy of import
controls should not necessarily be taken as advocacy of import cur-
tailment and little-England protectionism. It is encouraging to
note that some of the Cambridge economists, such as Wynne Godley,
now seem to be advocating a much wider and more flexible version
of import controls than before. The essential idea of import
controls as state control of trade should be given much wider
publicity in the movement.

IS THE STRATEGY FEASIBLE?

Opposition to the strategy comes from both the right and the far
left. Different economic arguments are employed by these groups.
The right invokes the market economics of the undergraduate text-
books: 'leave it all to the forces of supply and demand; to
"interfere" is to move away from the glorious equilibrium of Pareto
optimality'. This assumes, of course, that the model of the perfectly competitive market actually applies to the real modern world,
and furthermore that the virtues of perfect competition are such
that they should be the objective of economic policy. It assumes
that firms have, or can have, complete knowledge of all the relevant
market parameters. It assumes a large number of small competing
firms.
    This model is neither realistic nor relevant. Perfect knowledge
can never occur in a market economy. And capitalism today is dominated by a few giant firms. The model of perfect competition is
as obsolete as the horse-driven carriage. Neither should we use
Friedmanite methodology to salvage the model on the basis of the
claimed accuracy of its 'predictions'. The model 'predicts' full
employment; and that, quite clearly, is no longer with us.
    The far left invokes Marxist arguments and appears to be more
realistic. It is asserted that the 'law of value' is dominant under
any form of capitalism. Unfortunately, however, this 'law' is
rarely explained. But it appears to be a sort of 'hidden hand',
forcing prices into line with quantities that, in some way, are
derived from embodied labour values. The crude version sees prices
as being in proportion with these values, the sophisticated version
sees them as being derived from them according to some mathematical
function, given by the solution to the so-called 'transformation
problem'. (5) However, all rigorous demonstrations of this transformation assume that the rate of profit is the same in every industry, whether it is dominated by small or large firms. Clearly,

this will not be the case in an oligopolistic economy such as
Britain. Neither can we assume that the ratio between the rates
of profit in large and in small firms is fixed in some way. Oligopolistic economies contain an element of interactive indeterminacy
which defies a fixed structure of profit rates. (6) The hidden hand
is not only hidden but extremely shaky.

The second set of Marxist arguments involve some sort of theory
of capitalist collapse or decline. The most popular is Marx's
theory of the tendency of the rate of profit to fall. This has been
criticised by Sweezy, Harrison, Steedman and many others. (7) Other
theories, although there have been many, have generally been found
wanting and never gained major recognition. The result of this is
that we cannot rely on any inbuilt tendency within capitalism that
will lead to collapse or automatic decline. In principle there is
no crisis, no downturn, and no prolonged period of stagnation from
which capitalism cannot recover. The overthrow of capitalism will,
and must be, primarily a political act.

It is also strange to find the far left putting forward the view
that, under capitalism, the solution to the crisis is to cut the
wages of the working class. This view is pre-Keynesian and ignores
the role that wages and salaries play as effective demand in the
economy. No doubt there is a wide section of the capitalist class
who would like to see wages kept down, but to suggest that this
could restore both investment and profitability ignores arguments
in economic theory that have been well rehearsed for forty years.

If wages were to rise or be kept constant in real terms would
this mean an erosion in profits? It is startling that much Marxist
literature comes to the affirmative conclusion with little or no
hesitation. Ironically, such thoughts are Ricardian rather than
Marxist, for they assume that output is given and constant; the
cake is fixed and the only struggle is over its distribution. What
is ignored is that higher growth and output could, in principle, be
achieved by increases in productivity. Considerable evidence exists
to show that huge variations in output are possible with the same
capital equipment and the same size of labour force. Furthermore,
the higher levels of productivity are not associated, necessarily,
with greater repression of the working class, nor greater direct
coercion in the sphere of production. Neither evidence nor history
bear out the scenario of the far left; progressive governments have
existed in the past, and managed to deliver real reforms. Despite,
for example, Allende's political mistakes, his Government did
materially improve the condition of the Chilean working class
before the coup.

The issue of productivity must be central to a consideration of
the Alternative Economic Strategy. Some interpretations of the
latter have assumed that the simple quantitative augmentation of
resources allocated to investment is the central problem of the
British economy. Investment is, indeed, the central problem, but
it is not simply one of funds and resources. As Purdy has pointed
out (in the work referred to above), what is most startling about
the British economy is that investment in the British economy is
considerably less efficient than that in its main capitalist rivals;
a given investment in plant and machinery will, on the average,
yield a lower increase in output per annum in Britain. Investment

in Britain is not only deficient in the quantitative sense, it is
deficient in the qualitative sense as well.

The point is that the Alternative Economic Strategy cannot be
conceived as simply an alternative policy for centralised statist
action. It also involves elements of political mass mobilisation.
Despite the inadequate treatment of the investment problem by many
advocates of the Strategy, one of its central ideas, that of
planning agreements, does offer the beginnings of a solution.
Planning agreements can shift the balance of forces towards the
working class within the factories, and provide the essential link
between macro-economic planning on the one hand and working-class
mobilisation and workers' control on the other. A collective effort
by the working class to seize more control of the processes of investment and production could involve a massive increase in productivity and creative capacity. This is an important reason why
planning agreements should be emphasised.

THE APPROACH OF THE TRIBUNE GROUP

It should first be made clear that the Tribune Group in parliament
is neither a homogeneous nor a disciplined body. It has not got a
comprehensive or coherent politico-economic programme. There are
wide differences of opinion within the Group. For example, some are
opposed to any sort of incomes policy under capitalism, but others
do not rule out support for a socialist incomes policy under this
system, and some even go so far as to give support to various phases
of the post-1975 'Social Contract'. But the Group is, it appears,
unanimous in its association with the Alternative Economic Strategy.

Unfortunately, as we noted above, there is no single rigorous
presentation of the Strategy which can be associated with the Group
as a whole. There are simply a number of individual presentations.
(8) But even if the Tribune Group had managed to produce a collective economic policy statement an evaluation of that would not
be enough. It would also be necessary to examine the political
practice of the Group in relation to that Strategy.

What has been the political practice of the Tribune Group in relation to the Alternative Strategy with which they are associated?
Almost exclusively, their practice has been concentrated on repeated
attempts to get the Strategy adopted purely as an item of legislation. They have concentrated on the battle to get certain bills
passed or amended to the exclusion of almost every form of extra-
parliamentary political activity. Attempts from within the Group
to get it to adopt a broader perspective, including extra-parliamentary activity, have failed. Audrey Wise, for instance, continually urged the Group at its weekly meetings to establish some working relationship with the 'Tribunite' left in the trade unions. But
the horizons of the Tribune Group do not seem to extend beyond West-
minster.

The implicit conception in the practice of the Tribune Group is
to regard the Alternative Economic Strategy as simply an alternative
set of policies to be adopted *within* the existing structures of
power. It assumes the immutability of the existing relationship of
forces between social classes and political groups within capitalist

society. It does not combine with a challenge to the prevailing
bourgeois hegemony; the working class remains subordinate.

The ultimate damning paradox of this conception is that it fails
simply within its own terms. When it came to a crunch like the
economic crisis of 1976, and the Labour government accepted a
package of cuts imposed by the International Monetary Fund, the
Tribune Group had no base to appeal to outside parliament. It had
neither the will nor ability to mobilise resistance to the sell-out,
in the constituency Labour Parties or trades unions. It had to
accept the purely electoral logic which was imposed by the lack of
an extra-parliamentary dimension: the issue was to defend or not to
defend the Labour government. The Group had no material force to
push the government on a new and radical course. Its only power was
as fuel for the voting lobbies.

So when the government put its measures of austerity to the House
of Commons the Tribune Group was bound to see the main issue as the
survival or non-survival of the government. In the words of a
'Sunday Times' article on the crisis of 1976: 'The Left became the
most influential proselytisers for the package [of cuts] that they
had originally opposed. ... [The Tribune Group were told:] "You are
just going to have to close your eyes and walk backwards into the
lobby." And they did just that.' (9)

REJECTION BY THE FAR LEFT

The far left has been unanimous in its rejection of the Alternative
Economic Strategy. At the start it was dubbed as reformist and
judged as doomed to fail. It was seen as an attempt to patch up
capitalism rather than a means of mobilising the working class for
fundamental political and economic change.

There is a latent ambiguity in this attitude. The far left in
general, and the Trotskyist left in particular, rarely declares opposition to reforms, such as the reforms that are included in the
Alternative Economic Strategy, and even pledges itself to struggle
for particular reforms, but believes that their attainment under
capitalism is impossible. At the same time its repeated declara-
tions that the reforms themselves cannot be attained have the
natural effect of damping the ardour of those that are engaged in
struggle for the reforms. In effect, therefore, they result in effectively opposing both reformism as a strategy *and* the particular
reforms themselves.

The only sensible way out of this dilemma is to campaign for the
positive reforms, whilst suspending judgment on whether or not they
can be achieved under capitalism. The far left should not be dogmatic about the possibility of certain demands being realised under
capitalism. For instance, elements of the Trotskyist 'Transitional
Programme', a programme explicitly framed for the impossibility of
it being achieved under capitalism, have actually been implemented.
For example, in Belgium there is a sliding scale of wages, and in
France 85 per cent of finance is under state control.

To pursue a reform whilst suspending judgment on its possibility
is not the same thing as reformism. The latter is a strategy that
is founded on the belief that fundamental social and economic change

can be achieved through legislation in parliament alone. An analysis of history, and of the structures of power in modern capitalist society, shows that a reformist strategy is doomed. (10) But that does not mean that we should reject the Alternative Economic Strategy, for if that were allied to a strong extra-parliamentary campaign then, as we have argued above, it would certainly be feasible.

It is almost forgotten that on occasions Trotsky himself had a more realistic and adequate attitude to such packages of reforms. He argued that his followers should support and campaign for the 'reformist' Belgian 'De Man Plan' in 1935. (11)

It is clear, therefore, that both the Tribunite consensus and the far left conceive of the Alternative Economic Strategy in reformist terms: the former to embrace and the latter to reject it. This conception is to be questioned.

THE ALTERNATIVE STRATEGY AND MASS MOBILISATION

Is it realistic to place the Alternative Strategy in a reformist mould? In my view it is not. The main proposals of the strategy are, in fact, incompatible with reformism and cannot be achieved through a reformist strategy centred on parliament. The veracity of this latter statement is not undermined by the strong probability that the majority of the Tribunite advocates of the Alternative Strategy are not aware of its truth. This would simply confirm the narrowness of their parliamentarian perspective. Quite simply, the Alternative Strategy could *not* be put into practice merely as a legislative enactment.

Take import controls as an example. If a Tribune-style package of import controls were adopted by parliament then the socialist movement would face at least sabotage and black market evasion of these controls. The recent revelations of Rhodesian sanctions-busting by British companies should convince everyone of the unwillingness of capitalist interests to keep in line with legislation and even mildly radical government intentions. Legislation for state control of imports would have to be backed up by a grass-roots popular movement, to monitor the behaviour of capitalist enterprises and to put on the necessary pressure to ensure that both letter and spirit of the legislation is enacted.

The well-financed campaigns by sections of capitalist industry to resist moves towards nationalisation, or even to scotch nationalisation proposals before they are fully discussed or formulated, demonstrate the power of the capitalist establishment to prevent such radical legislation. There is little doubt that similar or more intensive acts of resistance would occur at the stage where measures to nationalise the commanding heights of the economy reached the statute books.

Planning agreements, to take another example, involve a proposed compulsory procedure through which the management of a particular firm, its work-force, and the government, would reach an agreement over investment and industrial development. The very nature of these agreements requires the conscious mobilisation of working people, and the sort of agreement that is reached will depend very much on the balance of class forces between the work-force and the management within the firm, and between the labour movement and the capitalist class in the country as a whole.

In short, therefore, the Alternative Economic Strategy is not feasible without an extensive mass mobilisation of the working class and their allies. A reformist version of the strategy simply will not work in practice. This same conclusion is reached in an important recent work: (12)

A government committed to the *success* of certain planning objectives directed at private enterprises is politically hostage to sabotage and evasion. The policies proposed by the various Left-Labour strategists presupposes a massive exercise of state powers of coercion, inspection and regulation. A government even with a substantial and committed majority would face legislative obstacles, judicial resistance, and the opposition of the higher organs of certain ministries (notably the Treasury). The normal means of legislative enactment and administrative action are unlikely to overcome the combined resistance of enterprises, political organisations, and the state machine. The creation of special state institutions and the support of extra-parliamentary organised forces (trades unions, workers' committees, etc.) not restricted by narrow constitutionalism or legality would certainly be required. In other words, to implement such programmes a Labour government with a left majority in Parliament backed by strong organised mass support would be necessary.

THE ALTERNATIVE STRATEGY AS A MEANS OF POLITICISATION

However, the authors of the above lines (B.Hindess, P.Hirst and A.Hussain) go on to dismiss the Alternative Economic Strategy, at least in the Holland-Benn form. They argue, correctly, that mass mobilisation is a necessary precondition for the implementation of the strategy, but then they add the remark: 'Given the existence of these means [i.e. strong organised mass support], it would be absurd to limit the political objectives of such a government to the schemes of Holland or the other Left-Labour industrial strategies.'

At first sight this seems plausible. A necessary condition for the implementation of the strategy is an organised popular movement. But if such a movement existed why should it limit itself to the proposals within the present Alternative Economic Strategy? Indeed, it should not and would not limit itself. But does that mean that we withdraw all support, even critical support, for the Alternative Strategy here and now, in quite different circumstances? In my view the answer must be no. For what Hindess, Hirst and Hussain do not consider in sufficient depth is how we *begin* to create the very movement which is regarded as necessary.

Let us take two examples from history. As every socialist knows, the Chartists, in the middle of the last century, campaigned for universal suffrage and substantial reform of the electoral and parliamentary system. No doubt these reforms could not have been achieved 130 years ago without an extensive and organised popular movement of dimensions much greater than the Chartists actually managed to achieve. But if such a movement had actually been

created then it certainly would have been 'absurd' to limit it to
mere reforms of the electoral and legislative apparatus. This is
not intended to be ironical: such a movement would surely have gone
on to adopt demands for fundamental social and economic change.
But, if that is so, should we in those circumstances, and knowing
the limits of the Chartist movement, withdraw support from Chartism?
If Hindess, Hirst and Hussain were to travel by time-machine to the
1840s, would they duplicate their arguments against the Alternative
Economic Strategy against the Chartists? Fortunately time-machines
do not yet exist, so their further embarrassment is avoided. But at
least they should see the political error in their stance.

The history of the Allende government in Chile is also worthy of
reflection for the purposes of this discussion. The Popular Unity
Movement, headed by Allende, did, in the main, believe that it could
achieve fundamental social and economic change by electoral and
legislative means alone. In practice, of course, Allende did find
that he had to mobilise mass support even to stay in power in the
various political crises before the coup. But his narrow consti-
tutionalist illusions remained. What did this mean for those on
the left who saw the limitations of his reformist strategy, and
argued for a strong and organised popular counterpart to Allende's
constitutional power? Should they have duplicated the Hindess-
Hirst-Hussain train of argument? This would run as follows: the
programme of Popular Unity cannot be achieved without extensive and
organised mass mobilisation. If the latter were achieved it would
be 'absurd' to limit our objectives to those of Popular Unity.
Hence we do not support Popular Unity. If any grouping or current
adopted this position in Chile in 1970-3 then it would commit political suicide. Some far left groups did. By failing to give even
critical support to Popular Unity they removed themselves from the
political scene long before the aeroplanes of the generals bombed
Allende's palace and toppled the regime.

The Alternative Economic Strategy has many defects and its implications have not been fully worked out. But it is to be supported
because it is a means of breaking out of the economism and narrow
trade union consciousness and activity which has long been recognised as a major defect of at least the British working class. It
poses questions of power and policy which, in certain terms, are
feasible and realistic, and which begin the process of politicisa-
tion which itself is a precondition of the creation of a popular
organised movement. This is what Hindess, Hirst, Hussain and many
others ignore. Unfortunately there is a predilection on the British
left in the current period, for attacking the canons of established
left-wing thought, without recognising the positive and popular
elements that must be retained if progress towards building a movement is to be made. A bit of iconoclasm does indeed work wonders,
but unfortunately progress towards socialism is not measured in
ideas alone. The pursuit of truth and the rejection of falsehood
are indispensable activities, but they, of themselves, will not
build socialism, nor move a single stone of the capitalist fortress.

LUCAS AEROSPACE, VICKERS AND THE WORKERS' CO-OPERATIVES

At the risk of being hackneyed: we can learn much from the concrete struggles of the working class. Faced with the prospect of redundancies the workers at Lucas Aerospace began a struggle to defend their jobs. However, they were reluctant to acknowledge the social desirability of their employment in an industry concerned with the technology of military destruction. So, as an alternative, they developed a set of proposals for using the available technology for peaceful and socially beneficial uses. They drew up plans for a freight vehicle which could be used on both road and rail, an invalid carriage and many other items. This struggle, developing from the shop floor of a major industry, has naturally become allied to a national struggle for industrial regeneration and workers' control. The struggle at Lucas Aerospace was unrealistic without a feasible economic back-up at the national level. Hence it became fused with the Alternative Economic Strategy.

Since then the workers at Vickers, concerned at present with making such items as the Centurion tank, have also presented their plans for using their home technology for alternative and socially beneficial uses. The presence of a significant national lobby for an Alternative Economic Strategy, with all its faults, has been of direct and immediate aid. The alternative strategy at the national economic level has promoted the formulation of alternative uses of technology at the level of the firm.

In the mid-1970s there were a number of producer co-operatives set up by workers whose jobs or conditions were threatened by the poor performance of the respective firms under capitalist ownership. In characteristically sectarian fashion these co-operatives were dismissed by many on the left. These hostile arguments have been dealt with elsewhere. (14) But it is also necessary to note that the worker co-operative movement had to, and did, see itself as part of a general strategy for change, albeit ill-defined, at the economic level. The workers involved immediately saw the need for a policy commitment from the Government in order to make the co-operative project viable. This policy commitment had to be on the lines of a strategy for industrial regeneration which at least must take some inspiration from the ideas of Benn and Holland.

CONCLUSIONS

The first point that has to be emphasised is that the Alternative Economic Strategy cannot be judged simply as a collection of ideas. It also represents a slogan and a movement. Furthermore, it has important revolutionary implications. Even if the strategy is based on some wrong economic analysis, even if it is proposed by the Tribune Group in purely reformist terms, it is still necessary to support it. In the realm of actual practice, rather than in the insular world of ideas alone, it has practical implications which lead to the creation of a movement that can bring about fundamental social and economic change in our society. The strategy has to be supported and campaigned for, not because it does or does not present the right ideas, but because the *effect* of a push for its implementation does lead to the creation of such a movement.

In the late 1960s and early 1970s the left in Britain was on a fundamentalist binge. A new generation 'discovered' Marx, Lenin, Trotsky and Gramsci, and the truth was found in their classic texts. This truth was 'proved' by repetition and incantation. Now many see the error of these fundamentalist ways. But more recently an equal danger has arisen: that of reckless iconoclasm. There is much in the writings of the great socialist theorists that is worthy of criticism. There is also much in the thought and practice of the labour movement that has to be criticised and discarded. But many have taken iconoclasm too far; to the extent of making a profession out of attacking the canons of the left, without regard for the creative progress of the real socialist movement. Taken to its conclusion, this iconoclasm would leave us with little more than a Fabian mélange of the 1950s variety.

What fundamentalism and reckless iconoclasm have in common is a concern for ideas alone, without regard for the relationship of political forces and the battle to change material conditions. A movement is not built out of correct ideas alone, although, of course, correct ideas are desirable. It is built of necessity out of the imperfect movements, institutions and traditions of the past. To build a movement for fundamental social change in Britain we must build from the sort of movement that has campaigned for an Alternative Economic Strategy, and for workers' co-operatives, and for socially beneficial uses of technology (Lucas Aerospace and Vickers). (15) This movement is significant and positive, and there is little else to choose from.

We should be under no illusions about the low level of political consciousness of the working class at the present time. Whilst the far left continually warns us that the main problem is the hold of reformist ideas on the workers, the reality is that many, if not most, workers are against the socialist objective and many individual reforms. That is an unfortunate fact, but it is a fact for anyone who opens their ears and eyes.

In the struggle to change this regrettable state of affairs we are forced to use the tattered banners and slogans that are already established. These can be grouped, crudely, into two. On the one hand there is the banner of limited and economistic trades unionism. On the other is the banner representing a struggle for a realistic alternative economic policy. The latter is a banner around which we must group. This does not mean, of course, that we do not try to create new slogans and lead the movement in new directions. But to move from A to B it is necessary to start at A. And there are many on the left that have not yet done that.

NOTES

1 S.Holland, 'The Socialist Challenge', London, Quartet, 1975.
2 D.Purdy, British Capitalism Since the War, Part 2: Decline and Prospects, 'Marxism Today', October 1976.
3 A.Singh, UK Industry and the World Economy: A Case of De-Industrialisation?, 'Cambridge Journal of Economics', June 1977.
4 Cambridge Political Economy Group, 'Britain's Economic Crisis', Nottingham, Spokesman, 1974.

5   See for example, Marxian Epistemology and the Transformation Problem, 'Economy and Society', November 1974.

6   A verification of this can be found in any adequate textbook discussion of oligopoly.

7   P.Sweezy, 'The Theory of Capitalist Development', New York, MR Press, 1968;   J.Harrison, 'Marxist Economics for Socialists', London, Pluto, 1978;   I.Steedman, 'Marx After Sraffa', New Left Books, 1977;   G.Hodgson, The Theory of the Falling Rate of Profit, 'New Left Review', no.84, 1974.

8   S.Holland, op.cit.;   S.Holland, 'Strategy for Socialism', Nottingham, Spokesman, 1975;   B.Sedgemore, 'The How and Why of Socialism', Nottingham, Spokesman, 1977;   J.Eaton et al., 'An Alternative Economic Strategy for the Labour Movement', Nottingham, Spokesman, 1975.

9   S.Fay and H.Young, The Day the Pound Nearly Died, Part 3, 'Sunday Times', 28 May 1978, p.34.

10 See R.Miliband, 'Parliamentary Socialism', London, Merlin, 1973; 'The State in Capitalist Society', London, Quartet, 1973;   G. Hodgson, 'Socialism and Parliamentary Democracy', Nottingham, Spokesman, 1977.

11 L.Trotsky, 'Writings 1934-5', New York, Pathfinder, 1971, pp.210-19.

12 A.Cutler, B.Hindess, P.Hirst and A.Hussain, 'Marx's "Capital" and Capitalism Today', vol.2, London, Routledge & Kegan Paul, 1978, pp.282-3.

13 Ibid., p.283.

14 K.Coates (ed.), 'The New Worker Cooperatives', Nottingham, Spokesman, 1976.

15 See K.Coates (ed.), 'The Right to Useful Work', Nottingham, Spokesman, 1978.

Chapter 7

WOMEN WORK TO RULE
Beatrix Campbell and
Valerie Charlton

This essay attempts to review women's politics in the context of
some political developments within the Women's Liberation Movement
and the labour movement. At the centre of our review of the political priorities of both is the problem of the family and the
sexual division of labour in society (both social and domestic).

Our starting point is that the demands of the Women's Liberation
Movement, formulated early in its history and expanded in recent
years, now have limited utility - times have changed, and anyway
they never adequately summed up the movement; and that the priorities of the labour movement have not particularly advanced women,
indeed tend to presuppose and replicate women's dependency on men.

The poignancy of such a review is expressed in factors within the
Women's Liberation Movement and the labour movement:
1 The crisis of the left: This is manifest in the isolation of the
left in British politics during the 1970s, with the demise of a
coherent left strategy during the period of the Social Contract
followed by the left's anchorage in the purely apolitical and
economistic upsurge of militancy in 1979, in which the celebrated
strike movement at the beginning of the year contained no calculation of effects at the level of politics, and was indeed one of the
major factors in the undoing of the raggy, right-wing Callaghan
government. That this wages uprising did not, and could not, contain a political project as such was expressed in the lack of demands of the state in respect of the public sector (the crisis in
which was an important detonator of wages militancy) and in the
relative retreat from the political stage of all the industrial
groups which had engaged in confrontation with the government in
the last quarter of 1979, once their economic demands had been more
or less achieved. This subsequent lack of combativity was consum-
mated in the trade unions' non-exercise of bargaining power during
the election, when the Labour Party was excessively dependent on
trade union funds and active electioneering.

The demise of the left during the social contract was critical
for women. The left's abstentionism and dumb oppositionism resulted
in complete failure to wage an effective fight for the social wage
and for defence of the besieged social services. The way in which
this was particularly pertinent for women was that the WLM's demands

124

presupposed expansion of social services. A defeat for the social
demands of the social contract was a defeat for women. This situation also revealed a persistent tendency of the left to mobilise
around the individual wage, rather than the social wage and to rely
on wages struggles as labour's battering ram against capital.

We argue that such a priority does not necessarily advance
women's social position, because equivalent energy has never been
attached to the pursuit of the social wage or to support women's
financial equality in relation to men, not to mention the transformation of men's relation to children and domestic labour.
2 Changes within the WLM: our starting point is that the demands
of the movement have limited utility, and cannot, in the main, be
easily inserted in the concrete political practice of the women's
or labour movements. This is because, with singular exceptions like
abortion, or equal pay (which, however, we would argue is a problematic demand), they suffer from the following weaknesses:
(i)   they are too abstract;
(ii)   they cannot insert the central problems of the family and men
and women's relation to children and domestic labour into demands
within the social and domestic economy;
(iii)   they are limited, civil rights demands;
(iv)   where they concern sexuality and personal life they tend to
make abstract demands *for women,* rather than expressing a critique
of sexism and the sexual division of labour, in proposing political
action to transform the social roles and relationship of and between
both men and women;
(v)   the demands do not adequately express the spectrum of WLM political culture, nor do they make explicit the WLM's critique of the
left.

Our comments do not extend to the debate about socialist
(feminist) transition, but are rather concerned with practices
which could be assimilated within the activity of political forces
as they are now constituted. It remains to add that we believe that
an essential condition for the advance of women's politics is an
autonomous Women's Liberation Movement.

THE WOMEN'S MOVEMENT, FAMILY AND CHILDREN

The family debate in the WLM has settled down, unresolved. The collective experience swirls like burnt paper above a bonfire after
nearly ten years of adaptation, new consciousness and stretching the
boundaries of our own capacity to relinquish the protection of all
that was confining us.

The Women's Liberation Movement Conference in 1978 in Birmingham
discussed among other things, 'How we *oppress* each other', maybe the
wrong word, though feelings of oppression were perhaps inevitable
when 'sisterhood' i.e. goodwill, support and openness were found to
be insufficient to cope with all the permutations and variabilities
and contradictions between women.

All women do not experience oppression in the same way and
sisterhood cannot dissolve the differences. The Birmingham conference tried to open the discussion around the contradictions which
have preoccupied us for years - homo/heterosexual, black/white,

middle-class/working-class, old/young, children/no children.   But
the one which is definitive to the family debate is of course
children/no children.

At the initial explosion of the new feminism of the late 1960s,
the movement was heavily populated with disgruntled mothers, angry
at their predicament and looking for alternatives to the nuclear
family. Women who stayed within the family unit and fought to break
down the male/female division of labour and institute shared child
care and housework with their male partners had much the same
results as those who struggled with communal, collective living.
Mothers for whom either situation was impossible were thrust into
or opted for single parenthood, and joined the fastest growing group
on the poverty line. With or without nurseries, etc. the labour
involved in children is enormous.

The WLM attitude to motherhood has been: first and foremost,
avoid it; secondly, child care for all (twenty-four-hour if possible). The main bulk of feminist energy has concentrated on how
to escape it - motherhood is a disability of paraplegic proportions.

But a shift is visible on the horizon. There is a baby boom,
not least in the Women's Liberation Movement among feminists of
long-standing childlessness, and, what is more, some are getting
married. The sexual and domestic bravado of the late 1960s and
mid-1970s seems to have taken fright and fled back into the welcome
arms of monogamy and sexual dependence. It becomes clear that for
some women their childlessness is yet another compromise, a choice
that only women have to make. The approach of the left, on the
other hand, to children, and to the relationship between waged
work and domestic life tends to have been: if it moves socialise
it!

There has also been an assumption, at least implicitly in the
women's movement, and explicitly in the socialist movement, that
women's road to socialism was through full-time waged work. But
this did not take account of the constraints against this within
the family, and it did not take account of the feeling among many
women that the option of staying at home and being with children
may be no better or worse than exhausting, tedious, unskilled, badly
paid work. Nor did it take account of the fact that no one working
forty to fifty hours a week can *comfortably* cope with, never mind
enjoy, children. Solving the problem of children by putting them in
nurseries for long hours has had little resonance among men and
women who want children in their lives.

The double-shift does not hold compelling attraction, neither
does the prospect of children under five or three years spending a
fifty-hour week, i.e. ten hours a day, 8-6 pm in a nursery, however
good the nursery might be. And anyway, as soon as the child starts
school the problem reasserts itself, as school hours are not the
hours of full-time work. Half of the married women involved in
waged work do under thirty hours a week.

We have tried being independent without children, with children,
we have used nurseries, even instituted non-sexist ones. Fought
hard to remove sexual divisions in the home. Turned ourselves
inside out in efforts to shed ideologies of the family, monogamy,
jealousy, romantic love and dependence. Implicit in all our

strivings of the last years has been an adaption to the world of
work, rather than the adaption of that world to one that allows
time for children, leisure, politics....

OUR DEMANDS

What are the demands about work which would assimilate domestic
experience? What kinds of demands, or ways of thinking about demands, would express the concrete and complex reality of most women,
which includes waged work and domestic work and children?

The labour movement's strategies, and the left's current investment in its wages offensive, presupposes women's subordination and
dependence on men. This expresses historically the role of the
labour movement vis à vis the bases upon which capitalism assumed
a patriarchal form.

We know that the patriarchal form preceded capitalism and that
the capitalist mode of production existed in a contradictory relation to the patriarchal family, both the threatening its existence
and securing its survival:

1 By separating workers from their means of subsistence. Thus the
working class was left without the sources and structures of reproduction of labour power and social existence which have been available to it under the pre-capitalist economy.

2 By the creation of a free labour market, in which men, children
and women were potential sellers of labour power.

This forced the working class to rely on the wage. The history
of class struggle around the wage has to be understood through
analysis of capitalism grounded in patriarchal relations. An important part of this process was the intervention of the craft-
defensive male trade union movement in excluding women from the
labour process. A singular feature of this seems to have been men's
assertion of their wage as the family wage.

Clearly the banner of the family wage symbolised women's subordination, which in turn had a determining effect on trade union
struggles. It confirmed the disparity between men's and women's
earnings and the cheapness of female labour power. Veronica Beechey
has shown that the calculation of women's unequal pay can be understood in the context of dependency, since married women workers
'comprise a section of the working class which is not predominantly
dependent upon its own wage for the costs of production and reproduction of labour power'. (1) On the other hand it patterns the
forms of direct struggle between capital and labour in a way that
confirms the *separation between home and work. It is this
separation which feminists have an imperative to breach.*

In the following sections we will look at the way in which trade
union priorities replicate men's economic interests, and at the re-
emergence of the family into what might be called high politics in
a way that seems to suggest the reorganisation of the hegemony of
the family in the fact of its crisis.

Our argument will be broken into several sections dealing with
the family wage, equal pay ideology, the sexism of government pay
policy, problems with free collective bargaining and its relevance
for women, the 'family lobby', and - just for a laugh - some tenta-
tive proposals.

THE WAGES STRUGGLE AND THE FAMILY WAGE

How far will the current wages militancy advance the relative
position of women's wages? This must be a key question in any
political assessment of the wages movement.

The equation of the family wage with the man's wage has secured
men's privilege in the pay scramble and jobs market. Indeed, it
symbolises their finite responsibility as husbands and fathers.
Men's strategy in the waged work sphere historically has not expressed any responsibility as *active* fathers, because they have
none. The male wage/family wage equation also symbolises a waged
work system in which the full-time breadwinner is not a domestic
labourer. The ramifications of this go beyond the failure historically to equalise women's earnings. They affect the male-dominated
trade union movement's inclination to spread its struggles against
capital beyond the wage. The labour movement has managed to combine
a commitment to equal pay with a commitment to the family wage. You
can't have both!

The hegemony of the family wage in trade union ideology has never
really been challenged. This is expressed in popular discourse.
The equal pay case tends to focus on the worker's existence in the
labour process only. The wage is the price for the job, and all
workers doing equivalent jobs are presented as equivalent workers.
The family wage case resorts, however, to the actual social relation
between men and women, to prioritise men's earnings. Its reference
point is women's actual social dependence upon men, and it invokes
men's duty to support the family, on the one hand, and that family's
right to be supported, on the other.

Thus the left and supporters of women's equality banish from
their case the determinants of women's subordination, while the opposition, from the defenders of men's wages as the family wage, is
precisely about men and women's differential relation to the family
and to waged work.

EQUAL PAY - WHAT HAS CHANGED?

There are several problems involved in the calculation of the
relative incomes of men and women:
1 the exclusion of non-earning and women working part-time from
most comparisons.
2 The base rate is the basic component in wages, but the trouble
is that it does not tell you the whole story. This is important in
respect of women who tend not to qualify for the premiums and
bonuses for long service, shifts, and so on, that boost men's
earnings.
3 General statistics often do not reveal the detailed movements
within particular strata in the earnings spectrum, and, again, these
can be important in analysing trends in women's pay.

We would like to go into these briefly because they show quite a
lot about the state of women's wages.
(i) In 1968 women earned less than half the male average. This
rose to 58 per cent in 1975, deadline year for implementation of
the Equal Pay Act which was introduced in 1968. Among manual

workers, women's earnings in 1977 rose to 71 per cent of men's in
all industries. But among non-manual women in all industries, their
average was only 63 per cent of men's (TUC Women's Advisory Annual
Report, 1978).

These figures prompted the TUC Women's Advisory to comment that
despite the fact that the Department of Employment claims that discrimination has been removed from collective agreements, 'this is
difficult to believe'.

(ii) The relevance of breaking down the wage into its components is
that it shows how even if men and women's base rate were the same,
their take-home pay would not be. In 1975, manual women's pay was
composed of: basic rates and PBR (payment by results) 96 per cent,
overtime 3 per cent, shift premium 1 per cent; while for manual men
the figures were: basic rates and PBR 81 per cent, overtime 15 per
cent, shift premium 4 per cent. (2) During the period of pay restraint in the 1970s, the relative importance of the basic rate in
making up earnings has risen and the relative importance of PBR and
overtime and shiftwork has dropped slightly. Fewer people worked
overtime, and the rate of increase in overtime pay was smaller than
the overall rate of increase in total earnings. Overall then, there
was increase in the relative importance of the basic rate as against
the other components.

The political shift away from submission to pay restraint with
the reassertion of free collective bargaining by the TUC is likely
to change this, however, by restoring the weight of the non-basic
components.

Clearly this will have effect on the ratio between male and
female earnings of pushing up those components that boost men's
pay.

(iii) Looking at earnings distribution within industries and among
categories of workers there is evidence of a decline in women's pay
relative to men's in some instances. There is a trend women's share
of earnings to drop in many industries, particularly catering,
medical, and electrical engineering. (2) This is because the sexual
division of labour is very sharp and women are clustered in low-paid
ghettoes.

The most marked slump has hit women since 1975: 'Over half the
deterioration for manual women and two-thirds of that for non-manual
women has arisen since 1975' (Trade Union Research Unit, Technical
Note 40).

The conditions which thwart implementation of equal pay and the
erosion of the disparity between men and women's average earnings
are well documented and are confirmed in one of the most recent
equal pay studies, carried out by the London School of Economics'
Equal Pay Unit. (3)

This study points, among many things, to women's encirclement in
de facto women's grades, and shares a growing unease with the left's
reliance on free collective bargaining to hoist women's pay, something we will discuss later.

Since the beginning of 1978 the situation has deteriorated acutely. The New Earnings Survey for that year shows a *decline* in wome
women's wages as a percentage of men's. Women's gross hourly
earnings were 75.5 per cent of men's in 1977. A year later they
dropped to 72 per cent. A 1979 NEW (TASS) salary census confirmed

this.   Clerical women's pay rose by only 12.2 per cent compared to
clerical men's 15.2 per cent. Our cynicism on equal pay has been
vindicated. As an issue it seems to have been dumped. We believe
what is needed, however, is a new offensive!

TIME'S UP

Before leaving the review of women's pay, a comment on the question
of time.
     Women have a completely different relationship to time from men,
'much more progressive actually', commented a long-standing trade
unionist in the north-west, Betty Tebbs. This derives from their
qualitatively different relationship to children and domestic life
and labour as expressed in the number of women who work part-time.
From 1968 to 1976 the proportion of women working part-time rose
from 29 to 35 per cent - in manufacturing alone the numbers of women
working part-time shot up from 200,000 in 1961 to nearly 600,000.
This has been accompanied by an equally heavy rise in shift-work
among women manufacturing. In 1961 only 3,568 women were covered by
shift exemption orders, but by 1976 this had soared to 46,219. (4)
Apart from the increase in women working twilight shifts (geared to
their domestic labour), the numbers working double-day, night and
Sunday shifts (at least those governed by exemption orders) has
quadrupled over the last fifteen years or so. Between 1971 and 1974
the number of women with children under five who were going out to
work had risen 7 per cent to 26 per cent (and over 70 per cent of
parents with children over two wanted some child-care provision).
     So, full-time domestic labour is certainly declining. But the
difference in hours of waged work still expresses an institutionalised sexual division of labour.
     What does that look like, in terms of hours worked?

Under 36 hours a week: 1.5% of manual men
                          20.5% all women

36-40 hours a week: 46% all men
                          61% all women

over 48 hours a week: 27.8% manual men
                          (19% all men)
                          1.4% all women (5)

     Clearly, in the job-hours pay stakes women's prioritisation has
been with the hours. Because for women, time is at a premium.
Indeed women's prioritisation of time is legend within the labour
movement. However, until recently women's inability to commit themselves to a 'normal' working week has banished them to the swamp, in
terms of trade union organisation. Only now is the trade union
movement paying serious attention to the benefits of a shorter
working week, and then only because of the impetus provided by the
prospect of permanent and widespread unemployment.
     The tendency to cut the working week renders the part-time/full-
time divisions in pay and conditions 'increasingly artificial',
comments the TUC Women's Advisory Report, 1977-8, p.9.

Clearly, with this in mind, the distinction simply serves to dis-
criminate against a large section of married women by withholding
levels of pay, opportunity, contractual rights, etc. Capital has
always recognised control over work's time as key to productivity
and discipline. In some respects, the rampant absenteeism experienced in some areas of manufacturing expresses a de facto struggle
against capital's control of time, and for the right to time off.

Ford's succeeded largely in its battle to introduce penalty
clauses against absenteeism, in its confrontation with the workers
in 1978. The unions made no headway whatsoever in their demand for
a thirty-five-hour week (which stood first in the Ford women's list
of priorities for the 1978 claim). Management refused absolutely to
negotiate over hours, and it is clear that this is a major sticking
point for motor capital. The Institute of Workers Control Motors
Group points out in 'A Workers Inquiry into the Motor Industry' that
apart from generating higher output from a contracted work force,
the employers are currently trying to extend the working day.

Demands for a thirty-five-hour week were present in most of the
1979 claims, but little headway was achieved anywhere on this. It
was clear that the employers set their face against it completely -
it was usually one of the first components in the claims to fall off
the negotiating table. (Judging from the way the Ford strike was
represented in the media, it would be barely known that it was
anything other than a pay strike. Indeed even though demands on a
shorter week, paid leave and so on were an important aspect of the
claim, the strike did end up being a pay strike.) All this rendered
pretty hollow the declared commitment of the TUC only a couple of
years earlier to the thirty-five-hour week, a commitment on which it
has reneged in practice.

Flexitime is an example of employers trying to find a way round
women's domestic responsibility in the name of flexibility. However, the flexibility gets nowhere nearer establishing the right to
time off. Instead the labour movement has tended to treat women's
prioritisation of time as an index of women's backwardness.

The kind of approach that we might envisage could include:
1 Working no longer than school hours, with a target of thirty
hours a week.
2 The abolition of contractual distinctions between part-time and
full-time workers.
3 The right to time *off*. The right to *control* working time.

GOVERNMENT PAY POLICY

Pay restraint and incomes policies have been a feature of economic
life since the Second World War, generally taking the form of percentage or cash limits and occasionally more complex packages like
the social contract, or vain attempts to hoist low pay. The attempt
to impose a 5 per cent limit told us much about Labour's fidelity to
the woman's cause and to the low paid in general.

Percentage rises benefit the highest paid - the more you get the
more you get. If the full-time male average is nearly £80 a week
(New Earnings Survey, 1977) then 5 per cent brings about £4. If
the woman's average is £50 then 5 per cent only brings £2.50. Thus

the percentage gap would have remained static, and the cash gap would have increased. In that simple sense the government's pay policy would have discriminated against women.

We have referred to free collective bargaining already as being unlikely to improve women's overall earnings capacity in relation to men (though clearly it will raise the incomes of some women). These reservations have prompted us to review free collective bargaining as a strategy.

Restoration of free collective bargaining is, of course, associated with a wage offensive, and that wages offensive has been the chariot in which the left has ridden out of the political oblivion it fell into during the first phases of the social contract.

The questions we need to ask from a socialist feminist perspective are:
1 will the free collective bargaining-wages offensive strategy raise the level of women's incomes relative to men's?
2 What elements of the wage are accessible to free collective bargaining as it has been exercised hitherto?
3 Will it attack capitalism and advance us towards socialism?

Historically the pivot of free collective bargaining has been the family wage.

Taxation policy during the 1960s caused a serious breach in collective bargaining's capacity to protect the family wage by being by default heavily biased against parents, resulting from the elimination of reduced rates of taxation. Their abolition meant that 'in 1967 a married couple with three children came into the standard tax range when the household income was £23 weekly. By 1970, following three budgets a married couple with three children began to pay tax at the full standard rate when earning not £23 but £16.05.' During the 1960s the proportion of incomes paid in direct tax only rose from 9 per cent to 11 per cent for households with two parents and four children. But from 1969 to 1975 the bias turned heavily against the family. The 'normal' family, of two parents and two children, suffered the biggest rise in taxation, from 9 per cent to an enormous 20 per cent. (6)

The trade union strategy towards the end of the 1960s of increasing money wages had the effect of introducing many more workers to standard rates of tax because the government failed to amend tax thresholds. Only inflationary wage demands managed to keep pace with the erosion of workers' living standards. Cambridge economists, Turner and Wilkinson in 'Do the Trade Unions cause Inflation', pointed out that the trade unions' attempt from September 1968 to April 1971 to prioritise pay demands for the lower-paid 'was almost entirely cancelled out by taxation'.

The labour movement's then and subsequent passivity in the fact of the degeneration of the services for which more and more workers were being taxed meant that not only were wages booms not improving workers' general standard of living, but they were also not in any way addressing the decline in the services for which people were being taxed, i.e. the social wage.

It is already clear that in any new offensive, men's emphasis will be on their own money rises, rather than the other social demands included in any of the current pay claims. The men of the movement will be saying 'Give us the money'. What will the women

be saying? We estimate that the social demands in the 1979 wage
packages and the demand for a shorter working week, had much greater
resonance among women.

As a laissez-faire system of wage bargaining, free collective
bargaining does not fully assimilate the effect of state intervention in regulation of wages. The State is now a permanent mediator in the determination of levels of income, either directly
through the imposition of 'voluntary' or statutory pay limits, or
indirectly through taxation and manipulation of employment levels.

Furthermore the State is now the country's biggest single employer and is therefore an active presence in pay negotiations for
millions of workers, which gives the State a definite imperative to
hold down wages in the public sector. Feminism's demands presupposed economic boom and expansion of the state. It was an irony of
history that the women's movement was barely born before those very
conditions were dissipated.

Politically, free collective bargaining is heralded as a strategy
that aims to hit capital where it hurts. But it is only as a response to capitalism. Though there's a tendency when the strategy
works to say: 'it wasn't us ... we didn't cause inflation'. It is
essentially a response to capitalism, not a strategy against it.

To sum up: in our view free collective bargaining is not an effective socialist economic strategy against capitalism, nor is it in
any way a strategy for women's equality. As a political programme
it is a vain one as capital has clearly shown over the last ten
years, with its simple tactic of passing pay rises on to the consumer. The wages offensive cannot be sustained as a political offensive against capital because it never actually confronts the
problem of capital's control over the economy. Wages as compensation for the hardships of labour does not mitigate the hardship and
need not necessarily generate demands about the intensity or content
or products of work that would change the degree of exploitation or
capital's control over the labour process AND over consumption. As
a form of negotiation with capital it fails to incorporate the permanent presence of the State in the economy. As a galvaniser of
trade union solidarity it fails too. It is not a form of bargaining
that includes all workers or is on behalf of all workers. It is a
survival-of-the-fittest strategy. Nor can it advance the erosion of
hierarchies and divisions between workers. Rather it has a general
tendency to consolidate differentials.

All this leads us to the view that what is needed in order to
shift women's economic situation is a feminist incomes policy or
strategy, which would include:
1 attacking women's relation of dependence on men (this is already
expressed in the Women's Liberation Movement's fifth demand campaign
for financial and legal independence).
2 Outflanking the family wage and abolishing the concept of men as
breadwinners.
3 Eroding the differential between male and female earnings directly by, where appropriate, awarding proportionately greater increases
to women. In this sense feminists are firmly located in the movement among some on the left to erode differentials.
4 Attaching substantial energy to the fight for time. Only then
will the conditions really exist for transforming the sexual division of labour at home and in waged work.

POLITICS AND THE FAMILY

Mr Callaghan appealed to the nation's women not to allow their changed working situation to blow up the family, delinquency and the collapse of decency. His speech in May 1978 to the Labour Party women's conference launched the party into the Great Debate on the family, initiated by the Tories who have attempted to capture the family as their own sphere of influence in opposition to Labour's hegemony in the trade union movement. 'We are the party of the family,' said Margaret Thatcher.

The issue presents us with an interesting example of contradictions within Toryism vis-à-vis the role of the state. The social services spokesperson, Patrick Jenkin, initially raised the issue of the family in the context of the creation of a national family agency, but has since dropped this project, presumably recognising that it goes against the Thatcher ideology of laissez-faire, self-help and non-state intervention. These moves represent the culmination of a trend towards the re-emergence of the ideology of the family in politics.

In a Tavistock Institute analysis of past Tory, Liberal and Labour manifestos, identical positions to the family were shown. From 1918 to 1936 there was little interest in the family. It rose markedly from 1945 to 1950, declined somewhat in the 1950s and early 1960s. But by 1974 the family was referred to on every page of all three election manifestos.

The implication of the backlash is a will to respond to the connection between the family crisis and the changing role of women by willing a new retreat from waged labour and a return to their central role in the family. Long-term and substantial unemployment and the likelihood of a massive technological restructuring of the labour process which will produce yet more unemployment, which could be mitigated by the withdrawal of women from the labour force.

At the ideological level, the spectacle of domestic life is one of the most explosive dimensions of state and civil society is being treated as a kind of war on the home front, with the leaders of establishment politics digging in. The family spirit is equated with patriotism, as a national value, natural and eternal.

But it is precisely out of the contradictions within the family, and between the family and waged work, that contemporary feminism has sprung. However, it is odd that while women's liberation has focused so strongly on the family, sexuality and the sexual division of labour, it is in fact only our enemies, the right, the moralists and the mysoginists who have persuasingly inserted the family and personal life into their strategic objectives.

THE IMPACT OF THE FAMILY LOBBY

The core of the problem which family theorists over the last decade have been addressing concerns the effect of taxation on parents' incomes, the systems of child support in this country (which have still not confronted the individualisation of responsibility for children) and changing attitudes towards women in the family.

We propose, here, to concentrate on the response of the family lobby to family incomes.

Margaret Wynn's pioneering work has demonstrated the enormous costs to families of rearing children, and has challenged the non-correlation of tax levels either with family size, or with family cycles (i.e. the different costs involved in rearing babies as against adolescents).

The response to the relative emiseration of parents and children has produced a political shift away from the defence of poor families, which characterised the approach of the family lobby, to a defence of the family - all families. This is exemplified in the approach of the influential Child Poverty Action Group. Attention was directed to the poor as a sub-group of families, rather than to families per se - a policy which Frank Field, then director of the CPAG, now says was a mistake. 'A family lobby', he said, 'would have brought the benefits of the "sharp elbows of the middle class" in turning the needs of families into a political priority.' ('New Society', 8 June 1978)

This political shift is being resisted by some in the family lobby. The National Council for One-Parent Families fears that it will end up deprioritising poor families. As Paul Lewis, its deputy director has said: 'The problem of one-parent families are essentially the problems of women in a society geared to the male breadwinner. Lone fathers face the problems of women that men usually avoid.'

The evolution of elements of the family lobby, then, expresses a political shift away from categories of special need, and a return to defence of all families - a shift that ominously fits the mood in Establishment politics to reassert the virtues of the family as an institution, appropriately headed by 'the average family man'.

Broadly speaking the left is caught in the hegemony of the family, and has never risked a rupture. Its approach tends to treat the family as sanctuary from capitalism, marred only the drudgery of domestic labour.

The sanctuary approach, of course, dissolves the contradictions between men and women generated by relations of dominance and dependence.

The location of the problem in domestic drudgery appeals to the State for the socialisation of the family's functions. One of the most lucid and interesting examples of this is Alexandra Kollontai's formulae proposing the 'statisation' of family labour as a basic tenet of socialist transition.

However, what none of these solutions address is the sticking point - the sexual division of labour between men and women. The sanctuary notion de-politicises the issue because it assumes harmony where there is contradiction. The drudgery emphasis reduces the problem of the family to hard labour which can be resolved by family functions being socialised. This can either happen - as in contemporary capitalism to some extent - by their assimilation into the commodity market, or by the state.

Klara Zetkin and Kollontai may have been loved as leaders of women, but their sexual independence and sexual radicalism often left them besieged and politically isolated. The WLM runs the same risk of foundering on the rock of the family, and losing nerve in personal and sexual politics. At the moment, nowhere in our demands or in our literature do we express a clear view of the family. We

won't be rescued by the simple accretion of demands like the fifth,
sixth and seventh demands, which deal with financial and legal independence, sexuality and sexual violence against women.   The increment of discrete demands on 'personal life' doesn't effectively
give a liberationist tone to our previously equal rights type demands.

Over the next few years, former Confederation of British Industry
chief Sir Campbell Adamson will be chairing a special commission on
the family. What will we, the Women's Liberation Movement, have to
say? What we have tried to suggest is that first of all our approach has to involve breaking the separation between home and work
in our own thinking.

We don't think that an appeal to forms of Marxism that, in the
name of anti-economism, evacuate from concern with economic
struggles are much help.

We must think concretely about tactics which transform the conditions of waged work so that they assimilate the realities of
domestic life, and also conceive of the conditions of domestic life
that break the assumption that all families have two parents and a
male breadwinner (i.e. perhaps to base our tactics on the conditions necessary for the survival of a one-parent family).

This essay criticises the allocation of the politics of men and
the politics of women to separate universes. We do so because the
effect of this separation defuses the radicalisation of sexuality
and the family from within (by underestimating the dependency of the
structures of the family and waged work in a capitalist society).
By simply demanding equality with men at work we don't confront men
as men, or the nature of work. Men and women do not occupy separate
spaces in life - it is their relation to them which is qualitatively
different and it is that relation that we want to revolutionise.

NOTES

1 V.Beechey, Some Notes on Female Wage Labour in Capitalist
   Production, 'Capital and Class', no.3, 1977.
2 J.Hebden, Men's and Women's Pay in Britain, 'Industrial Relations
   Journal', 9, (2), 1978.
3 Reported in 'Department of Employment Gazette', July 1978.
4 TUC Working Party Report on the Under-Five's, 1976.
5 New Earnings Survey, 'Department of Employment Gazette', October
   1977.
6 Margaret Wynn, 'Family Policy', Harmondsworth, Pelican, 1972.

Chapter 8

ENERGY POLICY, THE ENVIRONMENT AND DEMOCRATIC CONTROL

Mike Prior

THE HEROIC AGE OF ENERGY SUPPLY

Energy supply has become, over the past few years, a controversial issue out of all proportion to its apparent statistical importance as a part of national income. The average family probably spends more on holidays in a year than on buying energy. Yet it is impossible to doubt the crucial role played by energy supply in the national economy.

The pivotal importance of energy is that it is the key to the extension of human control over nature. From the use of fire to protect and warm through to the most sophisticated nuclear power station, energy acts to extend human strength and bring greater areas of nature under human domination.

This control was, for several millennia, confined to a precarious and haphazard existence. The major energy sources outside human muscle were dependent either upon wood for burning or conversion to metallurgical charcoal, an energy reserve which could easily become exhausted if over-exploited and could only be replaced at the slow pace of tree-growth, or they used the unpredictable and unstorable energy of winds. The pace of human social development was tied to these natural rhythms with a seemingly irrevocable force.

These constraints need not, and did not, prevent the growth of highly complex societies and vast trading empires. Nevertheless, they had important consequences. One of the most obvious was that the lack of a controllable, major energy source provided a block upon the pace of economic growth but also there were two profound social effects. First, there was a great consciousness of, and fatalism in, human dependence upon nature. The 'natural order of society' could be seen as just that, a human hierarchy extending out of the hierarchy of the natural world, with men and women fitting in between animals and angels with no specific break.

Human society, governed materially by natural processes, could also be seen as correlated with order in nature. The idea that 'when kings die, stars burn' was no metaphor, but a literal description of how human action and natural order were seen to co-exist. Although constrained in other areas, notably food production, it was more than anything else a low level of available energy which was responsible for this attitude as energy is precisely that which enables humans to control nature.

One facet of this was the perception of those human activities which could be seen as disturbing nature. Mining, a process of extracting metals from natural rocks with no apparent natural balance, was commonly regarded with both wonder and apprehension. The miner tampered with nature, removing without replacing, and was regarded from Bohemia to Cornwall as a creature half in league with the devil.

Second, the lack of a firm energy source produced a life of physical drudgery. The most important part of life after growing food was, for most people of whatever race, to gather wood for the winter and for cooking. The symbolic wood-chopping required of a visitor in a film Western translated in real life to an endlesss round of collecting wood and stocking it for the winter months.

For a considerable portion of the world, this search for wood-fuel still forms a major part of existence. Large parts of Africa are deforested and eroded as people travel further and further afield for the wood which, as charcoal, forms the primary cooking fuel for most people. In Brazil, for example, a third of the people still cook with wood, whilst in Africa, wood accounts for 60 per cent of all energy use.

The extraordinary nineteenth-century phenomenon of opening up, first the coalfields of Europe and North America and the use of this fuel in stationary engines, in rail transport and in generating electricity, and then the use of liquid petroleum fuel, thus provided a dual liberation, from the constraints of nature, and potentially from the drudgery and oppression of physical labour.

Because of liberation from both these constraints, accessible energy was seen as a progressive and as a *democratic* influence by all early socialists. The cruel and destructive features of capitalist industrialisation notwithstanding, it was apparent that energy formed the key to many aspects of social development, from easier communication to house lighting, which were essential for human liberation.

The release of human beings from the oppression of the rhythms of nature could be seen as linking quite easily with release from the oppressions of human society. The Promethean myth could be taken over unchanged except for the substitution of the gods by an all too easily identifiable class of earthly oppressors.

The energy form which concentrated this sense of the liberating and democratising force of accessible energy, was electricity. 'Socialism equals all power to the soviets and electrification of the country' was the most famous encapsulation of this belief, that electricity supply was not just a useful facility but a basic human right. Another, equally influential but now half-forgotten, example was the Rural Electrification Programme in the New Deal period in the USA and the Tennessee Valley Authority set up to tame the Tennessee River and provide electric power to the backward rural areas of Tennessee, Alabama and Georgia. Woody Guthrie's songs about the great US dams, making mines and mills across half the country hum with electric power, evoke exactly the triumphant sense of controlling nature and liberating people which the electrification programmes produced.

Many of the power authorities set up at this time in the USA were either state owned or functioned as some kind of co-operative, owned by electricity consumers. Although private utilities dominate urban power supply, these other concerns still supply large parts of rural America, for example, the whole state of Minnesota, which private capital would not enter.

The British electricity industry has never passed through quite such an heroic age, and public control and regulation of most forms of energy supply has long been embedded into the structure of the British state. The period of 'gas-works socialism' when energy supply was largely the responsibility of local councils has become totally submerged into the technocratic aura of the great state energy corporations.

But in its own, quieter and more municipal way, the spread of basic energy supply in Britain was an important step in social progress. The fact that gas and electricity production and supply was, almost from the first in Britain, a publicly owned function meant that, although the issue was more subdued than in the USA, the question of democratic control was - at least in principle - settled in favour of equal access and public service.

The other side of the coin in energy supply was presented by the production of fossil fuels, first coal and then oil. Almost uniformly throughout the world, these showed an extreme and rapacious form of capitalist development. Coal-owners and oil companies tended to operate under rather different market circumstances; the main problems of the former centring around a long drawn-out and bitter conflict with its miners, the latter being concerned to establish as secure a monopolisation as possible of any particular oil market and source of crude oil.

The long struggle to bring the oil companies under, at least minimal, public regulation is most obvious in the USA, from the anti-trust legislation, designed to break up Rockefeller's Standard Oil Trust, down to the current political battle over the deregulation of gas prices. The widespread belief that the gas supply companies of the southern USA deliberately withheld gas from the north in the bitter winter of 1976-7 and allowed widespread gas cuts, in order to force up federal price limits, indicates the suspicion with which the oil companies are regarded. The fact that the suspicion is probably well-founded indicates the business ethics which still dominate this sector.

Bitter and often violent relations also characterise the US coal industry, particularly in the West Virginia region where the guns have never really been put away.

However, in Europe both the fossil fuel supply areas have for many years been fairly securely contained under public control. There are only residual pockets of private industry in coal-mining, all heavily state-subsidised, whilst the oil companies have been, at least, state-regulated and often state-owned.

As most of the post-war period saw a glut of Middle East, African and, lately, North Sea crude oil, all flooding the European market, the regulation of the oil companies has proved a relatively benign matter. The pressure of smaller US companies, wishing to dispose of their surplus crude in Europe, forced down oil prices in Europe throughout the late-1950s and 1960s and established a permanent condition of over-supply. A long established statism meant that the formation of state monopolies, initially over gas supplies as in Italy, France, Holland and Britain, but extending in various aspects of the oil market, could occur very smoothly with little of the ideological and political problems which accompany state intervention in the USA. In France, for example, oil supply has been firmly under government control since the 1920s whilst the British government actually bought a majority holding in an oil major, BP, to ensure strategic control of supply.

This does not mean that in long-term conditions of shortage, as opposed to glut, the private oil companies can be relied upon to act in any even-handed fashion. The extension of public control over this sector must, however, be limited by the difficulties of influencing the largely US-owned oil majors outside national boundaries. The most important way of ensuring long-term control is to establish an independent state-owned company, able to explore and produce on equal terms with the majors. In British National Oil Corporation, plus a majority holding in British Petroleum, the British state should be able to ensure, at least, a minimum target of secure supplies.

The coal industry for long remained a kind of halfway house in energy supply. Based upon natural reserves, it enabled energy production to be liberated from direct reliance on natural forces, but it remained as a substantial human activity involving the direct labour of a large work-force.

The basic shift in fossil fuel supply from coal to oil and gas has accentuated the change in energy supply from a major human activity to the province of a technological elite. In 1913, the peak year for British coal production, one and a quarter million men worked in the mining industry whilst an unknown but large group worked on the transport and handling of this fuel. Today this has been reduced to a fraction, perhaps a tenth, as not only the mining industry but also associated transport facilities have declined. The small coal-yard which lay beside every railway station with its coal-wagons, has gone (along with many of the stations), to be replaced by a highly developed supply network of gas pipes, oil pipelines, and wires carrying coal-based electricity.

This change has altered the 'physical presence' of energy from a tactile solid to a clean, invisible fluid, and has also altered the foundations of British politics. The miners dominated working-class politics in Britain in two ways. Their sheer weight of numbers enabled them to present a powerful, if sometimes aberrant, influence in the Labour Party and the TUC. In addition, in a more subtle way, the particular social and production relations of the miner, his very direct and unalienated relationship with the product of his labour, perhaps even a trace of the old magical mystique of the miner, gave miners' politics a directness which cut through the more complex orientation of other workers. The almost hallucinatory revival of that old presence in 1972 and 1974 may still prove important, but never with the sheer weight of fifty years ago.

In short, within the European context, the issue of public control over energy supply seemed to have been largely settled two or three decades ago. Energy passed out of the arena of politics and became the property of highly technocratic, and often state-owned,

corporations like the Central Electricity Generating Board, Gas
Corporation, National Coal Board, Atomic Energy Authority, in
Britain, paralleling bodies like Electricité de France, Gas Unie,
ENI, and so on, in Europe. Even BP and Shell, in their European
operations, became almost part of this club, alongside the directly
state-controlled ENI and CFP, the Italian and French state oil
companies.

THE ENERGY CORPORATION: THE AGE OF ETATISM

This process, whereby energy became the exclusive property of a
monolithic state enterprise, has developed furthest in Britain and,
possibly, France. Countries such as Germany, Sweden and the
Netherlands have much more decentralised energy economies with a
stronger emphasis on municipal control, something to which we will
return. However, the national state corporation remains the characteristic British unit. The growing importance of the British
National Oil Corporation illustrates how a strong state involvement
in a new energy sector can develop without even a whiff of the
odours of socialism. It would, however, be a mistake to assume an
identity between these state energy corporations and private industry despite the many similarities, notably the formal hierarchy
of work relations and, often, the image cultivated by their external
public relations.

The basic difference is the most obvious, that they have received
a state-enforced monopoly over some market sector in order to carry
out a public service. The CEGB, for example, has a statutory responsibility to produce and supply the cheapest possible electricity, a requirement which is normally interpreted by the Board as
meaning a technocratic form of private industry in which the invisible regularising hand of the free market is replaced by conscious
cost minimising using the marginal cost theory of neo-classical
economics. The electricity supply industry is in fact probably the
only British industry which actually *does* practise marginal cost
pricing. However, various factors intervene to prevent an equation
with private enterprise, for however much these corporations try to
reduce their profit maximising state-enforced monopolies to some
version of market capitalism, the basic fact remains that this reduction is inevitably artificial. The CEGB, or the Gas Corporation
choose to behave like private industry and they may for long periods
behave like such. But the fact of conscious choice remains apparent
and crucially distinct from the necessity of an organisation
governed by the market. Sooner or later, and in recent years it has
been quite common, internal pressure or external government action
surfaces and requires some other course of action to be chosen.

A more subtle though equally effective element is the very
concept of 'public service' itself and the ideological effect it has
upon managers and workers. Much more so than the 'industrial'
nationalised industries, the energy corporations, including the NCB,
are imbued with a sense of working in the public service. Some of
the effects of this are beneficial, in that many of the managers do
feel that they stand in a different relationship to the public than
private industry, that in some sense they have a duty to perform.

At its worst this becomes elevated to an elitist refusal to accept
any outside criticism because it is alleged to derive from some
sectional interest. Only in the corporation, it is sometimes believed, does true, disinterested, dedication to long-term public
interest lie. At its best, it can motivate and enthuse otherwise
purely technical disciplines.

The energy corporations have acquired distinct similarities even
across national boundaries and fuel types. They are all technocratic, in that the corporate view is to regard all problems as
being essentially reducible to matters of improved technology.
Their involvement with technical matters over which they often have
a near-monopoly of substantive knowledge and the fact that they control the optimisation of the supply network, means that they become
very scornful and dismissive about external comment or analysis. In
particular, attempts by the government to alter their plans are resisted on the basis of being political tinkering in matters about
which politicians know nothing.

The question of the democracy and public responsibility of the
energy corporation will be considered below, when other problems of
energy policy have been considered. What, in summary, has been
argued to this point is that these bodies represent the highest
stage of a now-subdued popular demand to achieve equal access to
energy and to the possibility of human liberation stemming from this
access. They also represent an important pinnacle in both freeing
human society from a blind reliance on natural rhythm and, simultaneously, in causing an estrangement from nature.

The electric power-point or gas-connection allows night to become
day and winter to be summer. It also puts the consumer at the end
of a chain of physical transformations so elongated as to dislocate
all connection between the physical origin of the energy and its
consumption. More than anything else modern energy supply exempli-
fies the achievement of modern industrial society, the simultaneous
liberation and alienation of its population.

THE ENERGY CRISIS

It is not intended here to discuss technical options, or to analyse
the economics of energy supply in any detail, but some technical
framework has to be given. In particular we have to consider just
why the coming decade is often regarded as being one of energy
'crisis'.

The energy supply system considered above has depended for its
success upon two interlocking factors, the availability of cheap,
bulk raw fuels and the advantages of scale which derive from large
conversion plants and unified distribution networks. This was only
partly evident in the first stage of the energy revolution, the expansion of coal. The major advantage of coal was its availability
in bulk in certain localities. The fuel it replaced, wood, simply
became unobtainable above certain demands. However, coal did not
require extensive conversion and its transport was relatively
straightforward. Except in certain specialised chemical operations
such as the early synthetic dyestuffs industry, coal conversion effectively equalled coal combustion, an essentially similar process
whether carried out in steam boilers or household grates.

The introduction of oil both accentuated the possibilities of coal in the supply of bulk energy and also provided huge cost reductions in applications which coal could not enter. The first crude oil, from Titusville, Pennsylvania, changed hands at twenty dollars a barrel (about seven and a half gallons). It substituted directly for whale oil for use in house lighting and soon swept the market, in the process ruining the New England whaling industry. Thereafter oil prices pursued a switchback as demand and supply, monopolisation and new discoveries, followed in rapid succession. The bottom of the market was reached in 1930, when the combined effects of the Depression and the discovery of the East Texas oil-fields, caused crude oil prices in the USA to drop to 5 cents a barrel.

Thereafter, the cartelisation imminent whenever three oilmen sit down together, assisted by government regulation, stabilised the world market to some degree. However, prices, particularly in Europe under the impact of Middle East and African discoveries, dropped steadily in real terms throughout the 1950s and 1960s, with crude oil prices floating around two dollars a barrel.

This was achieved by an enormous increase in the scale of oil refining and transport as well as by the opening up of new oil fields. The use of larger and larger tankers, oil-refineries and pipelines achieved huge savings in the unit costs of production. The process, it seemed, had no end as half-million-ton tankers were planned to supersede mere quarter-million-ton tankers, and as ever larger refineries were projected.

Electricity supply paralleled this growth. Shortly after the war, fifty MW electrical generators were common; now 660 MW sets are standard while some giant US machines are as large as 1,000 MW. An average household may have a peak demand of five or six kW, so these modern generating stations, containing two or three turbo-generators, can supply a city of perhaps a million people. As well as generation, electrical distribution too has enormous scale advantages. The cost of putting an electricity cable into a home or factory is scarcely altered if double or treble the power is taken. In the initial period of development, the main problem is hooking everyone into a single grid along which electricity can be channelled from many different generating stations.

The establishment of such a 'super-grid' is the highest point of technical achievement by the British CEGB and it remains a remarkable piece of engineering. And accompanying such feats was a consistent lowering of electricity prices. In the USA, they fell steadily in real terms, from 9 c/kWh in 1940 to 3.5 c/kWh in 1970 (in 1967 prices). In Britain, electricity cost 20 per cent less in real terms in the early 1970s than in 1948.

The great OPEC oil price rises of 1973-4 were a major setback to this steady expansion of cheap energy. It is important, however, to appreciate the difference between the short- and the long-term effects of this price rise.

In the short term, the price increases, which raised crude oil prices up to about twelve dollars a barrel, obviously produced a powerful deflationary shock to those countries dependent on imported oil and it created a serious problem for international financial institutions in the financing of oil-induced balance-of-payments defi-

cits. The deflationary shock undoubtedly assisted in deepening and
prolonging the world economic recession with which it coincided. It
would be wrong, however, to over-emphasise the overall effects
simply of the price rises.

Crude oil, although a vital raw material, only formed a small
part of any national economy and the price rises could be absorbed
by diverting, in rough terms, less than one year's normal economic
growth for most countries. It also became clear that the recycling
of the 'petrodollars', that is the use of unspent oil revenue to
finance oil-importers' payments deficits, could be accomplished by
extending the activities of existing institutions.

The OPEC crisis of 1973-4 proved relatively short-lived and was
succeeded by several years in which the real price of oil fell
steadily. In 1979, a political crisis in Iran quite different to
the Yom Kippur War which sparked the 1973 action, but similar in
consequences, led to another round of rapid leap-frogging in prices
and another threat to limit crude oil supplies.

It would be unwise to speculate about the future of OPEC given
the inherent political instability of Saudi Arabia, Iraq and Iran,
the major exporters. It is easy however to overestimate their effective power. There are clear constraints to OPEC pricing and much
of the apparent dizziness of the 1979 price roundabout can be put
down to the sluggishness of prices in the previous five years.

In any case, UK oil reserves largely insulate the British economy
from OPEC except in so far as the government *chooses* to follow its
rises and therefore to generate tax revenues from Petroleum Revenue
Tax rather than choosing to price oil on the basis of production
cost as is done with gas. The most important consequence of OPEC,
and one that is by no means wholly negative, is that it has stimulated the search for oil alternatives.

The requirement to search for alternatives to oil derives from
two sources. The shock of 1973-4 was directed in part to national
security, to the fact that most countries had become dependent on
a handful of external suppliers for a crucial material input. It
has become clear that no government, capitalist or socialist, can
reasonably allow such a crucial external dependence to continue.

In addition, attention has been focused upon the dramatic interaction between exponential growth rates in energy demand and fixed,
even if large reserves of natural resources. Oil became not just
expensive but also finite. Just why the sudden price rise was required to make this fact plain is not entirely clear but its result
is evident. For the very first time, human societies have been
faced with the problem of how to alter their reliance upon a particular natural resource, as a matter of conscious policy rather than
as a gradual and only partly perceived consequence of underlying
economic and social pressures.

It is quite possible to argue that this pressure is misplaced,
that there is still a lot of oil left and that a too precipitate
rush away from oil is not necessary. There is probably some truth
in this. It is quite likely that oil will remain a major fuel
source for longer than is commonly accepted at the moment. But this
does not alter the magnitude and the uniqueness of the problem.
More likely it gives a realistic time-scale for it to be solved.

The difficulty in shifting reliance away from oil does not lie in any technical shortage of fuel; there is almost an over-abundance of alternatives. Various hydrocarbon reserves, such as the tar sands in Canada, oil-shales or heavy oil deposits, can multiply existing oil reserves several times. Coal is available to satisfy existing demand for several hundred years. Uranium and thorium can power conventional reactors whilst breeder reactors can extend this potential supply by sixty or more times. A range of solar energy technologies, direct solar heating, windpower, waves, biomass and so on are all technically quite easy to develop. The actual supply of raw energy is much less of a problem than is sometimes presented.

It is not even particularly serious that these energy sources are all likely to be rather more expensive than existing oil and gas. As we have seen, the actual statistical importance of energy in the national income is much less than its practical role. Energy is, so to speak, the necessary lubricant but is not, except in certain industrial sectors, a large material cost. A doubling in real unit energy costs, which is about the likely order of change, can be fairly easily absorbed over a period of a few decades.

What is difficult is the diversity and complexity of the conversion and supply systems for new energy sources.

Oil has the remarkable characteristic of being not only cheap to supply but also of being of universal application. Homes can be heated with it, cars run on it, power stations fuelled with it, chemical plants can use it as a primary feedstock. It is the most flexible energy source ever developed by human technology. All the other energy sources noted above are essentially rigid or can be us used in certain end uses only after expensive conversion. Coal *can* be converted to liquid fuels; cars *can* be battery powered; solar heating *can* produce electricity. But all lack flexibility and are more easily viewed as substituting for oil over limited ranges - coal in power stations and large boilers; nuclear in power stations; direct solar for domestic heating and so on.

All this requires that the energy supply trend of the last hundred years be set in reverse. An era of cheap and flexible fuel produces a situation where efficient use of energy at point-of-use and the use of a range of fuels, each appropriate to the application, is submerged in favour of a uniform supply from large centralised conversion plants, which can take advantage of all the cost reductions associated with big units. An age of expensive and inflexible new energy will act to produce the opposite; a situation where there is much greater emphasis on efficient energy use and a flexible supply chain using a variety of energy sources.

Or it will in principle, for what has emerged as a major stumbling block to change is the difficulty in finding the appropriate institutional method for carrying through this change. The great energy corporations, which emerged as the pinnacle of achievement of the old energy supply patterns, are not obviously the right vehicles for the required changes. Yet, in both political and technical terms, they retain enormous influence, having had given to them virtually all power of choice in return for providing, at least a good imitation, of the equal access to cheap energy which was the first and primary democratic demand concerning energy.

The 'energy crisis' as considered here is rather the reverse of what is normally proposed, in that it is connected with a crisis in

energy conversion rather than in raw material supply. The problem
is not that of the oil running out, though this provides an essential context, but rather is concerned with the social implications
of the conversion process necessary to provide replacements for oil.
The raw energy, whether in the form of coal, solar or uranium
presents no essential supply problem. The 'crisis' which has developed is that no capitalist society has yet been able to resolve
this dilemma over energy conversion; decisions about the energy
economy have become more difficult to make as the protagonists of
various viewpoints force a stand-off in which no choices are made.

One of the most significant features of the quite furious battle
over energy supply, which has been waged over the past five or so
years, is that it has contained only a small 'political' intervention, if by political is meant political parties. In particular,
it has involved only minor commitment by the socialist movement
except in certain rather particular cases. As a result the debate
has acquired a rather apolitical flavour.

This is true of the most extreme positions, which are worth considering not because they define on the true complexity of the issue
but because they set boundaries to the choices.

THE TECHNOLOGICAL DREAM-MACHINE

The first option, the extreme nuclear technical-fix has been an implicit part of the baggage of most of the major electricity supply
bodies, Electricité de France and the CEGB are good examples, for
several years. A full intellectual articulation has come from, in
Europe, such men as Hafele of the International Institute for
Systems Analysis in Vienna (an interesting body which brings together medium-level technocrats from capitalist and communist
countries to analyse and model technical change) and from such as
Alvin Weinberg of the Energy Analysis Institute at Oak Ridge in the
USA.

The essential vision is that of an all-electric energy economy
based on nuclear power, coupled in some versions with the use of
nuclear reactors to produce high-temperature heat to gasify coal
or split water to make hydrogen. The basic energy supply unit would
be the 'energy park'; a large energy complex with several nuclear
reactors of various types, fuel cycle facilities such as reprocess-
ing and fabrication, waste fuel treatment and storage and, possibly,
associated chemical plants producing hydrogen or methanol for transport fuel. Such 'parks' would supply a significant fraction of a
country's energy; they might indeed be transnational with some kind
of international inspectorate or operating agent. Weinberg has
suggested, only half fancifully, that what is required is a new
priesthood dedicated to the service of society by producing energy.

Energy parks and an all-electric economy in general are of course
a long way off and can only be described in the broadest terms.
Nevertheless they form a clearly discernible part of the energy
strategy of many influential bodies, the most important of which in
Britain are the Atomic Energy Authority and the CEGB.

There are any number of technical problems about the all-electric
economy, some would say enough to question the whole strategy right

from the start. But the main questions to be raised are social, that is what kind of society requires such an energy economy, and in turn what kind of society is produced *by* it.

The advantages are clearcut, for provided the fast breeder reactor can be controlled and, at a later date, fusion reactors can be developed (and these are big provisos), the natural resource base of energy can be extended to the point of being almost inexhaustible, for fusion reactors can be run almost wholly on water. Energy supply could be reduced to a single set of wholly technical matters; how to take enough electricity to all consumers and how to adapt energy usage to this single supply.

It can be seen that this strategy is an attempt to proceed further down the road which abundant oil supplies opened, that of providing all energy wants from a single, flexible fuel, in this case nuclear electricity. It is, in essence, the final version of the vision first offered by the Calder Hall power station in the 1950s; clear, silent power produced from gleaming spheres by a few men in white coats. No fuss, no miners, no remote oil-fields. Everything under the control of human science, on tap at the press of a button.

It is easy to see why this strategy is so favoured by a large energy corporation such as the CEGB or the AEA, for it offers the ultimate 'technical fix' in which all decisions are reduced to that of technical optimisation, and in which there is almost autonomy both from politicians and from external raw material suppliers.

The huge quantities of cheap Middle East oil caused the vision to fade, along with a series of technical problems which made nuclear power seem less and less cheap. But in the early 1970s, it was possible to view the era of cheap oil as simple a detour on the road to the all-electric, all-nuclear economy.

It is probable that it is this situation which comes closest to the vision of the early socialist prophets, in which inexhaustible energy would enable human activity to proceed undisturbed by arduous labour; in which all unpleasant physical activity would be taken over by ubiquitous machines; in which transport would be free, quick and clean; in which release from required physical activity would be automatically complemented by an increase in mental and physical recreation.

This has been part of the ideological dream-machinery of both left and right for many years. Huxley's 'Brave New World' was a response to it, forty years ago. The electric-economy represents, however, its most precise technical configuration, the first attempt actually to compose the nature and the chronology of such an energy-path.

Most probably it is a path which until recently, would have been accepted, almost automatically, within all advanced industrial countries. However, the twenty year gap between the nuclear-visionaries of the 1950s and the disillusioned 1970s have brought a rather different set of perceptions into play. These can be encompassed, though not defined, by the environmental movement.

THE CURDLING OF THE CREAM

This essay will use the word 'environmental' to classify what is, in fact, a very wide social movement containing elements which politically span the spectrum. However, despite the disparity of views, it will be argued that there exists a clear and consistent environmental position which can be considered independently of the precise aims of particular groups. (Though this should not be taken to mean that the environmental movement is undifferentiated within itself.)

Such a claim will surprise some, who tend to view the environmental movement as a disparate and endlessly changing set of groups, essentially based upon a negative view of opposing all progress. This view, it should be emphasised at the outset, is totally wrong. Whatever the rights or wrongs of particular issues, the environmental movement has over the past years developed a systematic and highly developed critique of modern society; a critique which has gone largely unanswered except for distortion.

The environmental case can be summed up in the famous phrase, as being 'care and maintenance of a small planet', but its implications are extremely complex. The central issue is the relationship between human society and nature, and how that relationship shapes and determines relationships in society between people. In particular it is concerned to redirect the primary direction of change within industrial society. It recognises that social existence rests upon nature: that all the advances in science and technology ultimately give only control not independence, and even then control that is constrained and limited.

This remains as true, in principle, today as it was for a feudal village. However, whereas the feudal village or, for that matter, a modern Bengal village, lived and lives with nature as a rhythmic flow, the relationship of modern industrial society is that of living from stock. The ebbs and flows are evened out by the massive ability of modern technology to open up natural resources on a wider and wider scale.

We have already noted the consequences of this in energy; the simultaneous liberation and alienation of human beings from nature, and have commented that it has been, in general terms, regarded as a progressive and democratic trend. It is not necessary to abandon this position entirely in order to accept the environmental critique but it has to be modified. In particular it is required to examine seriously the implicit relation between technology and progress and the belief that nature exists as an endless source of wealth which is only hidden, or out of reach, because of a failing in human ingenuity.

Human society in advanced industrial countries is an increasingly complex and interlocking mechanism, which relies upon long chains of material supplies and transformation. It may be possible, in principle, to give up or substitute any one of the links in these chains, even to abandon whole chains. If oil reserves dwindle then switch to coal or nuclear power. If one material or process proves dangerous or unreliable then another can be found. All this is possible.

The practical problem is that human society has not so far demonstrated any ability to make these adjustments in anything other than, at best, a hasty and ill-conceived fashion, and at worst, in a spirit of short-term rapacity. The technocratic assumption that complex and technical questions are best resolved by increasingly centralised groups of 'experts' totally fails to account for the institutional and bureaucratic pressures under which all energy policy is settled. This is not a problem only in capitalist countries; centrally-planned socialist countries suffer the same defects. The basic issue is that it has become accepted that a modern, industrial society is one in which entire sections of knowledge in that society, relating to its technical basis, are almost entirely removed from the control and, in particular, the understanding of most of its people.

This segregation of society was initially passed in a spirit of social awe - the era when technology was regarded as a universal, if ill-understood, panacea. Its full implications have only recently become apparent in an age when it has been shown that technology offers no automatic utopia, when, indeed, it has been shown that the dual effects of a split society are, on the one side, an increasing suspicion and fear, and on the other, a persistent tendency for the experts to overestimate their own knowledge just because they are inside the magic technocratic circle.

Nuclear power forms a precise and central illustration of this dual impact. From initial awe, most people have passed to the stage of being, more or less, suspicious and frightened of nuclear energy. The degree of which this suspicion finds political voice varies, but as an underlying theme it is certainly present. The small circle of nuclear engineers have not only resisted this suspicion but have used it as positive proof of the danger in allowing democratic control of nuclear power.

We know, they have said, about the dangers of radiation or of core meltdown, not the masses. We, therefore, should make the decision because only we are not swayed by irrational fears. Yet it is only after thirty years of developing nuclear power that the full dangers of low-level radiation are emerging from such as the Hanford and Rosyth naval yard studies, or the full complexity of controlling reactor dynamics has been shown at Three Mile Island. The 'experts' appear to have consistently underestimated these matters, believing that their superior knowledge could not fail.

Other issues can easily be discovered, for example the now-emerging fact that high atmospheric lead levels, derived from increasing road traffic, have affected the mental state of many urban children, the concern over chemical-induced cancers or the catastrophes like Flixborough or Soweso. None of these things were regarded as 'possible' by expert opinion. All, with hindsight, have shown to derive from faulty technical knowledge.

One of the most striking and perceptive arguments of the environmental case is its challenge to the idea that we *understand* the effects of technological change. Instead of the implicit assumption that the physical effects of any new process are simple linear progressions which can be easily predicted, a much more complex system has to be substituted, which can encompass a maze of non-linear interactions. A good example of this new model is the effect of DDT and similar pesticides. These can build up from very low levels

in the treated plants to much higher concentrations in the body fat
of animals, to the point where they have caused sterility in some
bird populations. The low initial concentrations caused these prolonged side-effects to be discounted by early authorities but the
complex features of an ecological chain produced an effect of local-
ised and severe concentration.

Much of the environmental argument is based upon the suspicion
that analogous processes are occurring throughout modern industrial
society both in the physical and the social environment. An example
of the latter is the failure to understand what happens to social
structure when the built environment is suddenly and dramatically
changed from close-packed slums to wide-open council estates. Most
cope with change, often welcome it, but some do not, perhaps concentrated on large or single-parent families. The resulting social
breakdown can cause vandalism and a crippling of social life in ways
that are almost entirely unpredictable. At its most extreme this
attitude to technological change can become a semi-mystical rejection of industrial society, but this no more represents the main
force of the movement than any other movement's extremities.

At the heart of the argument is the question as to what extent
we can ever fully understand the consequences of major technological
change and, therefore, the extent to which risks should be taken in
the name of social progress. It is an obvious step to move from
this question to an answer which essentially espouses conservative
and selfish stagnation, but to criticise this is not the same as
providing a satisfactory alternative.

Just why these concerns have emerged so powerfully in the past
decade is an issue which requires much more attention than can be
given here. One origin is obviously the nuclear weapons protest
campaigns of the early 1960s. The awareness bred by the knowledge
that it has become possible for human beings to wipe themselves out
and the terrifying consequences of nuclear fallout from weapons
testing - the first time that a new technology had literally pol-
luted the world - undoubtedly sparked a more general concern with
the consequences of an industrial society.

Another factor has been the apparent failure of technology to
cope with the poverty of much of the world's population. This, it
should be said, has proved a double-edged weapon for one of the most
biting arguments against some environmental manifestoes has been
their failure to accept that *any* industrial development could
benefit the underdeveloped countries.

But whatever their origin, the environmental movement has become
a powerful force, probably rather underestimated in this country,
but in other areas, notably Germany, Sweden, France and the USA,
they have become major political influences.

THE ENVIRONMENT AND INDUSTRIALISATION: CONTRADICTIONS AND
RESOLUTIONS

It is clear that the environmental critique is one that has, at
least, to be answered, if not accepted, within socialist theory if
for no other reason than that it has an increasingly influential
position in policy discussion.

One stumbling block is that this is not a class issue, not at least in any primary sense. It is impossible to locate any class conflict which lies at the root of the divergent positions - they derive from differences which are located somewhere else in the span of social conflict, essentially between technological elites and those who are suspicious or frightened by such a technocracy. As a result the environmental movement can develop politically in a number of ways, towards socialism or liberal capitalism or even towards a kind of mystical fascism.

The common socialist response to this is to use this fact to reject the issue from the sphere of politics, to assign it a peripheral place of concern only to the middle-class 'environmentalists'. Alternatively while recognising the serious issues involved, they attempt to assign spurious class values, that, for example, 'big business' lies behind the building of nuclear power stations. So of course it does, but nuclear power has been a consistent loss-maker for the companies involved and most show little active enthusiasm for promoting nuclear power. Moreover, the names of such as General Electric, Combustion Engineering, or Siemens can be found promoting wind machines or coal-conversion processes as frequently as nuclear power. It is as easy, or easier, to make a profit from coal-gasifiers or solar-panels as nuclear reactors and there seems no obvious reason to suppose 'big business' has a resolutely pro-nuclear position.

In practice, left involvement in environmental issues, in particular the anti-nuclear campaigns, has sometimes tended to become reduced to support for the sake of aggravation. Mass mobilisation against *anything* must, it is reasoned, be supported. The argument, though cynical, is not wholly invalid and in any case, a part of left support for these issues has always derived from a genuine agreement with the environmental position, even if the lack of a clear socialist justification has made this allegiance a touch abashed.

The question remains, however, of just how does a socialist practice, contain and resolve the issue discussed above.

There is, it must be admitted, a basic difficulty which touches upon the unresolved and often contradictory position which socialism adopts towards the process of industrialisation. We have already noted that early left attitudes towards energy production were that it was a democratic and liberating force. This, in general terms, was the usual attitude towards technology and industrialisation; that, whatever the short-term problems, technology played a vital part in developing human potential and could not be opposed. Such attitudes were not developed without an appreciation of the actual miseries of the new industrial process. The miseries, however, were always assumed to derive from social relations of ownership; the technology itself remained a progressive force, indeed in some sense, *the* progressive force in so far as it was the necessary changes of the forces of production which produced tensions forcing change in the social relations of production.

Similarly, though much more tenuously argued, the alienation of the individual within industrial society was seen to arise not from factors of technology but from a failure to own or have any social commitment to the final product in a manufacturing process. By

careful use of language and the introduction of appropriate cau-
tions, it remained possible to conduct searing polemics against the
effects of industrial society without ever directing that attack
against technology itself.

The strongest proponents of this were those, such as Bernal, the
famous communist scientist, who would assert that science, as such,
is socialist and that socialism equals science removing technical
progress almost entirely from the realm of social relations. The
point, it could be said, of socialism is that it enables science to
develop faster and therefore benefit society at large more quickly.

Although rather muted in such an extreme form, this position has,
by and large, remained part of the standard intellectual equipment
of the movement ever since. Technological change, whether micro-
processors or nuclear power, remain, in themselves, neutral; what
mattered was forms of ownership.

There are, obviously, a number of criticisms which can be made
of this attitude which, in a number of ways, has prevented the development of any proper socialist treatment of technology. One
example, not considered further here, is the difficulty of making
a substantial critique of certain modes of industrial activity, such
as the production line, and the lack of pressure for changing the
nature of industrial work except as a result of vague derivations
from nationalisation.

Another problem, and one that does concern us here, is that
technological change becomes considered as separate from social
forces; an inexorable scientific process that can be hindered or
retarded, but is on a separate plane to the relations of production.
This may have approximated to reality in the nineteenth century when
industrial and technical development was a fairly linear procedure,
that is, the way in which technology moved forward from one process
to an improvement was straightforward and fairly predictable. It
has, however, grave defects today when, over wide areas, different
lines of technological change can derive from social choice. Energy
supply forms a prime example of this. We can actually choose
whether to supply our future energy needs by developing nuclear or
solar technology; there is no underlying technological imperative
which suggests the necessity of one rather than the other. Moreover, whilst not impossible, it is not easy to visualise these
technologies developing simultaneously, they are to a considerable
extent incompatible.

The one involves removing energy supply almost wholly from individual or social control and giving it to a small, centralised
elite. The nexus of problems about safety, scale of production,
safeguarding of fissile material and security of supply, seem to
make this almost inevitable. The days of believing in nuclear reactors tucked into each neighbourhood are long gone, buried under a
mass of economic and safety factors. Involved in this process will
be a loss of anything other than the most indirect democratic control.

The other extreme, solar technology, puts responsibility for
energy supply on to a much more decentralised basis, if not the
individual household then certainly the community. The use of solar
energy, a 'dilute' energy form, in the same sense as nuclear power
is highly concentrated in the energy density of its reactor core,

requires a diffusion of responsibility away from the centralising tendencies of past decades.

These extremes are just that, and a variety of other energy sources, notably coal, exist which can be used in ways which tend towards either extremity. Coal, for example, can be used in huge central power-plants or in local district-heating schemes. Nevertheless, posing the issue in terms of extremities of choice does illuminate the underlying policy choices.

Energy sits astride one of the major dilemmas of socialist policy, that of the contradiction between centralised planning and decentralised democracy. The difficulty we face is that two, quite separate, traditions of socialism come face to face without any clear guide to their reconciliation. One is that which regards progress as synonymous with technical efficiency and defines at least part of the socialist goal as being the creation of a society in which human beings are no longer ruled by an oppression of physical labour. The other regards human labour as being, in some sense, a vital part of human activity with the socialist aim being the reunification of that labour with nature, the fulfilment of human beings by dissolving differences between work and leisure, natural and artificial.

In one tradition, the provision of boundless energy from unseen, automatically controlled machines forms, by and large, a desirable part of the ultimate society; in the second, this ideal would be a vision of dehumanised society, tyrannised and crushed by its own creations.

These are not theoretical constructs but underpin a good deal of the popular sentiments for and against many major energy developments. Our problem is how to resolve the apparent contradiction in our own traditions, which at present makes left energy policies face in two directions.

There is no point in attempting to resolve the problem by attempting to justify any version of a particular future utopia. Energy supply *may*, in some distant millennia, be derived from the sci-fi personal energy pack, conveniently carried at the waist and drawing power from cosmic force-fields. It may not. But clearly there is little chance of deciding which of the various energy choices confronting us is most likely to lead us towards this delightful goal. In other words, the decisions we take must conform to the problems which we can define now and must be made within the constraints of today's society. These may seem obvious strictures but they are often lost sight of by proponents of both the extreme 'technical-fix' and the extreme environmental solution.

In addition we should realise that no final resolution of the contradiction noted above may be possible. The problem is not one of choosing between pastoral or urban, art or nature, efficient centralism or democratic dispersal. In different ways, these poles are likely to exist as competing tensions within any likely human society. The issue is to try and restore balance and to promote a social organisation which can cope with the tensions without either being pulled apart or dominated by one polarity.

ENERGY POLICY

The technical situation we have described is one in which a clear
choice exists between moving towards a highly-integrated all-
electric economy based on nuclear power, and a more decentralised
energy economy in which a diversity of fuels are used and in which
the historic trend towards a homogeneous supply network is reversed.

   Each choice faces formidable technical problems, the new solar
and coal-based technologies as much as the nuclear systems, though
it is probable that these can be overcome. Neither provides any
real chance of 'cheap' energy: there seems every prospect of rising
energy costs with either route. Each produces associated environmental pollution problems; low-level radiation and safety hazards
in the case of nuclear power, air pollution and trace carcinogens in
the case of coal processes. Each can be regarded as satisfying the
requirements of long-term national security of energy supply if it
is assumed that the fast breeder reactor can be satisfactorily developed. In short, it seems as if there are no general technical
criteria which can enable us to choose between them. There are any
number of particular technical judgments, but these are not substantial enough to dominate the issue. Unlike previous eras, the
basis of choice must rest upon social judgments.

   These social issues are, of course, the nub of the discussion.
The following are offered as being significant in the context *both*
of energy supply as such and also of energy supply as a vehicle for
social change.

   A future energy policy must recognise:

1 that human consumption of natural resource stocks cannot continue
to increase at past, exponential rates of growth. Energy forms a
major part of such resource use and therefore energy conservation
and efficient resource use must form a central point of any energy
policy.

2 That the social perception and understanding of industrial
technology has shifted radically over the past few decades from a
position of general approval to one of vague fear and unease. There
is a real sense in which social life and industrial technology seem
out of harmony with each other.

3 That the centralising of energy supply into monopoly state corporations has engendered a form of technocratic bureaucracy which
needs to be counterbalanced by a more democratic and decentralised
institutional form.

4 That energy needs to move forward from a state-dominated but
market-orientated system to one in which energy can be supplied on
a basis which recognises its character as a major element in satisfying human needs. It needs to be removed from the confines of
state commodity production to one of production for use. Energy is
an area where this is a real policy option because of its special
characteristics of supply, containing large elements of natural
monopoly, and because of its long history of state control.

5 That energy supply systems and fuel types are slow-changing with
several decades required for substantial changes. This means that
energy policy must be tailored to moving society now in directions,
the destination of which are not likely to be reached for a long
time.

The most publicised policy-choice in Britain is that about the future of nuclear power. From a socialist standpoint, there is little doubt that this choice must come down on the side of, at least, drastically slowing the pace of nuclear power-station building. The reasons for this stem partly from the environmental and social issues mentioned above and also from the very doubtful economic case for nuclear power even in terms of centralised electricity supply. This is not to rule out the long-term possibility of nuclear power playing its part in the next century. It would, however, be a markedly more subdued role than at present envisaged by British electricity suppliers.

The fact is that electricity generation is not the crucial energy problem of the next ten or twenty years. There is large over-capacity in the industry and coal-firing could easily accommodate any additional requirements to the end of the century. The basic problem in British energy policy is a strategic one of how, in conditions of short-term energy abundance from British oil, gas and coal reserves, to move towards a situation, which can be foreseen in twenty years' time, of gradually tightening supply constraints. The two crucial areas are transport and domestic heating.

ENERGY FOR TRANSPORT

In 1977, transport took 22.4 per cent of total energy consumed, largely in the form of liquid petroleum fuels but with some use of electricity in rail transport. These liquid fuels, petrol and diesel, are now sold, in real prices, at levels a little below that of 1973 despite the massive oil price rises of 1973-4. This situation has developed in part because general inflation has eroded the real price of crude oil, partly because the oil companies have kept prices down in an effort to increase capacity utilisation of their refineries, which are currently operating at only about 60 per cent of full capacity and partly by the government not increasing its tax on petrol by enough to compensate for inflation.

The drop in direct government revenue from petrol taxation has been offset by the revenues from North Sea oil. These were very substantially increased by the OPEC price rises as the government chose to regard North Sea oil as being sold at OPEC market prices rather than at some figure related to production cost. However, the result of the three factors, noted above, is that motor transport has, in real terms, become steadily cheaper over the past four years after the initial shock of large price rises. This simple economic fact has been a far more decisive policy act than all the public exhortations to save fuel by driving more slowly or socialising transport patterns.

This condition of relative abundance of oil products and a reasonably constant real price is likely to continue in Britain throughout the 1980s if external forces are allowed to continue dominating the market. There is every incentive to the oil companies to bring North Sea oil ashore as fast as possible in order to maximise return on the massive fixed investments and, as mentioned above, another OPEC price explosion is not likely. In any case it would be unreasonable to leave national policy on oil use to the chance of decisive OPEC action.

Sometime in the 1990s, the exact period cannot be located with
any precision, British North Sea oil will cease to cover consumption
and we will either again become dependent on oil imports, which will
by then be coming from a world market also facing supply shortages,
or coal liquefaction will have to be developed for replacement
liquid fuel. In each case the result will be sharply rising prices
combined in the latter case with massive public investment.

It should be emphasised that this is not a sector in which the
government is powerless. A considerable volume of North Sea oil
belongs, at least nominally to the state oil company, BNOC, and such
matters as exploitation rates and landing policy can be directly
controlled under the Submarine Pipelines Act. One of the major
tasks of Tony Benn as Energy Minister was to enforce these legal
rights of control and give them the backing of a genuine degree of
state expertise and involvement. This has not been at all easy, but
several decisive acts, such as moving to forbid flaring of excess
gas from the Brent field even at cost of shutting down oil production, and enforcing a system of preferential licensing, have
brought the oil companies under much closer control. The issue now
raised is whether these acquired powers should be used in an interventionist fashion or whether as in other energy areas, a quasi-free
market should be allowed to develop in which state enterprise acts
as a facsimile of a private corporation. By adopting the price set
by an external cartel, OPEC, as the internal price used for such
purposes as tax calculations, the government has already gone along
the latter path.

Nationalisation of oil company assets, such as refineries and
even petrol filling stations, would be a largely redundant act in
these circumstances. It would involve very heavy compensation to
foreign companies (the possibility of nationalising without compensation or in the form of tied bonds is hardly worth mentioning given
the vulnerable position of many British oil assets overseas), and
would in effect substitute, for a fixed capital investment, a
massive money debt which would always be liable to disturb the
foreign exchange market. In any case, control over all aspects of
refinery policy is easily available by simple government regulation.
It would be fairly easy, for example, to force refineries to invest
in facilities to produce more transport fuels by converting existing
oil-fired power stations to coal burning, a technique which has been
used in Italy. By gradually eliminating a major market for bulk
fuel oil, the oil companies would be forced into investment to
convert fuel oil into petrol.

The area which needs to be considered more carefully is that of
a national transport policy, which will attempt to shift the balance
away from individual transport towards public facilities and to
restrain general demand levels. This is true both for freight,
where more rational use can be made of rail transport and private
motoring. One way of achieving this would be by raising taxes on
petrol and diesel, and this is, within limits, a reasonable move.
However, the limits of action are relatively narrow in any likely
political context and, in any case, the heavy and sudden increase
of petrol taxation would be both regressive and specifically dis-
criminatory against the rural population.

More positive policies would have to come from direct interven-

tion in the field of public transport, in particular an increased
discrimination against the use of private cars in towns and in
favour of enhanced bus and tube networks. One immediate act would
be to act fairly sharply against the 'company car' a device which is
no more than a transparent tax dodge coupled with a built-in tendency towards large and underutilised cars clogging up urban streets.
A simple ban on tax concessions for company cars, which make up 60
per cent of car purchases nowadays, over some maximum size might
provide a useful base. Sweeping parking bans coupled with the increasing use of car-free zones would also move in the right direction.

This, of course, would interact fairly sharply with industrial
policy, in the shape of propping up a car industry which already has
large surplus production capacity, and with urban planning policy.
A removal of tax concessions for large cars might well precipitate
the collapse of, say, Rover and Jaguar, whilst car-bans in towns
requires a considerable degree of popular persuasion in order to
enforce to any effective degree. Roads can seldom be physically
blocked to cars but left open for buses, and mass disobedience is
virtually unpunishable.

The constraints upon effective energy policy in the transport
sector are in fact rather severe, and it may well prove the most
intractable of all consumption areas. The difficulty is that transport has become a highly individualised concern with a great deal of
personal convenience, not to mention public status attached to
possession of a car. This convenience has proved to be only slightly affected by fuel price in terms of miles driven, though decisions
about actual *type* of car may prove rather more easily influenced.
In the final analysis it is this privatisation of transport which
marks out the most severe restraint upon energy policy in the
transport sector. The normal socialist policy for more public
transport, more freight on the railway and other moves towards
communalising transport remain largely ineffective in the face of
this move towards privatisation. The large subsidies required, at
least in the short term, to expand public transport would be likely
to meet with great hostility from a population turned towards car
ownership as a justifiable and beneficial social goal. The effect
of this is to establish the preconditions for a market in energy
which the government can control only by the traditional instruments
of taxation and general regulation. It is difficult to indulge in
too much direct intervention to encourage public rather than private
transport without encountering insurmountable political hostility.
In this, perhaps more than any other energy area, the immediate aims
have to be confined to nudging public attitudes in a particular direction rather than making sweeping changes.

DOMESTIC ENERGY SUPPLY

The discussion of energy in the transport sector has illustrated one
important constraint on energy policy, that of the privatised nature
of the market which it is desired to regulate. Another problem to
the implementation of effective policy is the institutional
structure of the state energy corporations.

The major determining features of these bodies is that they have
been set up and given enormous powers in the context, as has been
discussed, of an energy supply situation where the main thrust of
achievement was to reduce unit costs by using large integrated
supply systems. This has been historically the position of electricity, and is currently the position of gas, where the main determinant in getting the cheapest domestic energy is whether one is
hooked up to the natural gas supply grid.

One result of this has been a notorious neglect of consumer
interest in all matters other than those concerned with security
of supply. The basic issue concerning the energy corporations has
been selling larger and larger quantities of energy, confident that
this policy would bring its own reward in the form of falling, or at
least stable, unit energy prices.

A classic example of this was the selling of electric floor
heating systems to many council housing projects in the 1960s and
early 1970s. The basis for advocating these systems was the cheap
electricity which would be available from the new generation of
nuclear power stations. As a result many new schemes went ahead
with relatively poor levels of heat insulation and without fossil-
fired backup heating, all of which enabled substantial savings in
capital cost. The cheap nuclear electricity failed to materialise
and, faced with huge heating bills, many residents turned off the
electric heating and resorted to paraffin stoves and the like, often
causing severe problems with condensation on walls.

It is this kind of mistake which highlights the institutional
problem of energy supply, for at the same time as the electricity
authorities were pursuing these misconceived plans, local authorities in Sweden, Denmark, Germany and the Soviet Union were adopting
an entirely different solution to the problem of heat supply by increasingly installing district heating. In these, hot water or
steam, sometimes co-produced with electricity, is obtained from a
central boiler and piped around to individual flats for heating and
hot water. Such schemes exist in Britain, but are relatively few
and have not been developed very rapidly in recent years, despite
acknowledged advantages of energy conservation.

The key difference between Britain and these other countries lies
not in climate or fuel costs, but in the powerful local energy
authorities that exist in many continental countries. These are responsible for all energy supply in a district, including electricity, and they have statutory powers over the planning of future
schemes. In Munich, for example, the local authority is responsible
for a large amount of district heating, generating heat from fossil
fuels as well as from burning municipal refuse, and also for electricity supply. Most of its electricity is purchased from bulk producers (who in Germany may be private concerns), but some is generated from the authorities' own combined heat and power units.

In this context, matters such as insulation standards and efficiency of energy use become much more important as the supply body
is much more closely integrated with the consumer and is, in the
final resort, under direct democratic control.

It is also possible to be much more flexible about supply forms
in a situation where power is devalued to a lower level. For example, solar heating is of limited value in Northern climates as a

stand-alone source to individual housing units. It rapidly becomes an economic proposition, however, when considered as a source of communal heating allied to alternatives such as refuse combustion and central fossil fuel boilers. The unit costs of such items as heat stores and back-up boilers decrease rapidly in such a situation.

The primary bodies for developing solar heating are, therefore, the local authorities, but without additional expertise and supply powers over other forms of energy supply, their task becomes very difficult as the national energy corporations can see solar energy as a competitor to their sales rather than a complementary energy source.

In this situation democratic control is not a pretty, but inefficient, principle, but a basic tool for achieving a national and efficient energy policy. Up to now, democratic control has always existed as a rather peripheral demand in the energy sphere. It has never been easy to see how democracy, other than in the most general sense of consumer choice, could play a part in energy supply. Ironically, this idea of consumer choice is now being used as a political block to the development of district heating. It would be undemocratic, it is argued, not to allow consumers the right to electric or gas heating, even when district heating offers a reliable and cheap alternative. As a result to guaranteed heat-loads necessary to prove the commercial viability of district heating have never materialised. The argument is largely spurious, in the sense that few consumers are particularly concerned about the source of house heat, only that it exists, and in any case, the influence of consumer choice over gas or electricity boards has always been very sparse. Nevertheless, it is a valid argument to suggest that any compulsory replacement for gas or electric heat should have a stronger element of democratic control than these bodies.

The local council forms the most obvious vehicle for this democratic control, as in many Scandinavian or German cities, where the chairperson of the local energy supply authority is either elected directly or is a member of the local council. In this context, it should be noted that domestic energy, unlike transport energy, exists already in an essentially public sphere. Moves towards communal supply are therefore much easier than in the privatised transport sphere.

CONCLUSIONS

This essay has attempted to outline the historical and social parameters which sketch in a socialist energy policy.

There are clearly many unresolved problems which emerge, particularly how to integrate the environmental argument into a movement which has, until now, largely accepted the progressive nature of industrialisation as an article of faith, and how to exert proper control over areas of activity which are, by choice, largely individual, but which impinge heavily on collective social existence. In one sense this is all part of a much wider problem, how to move towards some distant social goal when what exists is largely fragmented and privatised.

One point made quite forcibly is that it may be a mistake to view the solution as deriving from increasing the powers of state control and ownership. Paradoxically, one result of this may be to create technocratic monopolies forced to act like quasi-private concerns because they have no other constraints than technical efficiency as defined by profit maximisation and marginal cost pricing. Such overall national supply bodies have a definite function, and it is better that they should be state-owned but clearly this is the start rather than the finish of the issue.

Nor can it really be said that trade union involvement, as such, provides any solution. The extent to which workers' control could exist in the context of energy supply has not been considered here, but it is fairly clear that it could not supply the essentially counterbalancing role which is required to redress the tilt in power existing between supplier and consumer. Indeed, one of the less satisfactory development in trade union activities of recent years has been the de facto alliance which has existed between the technical trade unions, working in energy supply, and the corporations themselves, in promoting such matters as nuclear power. Such an alliance can lead to a situation where even the Energy Minister can find it difficult to penetrate the defences of bodies allegedly under his control.

The local authorities have been identified as being the key bodies in this issue, a conclusion which may surprise, given the tendency of such authorities to themselves become governed by bureaucratic norms. However, it may be that the gradual insertion of a more positive role in the energy field could be a catalytic factor in reforming this area of democratic practice.

Chapter 9

THE NATIONAL HEALTH SERVICE: WHOSE BODY IS IT?

Judith Gray and Andrew Forbes

The National Health Service has passed its thirtieth birthday with very little celebration. Indeed, an air of disillusionment and dismay hangs about this great institution; across the whole political spectrum, from right to left, nobody seems happy with its present operation. As the present economic climate forces the NHS even further into crisis, the inevitable voices are being heard questioning the desirability of a nationalised health sector. The whole concept of the NHS is once again under attack, this time from a Conservative government with concrete proposals to increase the private sector.

Popular criticisms of the NHS point to the huge waiting lists for operations, the bitter industrial disputes which have led to strike action by virtually every section of NHS workers, the general signs of a caring service being steadily replaced by a hasty and depersonalised processing of patients by harassed medical staff. Refusal to co-operate with health administrators' desire for inflexible standardisation of services has led to a recent series of sharp battles over proposals to close local hospitals – notably the struggle to keep the Elizabeth Garret Anderson Hospital open. The health planners' failure to take notice of the expressed wishes of the people they purport to serve contributes further to a general crisis of public confidence in the ability of the health service as it is presently structured to answer the needs of the community.

It has been all too easy for socialists to blame the present NHS crisis on the economic climate. Trade unions and leftist political groups have tended to see a massive financial input into the health service as a means of solving the problems. Campaigns have been organised around slogans such as 'Fight the Cuts', 'more money for better services', which tend to assume a direct relationship between amount of money spent and the quality of healthiness obtained. The danger for the left is to tie itself to defence of the NHS as a socialist institution, without appreciating its difficulties and shortcomings as an enclave within a generally hostile social environment.

The socialists who conceived and implemented the NHS in 1948 were rightly proud of its decisive break from private insurance-based schemes. The explicit hope was that this would allow health and

more broadly, social welfare, to be co-ordinated and planned to meet
real needs in a way that is otherwise impossible. 'A free health
service is pure socialism,' Aneurin Bevan declared in his book 'In
Place of Fear'. But in winning support from the medical profession
for this scheme, Bevan allowed the top echelon of the profession –
the hospital consultants – to maintain decisive control over the
decision-making process of the service. He nationalised a piecemeal
structure of voluntary hospitals, municipal hospitals, nursing and
paramedical services, without elaborating any new democratic
mechanisms which could counterbalance the autonomy of the doctors,
and reorientate the service along lines broader than the limited
ideology of specialist medicine. In effect, the state gave consultants a handsome salary and large financial resources to do as
they wished – as long as they provided a free service for those
referred to them.

In practice this has meant that many of the historical distor-
tions and inequalities in health provision that are due to the exigencies of the capitalist social formation have remained unaltered
by thirty years of the NHS.

INEQUALITIES IN HEALTH

Although there has been a general overall improvement in the
nation's health since 1948, there has been very little improvement
in the fundamental inequality in health between social classes. As
Nicky Hart writes: 'the relationship between health and wealth
stands more or less unimpaired. Everybody lives longer but it is
still the poor who die first.' (1) Even taking into account such
complicating factors as the change in relative size since 1948 of
social classes, and the tendency of those who fall ill to lose their
position in the class ladder, it is possible to demonstrate this
inequality clearly enough. As can be seen from the graphs in
Figure 1, the standardised mortality rates for various diseases and
ailments show a marked gradient across social classes, with considerably more morbidity amongst the lower classes. (2) The perinatal
mortality rates (deaths from stillbirth and during the first week of
life) show that the accident of being born into a poor family still
claims many lives. (3)

There are obviously many reasons why this should be the case
which are beyond the power of medical intervention in itself to influence – for example, the substandard houses in which the poor live
encourage illness. But the NHS has manifestly failed to perform its
social task, for it is precisely where the need is greatest that
health facilities are poorest and most sparse. Julian Tudor Hart
has called this the 'inverse care law': (4)

In areas with most sickness and death, general practitioners have
more work, larger lists, less hospital support and inherit more
clinically ineffective traditions of consultation than in the
healthiest areas and hospital doctors shoulder heavier case loads
with less staff and equipment, more obsolete buildings and suffer
recurrent crises in the availability of beds and replacement
staff. These trends can be summed up as the inverse care law:
that the availability of good medical care tends to vary inverse-
ly with the need of the population served.

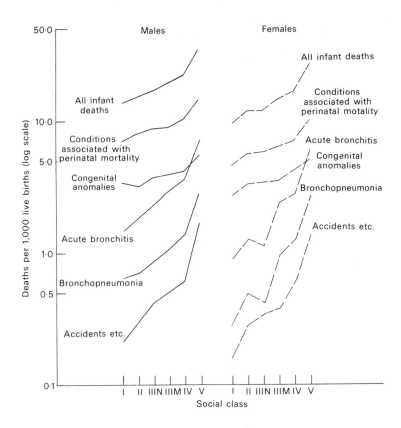

Figure 1   Infant mortality by sex, social class and cause of death
Source: 'Occupational Mortality 1970-72', London, HMSO, 1978,
p.158 (Crown copyright).

This maldistribution of resources has been perpetuated by the
tendency of doctors, at best if only to widen their career options,
to gravitate to the areas with the richest pickings. In working-
class areas a doctor's work is more difficult and often less clearly
medical. Chronic physical ailments are clearly connected to chronic
social problems, which a physician is ill-equipped by background or
training to cope with. This is where the fragmentation of welfare
services into separate compartments has the clearest effect. The
conception of medical intervention which the NHS inherited, in which
physical and social problems are considered more or less separately, has meant that there is hardly any co-ordination between social
workers, community workers and medical workers and little continuity
of care. There is confusion and often conflict between the various
departments of the local authority social services and the NHS, with
each separate administration attempting to shift responsibility on
to the other.
    The recent attempts to switch from institutional to community
care has often led to a reduction in NHS facilities without a commensurate development of local authority services.

With such a chaotic and confusing pattern of welfare responsibility, it is hardly surprising that people are bewildered and therefore unable to take advantage of those resources which are available
to them.   There is strong evidence that the failure to gain access
to the NHS, despite the lack of purely financial constraints, is
widespread, and again follows class lines.

British socialists have done surprisingly little thinking about
the specific problems of those who are the worst casualties of our
social system;   the very poor, who are not organised in effective
trade unions.   This includes the long-term unemployed, large
sections of the immigrant population and often women working at
home.   Being so materially disadvantaged, they have the feeblest
political voice.   Sociologists have argued that they are habituated
to ill-health and tend to be careless and indifferent to their
physical well-being. (5)   There is also a communication gap between
them and health workers;   whereas middle-class patients will consider themselves on an equal social footing to a doctor, and will
not be afraid to ask questions and demand answers, working-class
patients will be ill at ease with a GP's middle-class discourse, and
unable to formulate questions in the expected fashion.   They will
also tend to be far less educated about their bodies.   All this adds
up to a tendency for a large section of society not to refer themselves to health services except in acute emergencies.   Various
health researchers have called this the 'iceberg phenomenon'. (6)
Community surveys have found, for instance, that in Southwark 52 per
cent of people screened required further medical investigation and
possibly treatment.   In Camberwell, 57 per cent of women who had developed severe anxiety or depression over the year before the sur
survey, had not sought help from the NHS.   The bulk of the caring
services that the statutory bodies purport to offer is in fact
carried out within the community itself, with relatives, neighbours
and friends looking after the disabled or chronically ill in their
own houses.

Once these problems have been recognised, it becomes apparent
that the NHS is badly designed to meet the real needs.   Health problems as conceptualised by the medical profession are peripheral,
often chimerical, the product of a 'medical gaze' that goes no
further than the physical presence of a body.   It requires only a
brief glance over the past 100 years to see that the most important
factors influencing general health have not been the developments in
the acute medical services, but improvements in the quality of the
environment, in standards of hygiene and safety, in preventive im-
munisation and so on.

The areas in which the most fruitful and effective expenditure
of resources might be made are under-financed, under-researched and
badly organised.   Preventive medicine - early screening for disease,
health education, environmental health - is done in a patchy and inconsistent way in the NHS.   Community services, which would offer
support to those thousands who are already carrying the burden of
health care, are similarly primitive, relying on a small force of
district nurses, health visitors, social workers and home helps who
can only cope with the most severe cases, and who can only briefly
aid the work of families and friends in caring for their dependants.
The institutional facilities caring for the growing geriatric popu-

lation and the large psychiatric hospitals continue to be the poorest parts of the NHS in-patient services, despite central government's stated intention to give these areas high priority. (7) While brave words are written and spoken about better care for the elderly, the mentally ill and mentally handicapped, scrutiny of the figures shows that no actual shift in financial resources between the specialties is envisaged. The share of financial resources allocated to the mentally ill, for example, is actually projected to fall; this is against the background of an 83 per cent shortfall in the number of local authority day care facilities the government deems a 'national requirement'. Services for the elderly are being cut back by individual local authorities (for example, the Norfolk County Council) against a background of a 50 per cent shortfall in home helps and day centre places, and a 26 per cent shortfall in residential places.

The position of Health and Safety at Work legislation completes a picture of health initiatives which are not being concretised by the provision of money or back-up facilities. The responsibility for monitoring working conditions rests largely with trade union representatives in the workplace. Occupational health services within the NHS are not going to be expanded. The creation of the Health and Safety at Work Commission outside the NHS reproduces the traditional fragmentation of our approach to people's health.

This catalogue of misdirected facilities and inappropriately distributed resources adds up to a deep-seated structural malaise in the welfare services generally and the NHS in particular. As we emphasised at the beginning of this essay, the scope of the crisis in the welfare state goes beyond simple financial solutions. The task for socialists is to come to terms with the full implications of the Marxist concept of political-economy, and to develop policies that grapple with the complex interactions between power relations and economic forces. We must now turn from a discussion of the problems facing the health service to an analysis of the different strategies pursued by the medical profession, the labour government and the administration in their attempts to resolve the crisis in ways favourable to themselves.

THE MEDICAL PROFESSION

Doctors have never been important in Britain as a coherent national-political force. But since medicine began to provide effective answers to health problems they have gained a highly privileged social position, not to mention an aura of glamour and mystery, as people of high technical skill and ethical responsibility. The success story of the profession began with the great advances in public health during the late nineteenth century, when the construction of hygienic sewage and water works dramatically reduced the incidence of such diseases as typhoid and cholera in crowded cities. In a variety of ways, against opposition from business interests and political pressure not to encroach on the profitability of manufacturers and traders, the profession established reasonable standards of public and private hygiene.

But in the early part of this century the type of medical model

which gave precedence to establishing connections between disease
and environment, and which aimed at prevention of the causes of
disease, gave way to a new model based on the discovery of dramatically swift and effective cures for infectious diseases (e.g. peni-
cillins, the sulphonamides). The new breed of doctors concerned
themselves with the relief of individual suffering by means of controlling the mechanisms of pathological processes, and emphasised
curative and mitigative medicine at the expense of prevention. As
Professor Alwyn Smith notes: 'The primacy of the caring professions
arose during the era where the stereotypic illness was acute and
life-threatening and where intervention involved urgent and dangerous procedures carried out under the control of an undisputed
leader.' (8)

Though much was gained in terms of individuals' health, some
damaging features emerged. Medicine became less involved in
people's problems as a community and more of a service industry
geared to the needs (medically perceived) of individual 'consumers'.
The assumption grew amongst doctors that their technical expertise
should give them the right to undisputed authority in taking decisions about patient care. An image was cultivated of the doctor as
a scientific miracle worker thus encouraging public deference to
their activities and opinions, and passive public consumption of
health 'products'. The fact that doctors are almost all recruited
from the middle and upper classes adds a further dimension to the
elitism of the profession: a technicist medical ideology has been
married to a lack of sympathy and even a contempt for working-class
welfare problems.

The 'nationalisation' of health in 1948 simply established in
institutional terms the hegemony of hospital specialists over the
shape of British health provision. This has been expressed and defended by the ideas of 'centres of excellence', private practice
and, most crucially, 'clinical freedom'.

In the name of clinical freedom, doctors have developed strong
autonomous institutions to protect their interests. This is not the
place to delve into the complex network of professional associations, medical corporations (i.e. the Royal Colleges), trade union
organisations and statutory committees which represent various
sections and tendencies in the profession - suffice it to say that
it is in all practical respects self-regulated. Although theoretically under contract to the state, hospital doctors' professional
activity is controlled by independent bodies heavily dominated by
doctors. These various bodies control entrance into and (usually
only in cases of gross misconduct) exit from the profession, determine professional standards, supposedly guard against evils such
as over-prescription, control the distribution of doctors between
geographical areas, decide which hospitals are fit training institutions and negotiate salaries and terms of contract. Government control over such important matters as the deployment of medical manpower is severely limited, relying on the good will of the profession to encourage students to opt for undermanned specialties.
Often the lure of money tempts doctors into surgery or gynaecology
where there is plenty of opportunity to see patients privately, and
not into geriatrics or psychiatry, where there is a serious shortage
of specialists.

The public also has very little control of the deployment of resources by doctors. David Owen in a recent article calculated that
GPs each control annual resources worth £25,000, while each consultant spends an average quarter of a million pounds per year. (9)
The most glaring problem is that of drug prescription.

The relationship between drug companies, run as private business-
es, and doctors, who by virtue of the doctrine of clinical freedom
can 'freely' select from a great range of pharmaceutical products,
leads to a widespread use of expensive preparations of unproven
therapeutic value. There are wide variations in price for the same
drug;   for example, the price of an oral preparation of a cortico-
steroid could range from thirty pence for 100 5mg tablets, to £5.14
for the same number of a slightly different preparation with no
proven advantage. (10) Practitioners rely on the information that
drug companies themselves provide to advertise their products.
Faith in the assured efficacy of the complex and expensive therapeutic procedures has led to the spread of 'iatrogenic' diseases
(diseases *caused* by doctors) such as, most dramatically, the
thalidomide disaster. And the tendency to look to drugs as the
treatment of first preference - Senekot instead of wholemeal bread
for constipation, Valium as an instant response to stress - has led
to an NHS drug bill which has risen from thirty-nine million pounds
in 1949 to three hundred and twenty-seven million pounds in 1974.
(11)

On a wider level clinical freedom has meant that there are great
variations in the length (and therefore the cost to the NHS) of
hospital stay deemed suitable for the treatment of the same condition: in the Liverpool region in 1971 a patient could spend as
little as two days and as many as twelve in hospital for a haemor-
rhoids operation. (12) Planning and budgeting of resources becomes
an impossible exercise in these circumstances.

The doctors' response to attempts to rationalise their activity
has been to be conciliatory on the actual issues while maintaining
a firm grip on their autonomous institutions. The government scheme
of cash incentives to encourage GPs to practise in poorer areas was
accepted, but GPs retained control over the working of the scheme
through the General Medical Services Committee, which designated the
deprived areas and set the cash bonus levels and their presence on
local Family Practitioner Committees, where they could bar newcomers
from coming into an area where huge patient lists gave the present
GPs proportionally large salaries. (GPs are independent contractors
to the NHS whose basic salary is calculated by a head-count of
patients - the capitation fee.) More recently, the Resources
Allocation Working Party introduced a scheme to balance out the cash
given to each Health Region according to need and managed to keep
the implementation of this plan in the hands of administrators
rather than doctors. The idea is that the already rich and affluent
regions, such as London, should receive less money per thousand
patients to enable more to go to regions such as the North-West,
where facilities are poorer and mortality higher. But the influence
of consultants within each region has meant that the teaching hospitals have retained in some instances an undiminished share of existing regional resources at the expense of smaller hospitals and
primary health care facilities in the area.

Where the squeeze on the 'centres of excellence' has been mode-
rately successful this has accelerated doctors' efforts to find
private practice outside the health service. One of the great incentives for their entry into the NHS in 1948 had been the undertaking to maintain private beds in public hospitals at public expense. (13) The labour movement campaign against pay beds in the
past few years has produced a committee to oversee the phasing out
of private medicine from the NHS, but again the committee is strongly influenced by doctors, and is hampered by a commitment to distri-
bute pay beds only when the alternative arrangements have been made.
Obviously a consultant surgeon getting up to a hundred pounds per
private patient treated is not going to rush to offer the same
treatment for far less pay. Rather, as the pressure against private
practice increases, some consultants are accepting posts in a
growing private sector independent of the NHS. But here they become
involved in a contradiction: there are far greater restraints on
clinical freedom imposed by the necessity to keep patients' costs
down than so far exist in the NHS. The new government seems committed to reversing the trend of diminishing pay beds in the NHS.
This may turn out to be a crucial point of conflict with the NHS
unions.

The growing pressure for a system of monitoring the cost-
effectiveness of treatments is perhaps the most serious threat to
doctors' traditional freedom. The idea of a medical audit is gradually being accepted by the medical profession. More controversial
suggestions for controlling the safety and cost of medicines are
gaining ground. (14) These include the introduction of independent
testing of drugs for efficacy, the restriction of prescribing
certain drugs on the NHS to specialists only, and requiring that
the writing of prescriptions be done using generic names rather than
brand names so that only the cheapest would be supplied. But again
doctors are only prepared to concede the issue if they are given
autonomous control over the workings of these policies.

THE STRUGGLE FOR A NEW POLICY

The power of the medical profession within the NHS has meant that
central government has struggled over the years to exert any
meaningful control over health policy. The spectre of an endlessly
expanding demand for costlier and costlier health care finally
spurred the Conservative government in 1974 to restructure the
health administration. A third administrative tier was introduced,
so that we now have both Area and Regional Health Authorities in
layers below the Department of Health. The underlying intention has
been to enclose professional power within a tighter and more pervasive management bureaucracy. An immediate effect of reorganisation
was to give a dramatic impetus to the trend for the numbers of administrators and the cost of administration to rise markedly. In
the East Anglian Region, which nationally spends the least on administration, administrative costs in 1975-6 represented 14 per cent
of the total health services budget. (15)

Tom Heller (16) argues convincingly that we now have a power
dynamic in the NHS determined by the conflict between doctors and

management. The administration is basically orientated towards an
efficient 'delivery' of health care, which in practice means that
they attempt to make doctors' already existing priorities more cost-
effective without questioning the nature of the type of care de-
livered. The order of the day is bureaucratic trimming rather than
discussion of fundamental policy. Consultation over planning decisions involves (necessarily) the medical profession, but is half-
hearted in relation to other interested parties, such as NHS workers
and the general public. Consultative documents produced by District
Management Teams have often been hopelessly partial and imprecise in
the information offered to the public.

Heller documents how one local Community Health Council was given
less than three weeks in the middle of the summer holidays period to
comment on a proposed District health plan. (17) This is hardly
evidence of a real commitment to establish a rapport with the community.

So an increasingly expensive administration has produced ineffective plans with little attempt to find out the needs and wishes
of ordinary people. It is hardly surprising that this sector of the
NHS has come under attack from all sides. But the left should be
careful to dissociate itself from broad charges of administrative
overmanning and concentrate its criticism on the issues of the undemocratic character of the planning undertaken, and its resulting
failure to be appropriate and effective. In this respect, the activity of the professional management of the NHS during the present
crisis reflected the Labour government's failure to deal with the
situation adequately. The medical profession's general strategy of
only accepting reforms which do not challenge their sizeable control
over health policy was not met by an equal determination to seize
more control by the Labour government.

The attempt to impose massive cuts on the health service has, to
date, been largely unsuccessful due to the combined opposition of
all sections of health workers. Unfortunately, the left's reluctance to involve itself in a discussion of peiorities when faced
with a cutting back of the health budget has meant that the worst
cuts have fallen on the traditionally weaker sectors. For example,
staff levels in psychiatry and geriatrics remain critically low. On
another level, an effective fall in the standard of living of nurses
can be compared to the 30 per cent wage settlement negotiated by
doctors.

Faced with insufficient progress in the frontal assault on health
spending, the Labour government turned to a more ambiguous policy:
that of the move to community care. By adopting some of the concepts evolved by radical critics of technological medicine, in particular the call for a more community-based caring service, they
hoped to gain a popular base for such economies as shorter hospital
admissions and less institutional long-stay beds for the elderly.

Health workers have been naturally suspicious that the rhetoric
contained in the DHSS consultative documents (18) is a subtle cover
for a simple intention to cut services. The failure to translate
the priorities into effective action, the superficial approach to
policies of prevention indicated by campaigns to change individuals'
life-styles, the failure to respond to the argument that proper community care would require more rather than less money, all rein-

force this suspicion. Whether the government is genuine or not in
its desire to promote a more humane and responsive NHS, it has produced only a set of isolated, partial, tactical policies and no
realistic strategy for progress along these lines.

The point for the left is not to dwell on the intentions of the
last government, but on the possibilities that Labour's flirtation
with a community health perspective have opened up. What is needed
is a coherent policy to force a potentially reformist initiative
along revolutionary lines. The logical development of moves to reorientate the NHS towards prevention and communal care should take
us far beyond the economics of hospital budgeting.

Ideologically, we should work to popularise the concepts of
health-damaging and health-promoting economies. The Unit for the
study of Health Policy at Guy's Hospital has provided in a recent
study (19) a powerful formulation of these ideas. It is a matter
of perspective: primarily a perspective of situating the sources
of our ill-health in the effects that our particular economic system
has on our life-style and social priorities.

Proponents of social democracy - and these come from all the main
parties - advocate indiscriminate economic growth on the basis that
this will provide the means to finance social justice. But growth
in the capitalist free market in effect finances many of the most
damaging social developments. A few examples are: the promotion
by the food industry of an unbalanced diet; the production of an
environment dominated by poisonous fumes and distressing noise
levels; the encouragement of self-destructive habits such as
smoking and drinking; accidents and illnesses caused by substandard
or downright dangerous work conditions.

A health-promoting economy would aim to create 'an economy where
the healthier choices were the easiest choices'. (20) This would in
essence be an economy where an element of national planning co-
existed with a trend towards more self-reliant, smaller, ecological-
ly-conscious communities. If the political commitment was made, the
NHS could take the lead in researching into the exact relationships
between environment and health and involving people in educating
themselves about avoidance and prevention of illness.

In economic terms the feasibility of such a social transition
needs to be assessed by means of social budgeting. The criteria of
profitability should be widened to include the costs of counterbalancing the undesirable effects of unselective economic growth.
In this light, the argument that industry is productive while
welfare is purely expenditure can be undermined. (21)

Politically we need to start by challenging the established distribution of power among the people. The key notion is that of
democracy; by campaigning for a radical extension of popular participation in government the left can create the forum where socialist ideas and policy gain mass support. Practical opportunities for
beginning this process already exist in the National Health Service.

The major reorganisation of the National Health Service (1974) is
now widely acknowledged to have been mistaken. Even the Brunel
University research team which played a significant part in the
planning of it have provided evidence to this effect. The burden
of criticism is that the reorganisation gave too much power to the
centre and fostered hierarchical or bureaucratic patterns of manage-

ment. This should not be surprising to the architects of the system
since it was supposed to unify and delegate downwards and be accountable upwards. It was also designed to strengthen administration and management, but in a particular straitjacket of descend-
ing hierarchies of authority each appointing the one below.

What is needed in the future is the devolution of power in the
National Health Service. This would free the centre and enable it
to concentrate on neglected preventive issues. It would end the
imposition of single and over-simple solutions to complex problems.
Good health care needs imaginative innovation and careful evaluation
of different patterns. *Devolution* would enhance the possibility of
ongoing *evolution*. (22)

DEMOCRATIC FORCES

Trade unions

Despite the numerical superiority of health workers outside the
medical profession, the medical and administrative groups have retained most of the decision-making power.

At district level, District Management Teams contain three
doctors, one administrator, one treasurer and a nurse, but no other
health workers. Area Health Authorities now include provision for
two staff members, although they are outnumbered by the professionals already on the Area Health Authority. In some areas, however,
this provision has not materialised due (in some cases) to lack of
guidance as to how these two staff members are to be selected or
elected.

Joint Staff Consultative Committees exist in most areas, but many
have become defunct. One issue raised by some unions, particularly
ASTMS, was that of the desirability of sitting on such a committee
alongside non-TUC affiliates. This resulted in a boycott of many
JCCs by ASTMS members. A second stumbling block was the question of
its role - to what extent would the Joint Staff Consultative Committees overlap with individual trade union functions. This resulted in some areas in Joint Staff Consultative Committees merely
discussing 'coffee machine' issues.

Thus the need for recognition and negotiating rights and the
struggle over trade union recruitment in the professional associations have all led to trade unions retaining a jealous separate-
ness, and has led to an unwillingness to co-operate in joint
ventures, a rivalry and suspicion which prevents progress along any
lines other than purely sectional ones. There are obvious examples
where locally trade unions and joint shop stewards committees or
action groups have overcome such sectionalism, but these are exceptional.

In the past poor levels of unionisation, weak union structure,
small units of health service facilities, and the general acceptance
of a subservient submissive role combined with concepts of pro-
fessional-union incompatibility have contributed to the weakness of
trade unions in the decision-making processes of the NHS. In addition, the vast majority of workers in the NHS are women who were
poorly paid and often attracted to the work by a commitment to

relieve suffering, which seemed to rule out the possibility of
strike action.

However, concentrations of health service units and a realisation
that wage levels were low in comparison with those outside the NHS,
combined to make possible the greater unionisation of the work-
force, and the improved structure of these unions, particularly
NUPE, has led to the increasing power of unions in the NHS. Attempts to improve productivity as part of the managerial offensive
within the NHS (which reached its zenith in the 1974 reorganisation)
led to bonus schemes being introduced. This resulted in an increased number of meetings and discussions around pay and conditions
of work and contributed to the establishment of a collective machinery. (23)

Improved wages and conditions of work have resulted from this
growing militancy and the use of strikes as a legitimate weapon.
However, there has been less progress in other spheres. Those
interventions which have gone beyond the economic issues have been
limited, usually defensive, and in very few cases positive and innovative.

Recent campaigns against the provision of pay beds within the NHS
opened a debate, previously carried on in left circles such as the
Medical Practitioners Union section of ASTMS and the Socialist
Medical Association, to the public and presented an alternative
stand to that of the powerful consultants' groups. Unions undertook
industrial action in pursuit of their demands for the removal of
private beds from NHS hospitals. As a consequence, pay beds were
being gradually phased out, at least up to the demise of the Labour
government.

However, in this case, industrial action was the only means by
which trade union members could influence the outcome. This is
because there is virtually no legitimate entry into local decision-
making except recently via the above-mentioned staff members on the
AHA, and indirectly through trade union representatives on the CHC.
A further demonstration of the powerlessness of the unions is provided by their failure to negotiate successfully for adequate occupational health service provision to protect the health of workers
in the NHS. (It also demonstrates the lack of priority of health
and safety issues within the trade unions generally.) Even the
Tunbridge Report, in 1965, went down on record in its castigation
of the NHS for failing to provide a lead for other industries in
respect to the health of its workers.

Because of the unequal distribution of power and lack of entry
into the decision-making and information systems, and also because
the trade union movement more generally has tended to be a negative
rather than a positive planning agency (and moreover has tended to
put most of its emphasis into wage battles), trade unions have
tended only to react to decisions taken by the major power-groups
within the NHS. In today's atmosphere of cuts in the service,
unions fight to protect their members' interests against closure of
various facilities and reductions in staffing levels. This leads to
an acceptance of present patterns of health service delivery. Trade
unions struggle to maintain and even increase expenditure in high
technology, in acute services and in coronary care units, when
evidence disputes the benefit for the patient of such services.

In any case there is little tradition within the NHS trade unions for the raising of general or specific health care issues, and if anything there is a reluctance to get involved in questions of priority or of questions relating to the best methods of delivery of health care. Nurses, for example, following the medical lead, are often antagonistic to the advice of such groups as the National Childbirth Trust and are suspicious of their support to women ante-natally and in labour, seeing it as an unwarranted interference leading to women being more demanding and less accepting. (24) Other health workers, including nurses, take a repressive stand towards mentally ill patients, arguing for locked wards to protect themselves and help their routine, rather than looking at what is best for the patient.

In many general wards the routine of early waking (sometimes as early as 6.00 a.m.) and strict visiting hours is enforced and the spectacle of a sleeping patient being roused to take a sleeping tablet is a commonplace. Induction of labour in maternity wards for medical convenience, strict medical and nursing control of child-birth, the forcing of women to accept pain-killing injections when they know that their own control over breathing and relaxation will be more difficult, these are all well documented events.

In countless instances health trade unionists and health workers outside unions are not concerned with exploring health care from a patient's point of view. The assumptions are that these are not issues legitimately taken up by trade unionists, because their function is to defend the interests of their members in a sectional way.

If it is legitimate for trade unions to campaign against the closure of the Elizabeth Garrett Anderson Hospital on the grounds that a women's hospital is needed from the point of view of patients (no redundancies were planned); if it is legitimate for trade unions to campaign against private beds in National Health Service hospitals on the grounds that it detracts from National Health Service care and that it is socially unjust; then it should be equally legitimate for the trade union movement to be concerned in other broad questions of patient care.

Socialists within the trade union movement should be arguing that unions have a special responsibility to formulate long-term plans for the appropriate patterns of caring facilities, and that they should then develop their power to ensure these plans are actually implemented. These plans must be in the interest of both the community and union membership and this may well include considerable changes in the actual deployment of labour within the service as a whole. If what is advocated is a shift away from institutional, high technology, curative medicine towards community care this will have implications for staffing patterns requiring different train-ing, career structures and pay. Unions must be involved in such discussions in the same way as in Arezzo, Italy. There, unions and the community as a whole were involved in the many discussions which led to the virtual closure of a psychiatric hospital, the setting up of psychiatric hostels in the community, the setting up of community psychiatric teams, the abolition of ECT and the reduction of pre-scriptions of drugs for mental illness, together with a fundamental questioning by the whole community of the meaning of mental illness.

There is already a tradition of 'caring' in health workers; those who choose such occupations do have a commitment to helping people and this should be extendable to discussions about patient care issues more easily even than in the equivalent industrial arena where discussion is already taking place around the issue of socially useful work.

Increasingly British industry is unable to develop without the full involvement of trade unions in planning decisions. This is also becoming increasingly true of the NHS. Trade unions are consulted about the change of use of hospitals, for example, and about issues which are thought to involve the interest of their members. It is a short step away from this to discussing the policy issues which lie behind the change of use of the hospital. Those trade unions supporting the campaign against the closure of the Duchess of York Hospital in Manchester are not only concerned about staff interests but also the welfare of the children, for whom no adequate alternative hospital provision has yet been made. They are concerned too about the cost of transport to and from alternative hospital provision and the whole question of easy access of parents to their sick children.

In general trade unions have passed resolutions supporting contraception, abortion, well-woman clinics, priority for primary care, elderly, the mentally ill and the handicapped, and many other issues at national level. National policy is influenced in this way by the TUC, which has a health sub-committee and by trade union access to both government and trade union committees of MPs. It is, however, questionable whether these bodies have played a leading role in the shaping of the NHS. The gap is far greater however at local level where there is lack of detailed discussion and planning and involvement. It is at this level that positive plans could be most easily put into operation and where lobbying by an alliance of trade unionists and community interests would be most likely to succeed.

Developments in the Lucas Aerospace dispute could act as a precedent. Unions found themselves fighting to protect jobs which at the same time they knew to be destructive - making high technology goods which were ecologically disastrous or weapons. Their campaign involves the right to socially useful work, mentioned earlier. Similar developments could be envisaged in the National Health Service; the beginnings are already there.

Voluntary bodies and self-help

Medicine as practised in developed countries is increasingly being labelled as a threat to health, not only because of malpractice, iatrogenic (doctor-caused) disease and inappropriate treatment, but in the wider sense of diverting attention from the real causes of ill health by attempting to persuade people to adapt to them, rather than change them. There is therefore growing hostility towards a professional and physician-based health care system that 'expropriates the power of the individual to heal himself or shape his or her own environment'. (25)

Self-help groups can be seen as one way of challenging the power

of the established health professions. 'If participatory care gains
wide acceptance, it will be accompanied by a revolution in the
social structure of medicine. The rigid hierarchical structure in
which all knowledge and planning flow downwards from the physician
cannot survive the transition to participatory forms of care.' (26)
Some see the rapid increase in the number of self-help groups as a
'social movement' or even as one manifestation of a new era of
'self-determination'. Vattano considers self-help groups to be
'signs of an evolving more democratic society'. (27) Others see the
movement as essentially reformist, patching up the inadequate health
and social services and threatening with its armies of unpaid
labour, those who work in these services. In fact, all these
positions can be embraced from within a general movement which has
several components. Self-help and voluntary groups can perform one
or several of the following functions:
1 Those within the group helping each other on the basis of a
similarity of problem.
2 Those within the group helping others mainly outside the group
on the basis of a perceived problem (of the others).
3 The group lobbying for the interests of either themselves or
others or both.
4 The group challenging fundamentally some aspect of health delivery or the health care system.
  Each of these functions needs some closer inspection.
  The *first function* is the most common within self-help groups
proper, but less common amongst other voluntary groups like WRVS.
The fundamental idea is that those in the group have a similar experience and can collectively discuss it and give support to those
in the group. Support includes a recognition, help to overcome the
stigma of the problem (e.g. cancer), a continuing commitment, continuing help but without the 'us and them' distinctions; in some
cases a redefinition of the problem; and in some cases a new way
of life. (28) There may or may not be a challenge to professionalism. Women and health groups do challenge it; (29)

  Professionalism in medicine is nothing more than the institutionalisation of a male upper class monopoly. We must never confuse
  professionalism with expertise. Expertise is something to work
  for and to share: professionalism is - by definition - elitist
  and exclusive, sexist, racist and classist.
But most groups do not really question either professionalism nor
the present health care system. Some groups performing this
function are totally separate from the medical profession whilst
others are seen as distinctly threatening by the medical profession;
but many do have connections, for example Alcoholics Anonymous.
  The women's Community Health Centre (Cambridge, Mass.) defined
self-help as: (30)
  Women sharing experience, knowledge and feelings - women supporting each other and learning together. Self-help begins by
  working from a practical base, starting with learning from
  physical self-examination, finding out what we *do* know and exploring from there.
    Self-help groups are action orientated. One self-help group
  might investigate the menopause, another human sexuality, another
  lesbian health issues, another might train as paramedics and

health counsellors. The possibilities are endless, depending only on our own creativity and needs.

Self-help is women relating to ourselves in order to demystify health care, the professionals and our own bodies; it involves being able to make personal choices based on our won very valid experiences and knowledge. Self-help is a positive action by which we can change our own lives and those of our sisters.

Self-help is a political act. It is deeply challenging to the existing health care system. Through sharing our knowledge collectively we have developed skills - we, not only 'the professionals' will know what is done to us medically and why it is done. We do not take the place of the doctor but we *do* reverse the patriarchal-authority-doctor-over-patient roles!

At its best this community of interest, sympathy and action points the way to the community of the future; self-empowerment, and personal growth. At its worst this function can remove some of the most important aspects of nursing care into the voluntary field, thereby restricting the extension of this kind of care into professional groups.

The *second function,* that of helping people outside the group, is common to many groups, but exclusive to some like WRVS. In a sense it poses the greatest problem. Many such organisations are written off as 'charitable do-gooders'. They are seen as salving the conscience of the rich, ridden with Victorian attitudes towards welfare (the 'give them clothes but never money' attitude). Certainly at a time of National Health Service and Social Services cuts they can be accused with some justification of plugging gaps in those services. They have been seen as agents for depressing health workers' wages and even as strike breakers.

A criticism little heard, however, is that they remove certain 'human' aspects of caring from nursing (like chatting and giving out meals, taking patients for walks, etc.) leaving nursing to include only the most stark and painful tasks. Yet this criticism is often voiced by nurses.

Some of the good aspects of this function are displayed by such organisations as Battered Women's Aid which have set up services and facilities which give examples of better methods of care, challenging sexism, bureaucracy and often containing the element of 'helping people help themselves'. Another example of this is the Liverpool 'Home Link Scheme' which was originally a community-development educational venture funded by a Dutch charity but which resulted in women in a working-class council estate in Netherley setting up their own playgroups, a vegetable co-operative, and getting qualifications and jobs for the first time. The Waterloo Action Project and the Pitt Street Settlement in London have both set up women and health groups (paid community health workers being involved) which now discuss many aspects of women's health and also have started to provide some critique of local health facilities.

At its best this function points to new and better ways of doing things which could then be used as examples for the existing services and the planning bodies of the National Health Service and Social Services should benefit from these inspirations. At its worst this can let the authorities off the hook and threaten existing workers. A dialogue between those working in the service and

and those outside would perhaps lead to ways of getting the best
with a minimum of the worst.

The *third function,* that of the lobby, is not so common as the
first in self-help groups which, in many instances, put the emphasis
on *self*-help and less on trying to get services to take up issues
raised during their meetings.

However, groups like MIND, The Patients Association and the
National Childbirth Trust, make proposals at national and local
levels for changes in the National Health Service on issues ranging
from the rights of the mentally ill to the rights and facilities for
women in labour. Where such groups have taken up issues they have
had a real impact. They are seen as a threat not only be some
doctors but also by some nurses. However, the potential of such
groups in district health planning teams cannot be underestimated
and in planning at Community Health Council level, and in the Joint
Care Committees that we propose below.

The *fourth function,* that of the fundamental challenge, is overtly made by women and health groups, and less overtly by MIND, and is
encompassed by some aspect or other of groups' activities, e.g. the
patients' associations, the National Childbirth Trust, the Mental
Patients Union and many more. The third function, however, that of
the lobby, could well develop into this, especially if organisations
were to be involved in planning and began to realise just how difficult it was to shift certain power blocks within the National
Health Service.

Concentration on individuals and their problems is the essential
feature of self-help, but it does mean that self-help groups rarely
explicitly focus their attention on any broader structural features
of the shared situation in which they find themselves. The fact
that modern industrial production concentrates the work-force in
dense urban centres where 'homelessness, overcrowding, noise,
stress, loneliness, and other social problems are at their worst
and their most acute and where the emotional and psychological if
not physical health of the population is at its most fragile.' (31)

Some groups who do challenge the medical system, the 'illness
service', in its many aspects, do propose radical changes. Others,
such as *some* of the women and health organisations, write off the
medical system and concentrate on building alternatives outside the
NHS. (This is more true of the US women and health groups.)

All the previous three functions contain within them certain
aspects of a challenge to present 'care delivery systems', when seen
from the position 'the personal is political'. Challenges to the
bureaucracy of the National Health Service are producing exciting
developments; people are finding out for themselves what they want,
getting the self-confidence to make demands of the service, becoming
self-activating and community-activating. A new kind of democracy
is being seeded. Certainly the DHSS is looking to self-help to
provide the cheap cure to National Health Service ailments, certainly the Health Education Council is telling everyone to 'help themselves', but this need not blind us to the positive aspects of self-
help.

Nowadays community care is seen as the cheap panacea for many
problems ranging from care for the mentally handicapped to early
discharge for appendicectomy patients, and it is the basis of plan-

ning for the services for the mentally ill and to some extent elderly and physically disabled. This issue raises many questions rather
similar to those outlined under voluntary bodies and self-help. In
one sense the biggest voluntary body of all is the body of women
doing unpaid labour in the home. It is assumed by the planners of
health and social services that such a group of women exist in the
home and that they are just waiting to do this work.

At present, it is estimated that there are 300,000 single women
at home looking after relatives. Services are offered less to the
elderly if they do not live alone; district nurses call less frequently to the chronic sick if a woman lives in the home; the
health of the mother is the biggest determinant of whether the
handicapped child is institutionalised; and even housewives cannot
take time off to be ill, but go to the doctor just to keep going.
(32)

But most people would prefer to be looked after at home, within
a community they know. This is one of the most crucial issues in
the National Health Service today and yet there has been little
debate on it. Solutions from the left tend to be traditional;
'community care must be undertaken by paid, trained staff'. The
possibility of treating all people as individuals, removing any assumptions about women being dependent on men are written off as
'wages for house-work' and decried as institutionalising and fossil-
ising the position of women in the home, isolated for all time. No
real thought has been given to the possibility of everybody, over
sixteen, men and women, being eligible for social security or unemployment benefit whether they are married or not and the divorcing
of marriage from financial dependence. Except, that is, for the
consideration given to the question of legal and financial independence by some sections of the women's liberation movement.

On the other hand, a counterposing, although not necessarily
contradictory perspective, visualises the future as one of a shorter
working week, more holidays and more time, therefore, to develop
work in the community - perhaps unpaid - as part of the building of
a sense of community a sense of caring. This issue, the issue of
community care will remain in the arena of mere polemics unless
these ideas are developed on the left.

Community Health Councils

Consumer input into the reorganised National Health Service was felt
to be politically necessary, but was resisted by many within the
service. The Community Health Councils were added on to the new
structure to provide this input but in such a way as to make it unlikely for its function to be a meaningful one. CHCs cover
districts in multidistrict Area Health Authorities and areas in
single-district AHAs. Community Health Councils have between
eighteen and thirty members, half of them nominated by the local
authority, one-third nominated by voluntary organisations and one-
sixth nominated by the Regional Health Authority. The dilemma of
whether these bodies should be part of the management structure or
remain at a distance from it was inevitable.

The worry about being part of the structure is that Community

Health Councils would thereby be incorporated into it and be indistinguishable from the lay membership of the Area Health Authority. This could lead to their identification as part of the system not only by management, but by the public at large. They would, perhaps, be seen as less approachable and, more importantly, as less the representatives of the community more the representatives of management, explaining to the community the actions of management – a broker's role. (33)

The problem connected with remaining at a distance as at present is that Community Health Councils have no real power and very little money. (Budgets vary from £10,000 to £20,000.) The surveying of public opinion is very difficult in this situation and access to the information that they need for monitoring management is dependent on precisely that management that they wish to monitor. Communication with the public is imperfect and most people have no idea of Community Health Councils' existence and of what they are supposed to do. The corollary of being in a position (distant) to be 'activist' (Klein) is to be suspect and to be given none of the means to develop this activism.

Actual membership of Community Health Councils is more middle-class and middle-aged than the community they represent. Selection procedures for the *voluntary members* vary throughout the country. Each member has one or several partisan interests and problems arise in developing a balance between competing interests or ideas and how to arrive at solutions which are in the interest of the entire community. Powerful lobby groups can develop within Community Health Councils representing geographical interests or particular disease or client groups.

The local authority members of the Community Health Council may see themselves as primarily local council members with knowledge and interest in aspects of local politics but no real knowledge or interest in the National Health Service. For them it can easily be seen as just 'another committee'. When local councillors are elected they do not stand on health issues because the local authority does not manage the NHS.

Because of this and because the Area Health Authority is an appointed body with again no direct local accountability, there have been many proposals over the past forty years to make the management of the National Health Service more locally representative.

One proposal was that the Health Service should come directly under Local Government control, (34) and more recently a proposal that it should come under regional government. Further propositions include one to elect a specific district *health* authority at a separate election. This would ensure that only people who were interested in the Health Service would stand for election to this particular body. However, this would have the disadvantage that the other parts of local government such as housing and environmental health and social services would be still the province of the present local authority. The Campaign for a Democratic Health Service, which proposes this model, does suggest strongly that the local authority and the District Health Authority should have the same boundaries (coterminous), which would go some way to ensuring that there was a basis for collaboration.

At present Community Health Councils have observer status at Area

Health Authority meetings with the right to speak but not vote.
Another possibility, therefore, for Community Health Council involvement in decision-making would be for their members to have
greater representation and to have voting power. This would consolidate the 'broker' function, but, it is argued, could detract
from the 'activist' function.

The District Planning Teams of the Area Health Authority, which
were set up after reorganisation to make planning on certain patient
care categories (for example, the elderly, children, etc.), can
co-opt representatives of Community Health Councils, but so far many
planning teams have resisted this. Here again there would be opportunities for Community Health Council members to become involved
and knowledgeable about specific health care topics and therefore
they would be better equipped to make detailed proposals, but again
there is the fear of incorporation, the other side of the two-edged
sword.

The same arguments have been put up by trade unionists when
debating the Bullock proposals on industrial democracy, namely that
the trade union representatives would be 'co-opted' into the management structure, would enjoy the power of being on a managerial body,
would lose contact with the members, and would be involved in
running the 'system' and therefore compromised. It is argued that
it is necessary to keep the two sides apart, to keep class interests
opposed and not blurred, to ensure that trade unionists do not
become advocates of management. In rejecting these arguments,
whilst understanding the dangers and real difficulties posed by
them, a vision of democratic participation is needed.

It will only be possible for trade unionists to participate in
management (whether of private industry or National Health Service)
and for Community Health Councils to participate in Area Health
Authorities and District Planning Teams without the problems of
co-option if a structure of democratic accountability and reporting
back is devised, coupled with a model for their involvement in positive planning.

When Community Health Councils and trade unionists are seen by
the community and trade union members respectively as furthering the
interests of their 'constituencies' they will be regarded as relevant, but to do this they need access to the kind of detailed information which is only available if they are more solidly part of
the structure. They will, on the other hand, only be in a position
to further those interests democratically if they are in real
contact with their 'constituencies'. This will require, in the case
of the Community Health Councils, the funding of meetings and of
surveys, in other words the wherewithal to go out to the community
to find out what the people want; and, in the case of unions, time
off and finance to do the kind of detailed alternative planning such
as the Lucas Aerospace shop stewards were involved in recently.
(The problem of the Lucas proposals was that they did not arise
within any such structure and that they have been ignored by trade
unions and rejected by management and will only be implemented as a
result of a vast campaign and much conflict.)

Even more difficult for the Community Health Councils is the task
of raising the issue of the health of the community rather than ad-
hering to an illness-orientated approach. Ensuring ample coverage

of an effective curative service is important, but should not detract from adequate consideration of the preventive and caring
functions of the service, particularly community support. This may
require such developments as the linking of local authority members
of Community Health Councils with social service, housing and environmental health aspects of the local authority; a kind of m
mirroring of the joint care planning between the two authorities.

The achievements of some Community Health Councils in finding out
what people want from particular aspects of the National Health
Service (for example, maternity services in Liverpool South
District), joining up with voluntary bodies nationally (for example,
in this case, the Spastics Society), or Trade Councils (for example,
in Islington to campaign for a well-woman clinic), and achieving
real improvements in the Health Service locally, will inspire many
Community Health Councils to do likewise. The setting up of a
national body of Community Health Councils and the production of
'Community Health Council news' should spread the ideas and the
confidence.

Many of the above achievements of Community Health Councils have
been the result of informal alliances at local level. In the next
section of this essay we go on to discuss the development of these
alliances - the setting up of broader democratic structures.

BROADER DEMOCRATIC STRUCTURES

1 Patients' committees

The first patients' committee was set up in 1973, attached to
Aberdare Health Centre in Wales. It participates with the health
team in the running of the health centre in all its aspects. First
of all a general meeting was held to which all patients were invited. This elected a patients' committee which meets once a month.
The patients' committee discusses complaints about the practice, but
mainly talks about such matters as improvements in primary care
services, the hospital needs of the area, the starting up of a
screening service for the elderly, the care of mentally ill and the
transport to hospitals. The committee has also initiated a scheme
to create a system of street wardens with the intention of keeping
an eye on every old person in the town. This is supported by the
local council, the Community Health Council, local milkmen, postmen,
newsagents, social services, the pensioners association and the
National Union of Mineworkers. The committee also arranges social
clubs and gatherings.

One of the most important functions of the committee is health
education: information about preventive and positive health is
given; people are encouraged to improve their health status and
early signs and symptoms of disease are taught. Doctor Alistar
Wilson, who works at the health centre, writes: (35)

We do *not* consider that people expect too much of modern medicine
for many patients are prepared to accept a very low level of
general practitioner care, in shabby shops from doctors who
employ no staff, who have no time to listen, who take the quick
remedy of handing out pills for almost everything, for whom the

curative and ameliorative possibilities of modern medicine have
been superseded by the dogma of sticking medical labels on their
fellow human-beings (malingering is a favourite word). ... A
doctor must listen, question, examine, explain what he thinks is
wrong and discuss with the patient the proposed treatment. Often
no other treatment than counselling is required. Thus what is
being attempted is to use the untapped wealth of human understanding to fight disease and to teach the public the sort of
standards of health care they should *insist* on having. Greater
public understanding can produce levels of G.P. and hospital care
with subsequent improved public health and a big reduction in
preventable and therefore unnecessary illness and premature
deaths. The main way in my opinion to do this by involving the
general public in the running of all the health services and to
make the public conscious of the need to insist on the availability of the highest level of care, modern medicine can provide.
Patients' committees, I believe, are essential for this purpose.
Since then ten other patients' committees or associations have
been set up in various parts of the country.

Patients' committees are not recognised within the structure of
the National Health Service. At present their existence depends on
the goodwill of the general practitioners in those individual
practices to which they are attached. This could clearly lead to
problems if the committee made demands which the general practitioners were not willing to go along with. It also means that in
practices where the general practitioners are opposed to such a
democratic structure, there will be little chance of its being set
up.

However, despite these reservations, this coming together of
patients to discuss the health of the community represents a step
forward and there is great potential for extending knowledge, developing innovation, criticism and constructive planning. This will
be augmented by contact and collaboration with other local groups
such as trades councils, Community Health Councils, and voluntary
groups in the community.

Proposals for other broad democratic structures

Within any community the organised focus for collective trade union
activity may well be the Trades Council. Many Trades Councils have
taken up health issues both national and local. Some Trades
Councils have set up health sub-committees to examine in some detail
health problems. There has been a tendency for some of these to
centre around the field of health and safety at work. If these sub-
committees were to join with representatives of voluntary groups and
Community Health Councils on either a formal basis (by the inclusion
of such organisations in its membership) or on an informal basis (by
holding irregular meetings to which these representatives could be
invited), then an arena would be created for the discussion of community health needs and the formulation of alternative plans would
be possible. But, in addition, specific differences could be aired
and possibly solutions found to such questions as raised earlier,
e.g. unnecessary induction of labour, locked wards, etc., which at

present only seem to concern certain specific voluntary patient groups.

This forum would also provide the means for trade unionists to put forward *their* side of industrial disputes to gain the support and at least the understanding of such voluntary organisations. There is much conflict at present underlying what little relationship exists between health workers and some voluntary patient groups. There may well be much 'speaking bitterness' as happened after the Chinese revolution when the women voiced their feelings after decades of class and male oppression. Without this coming together, however, there is no possibility of progress in patient care.

The mechanisms for action of the joint care forum could be directly from the Trades Council to the TUC and so to the government; from the Trades Council to the Community Health Council (most Community Health Councils have a Trades Council representative) and so to the Area Health Authority; or from the Trades Council directly to the Area Health Authority, or indirectly through its representative actually sitting on the Area Health Authority.

The North-West leads the way

The North-West (regional) TUC has agreed to set up a joint care committee on the above lines comprising trade unionists and representatives of voluntary bodies and Community Health Councils. Positive alternative planning for the North-West health service is to be its main objective, although co-ordinating such campaigns as those against the closure of some NHS facilities may well be an important task also.

By concentrating on such developments we do not intend to denigrate the achievements of the Socialist Medical Association, which for years has provided a focus for left-wing discussion. But the Socialist Medical Association has remained a small organisation, and by acting mainly as a ginger group for the Labour Party has not involved people who would not identify themselves as socialists, but who, none the less, are concerned to change the National Health Service. Health Service trade unionists and members of voluntary bodies may not see themselves as socialists, but in challenging the present ideology of the 'National High Technology, Cure and Illness Service' they undermine ruling-class hegemony. We see the building of such broad democratic organisations as one example of the kind of detailed work required if a broad democratic alliance is to be put into practice.

CONCLUSION

This essay has dealt with the issue of control. We have examined the continuing influence of the medical profession in the control of health priorities and resources in the National Health Service. We have looked at the way in which the medical ideology of individual pathology holds individuals responsible for their own health and denies the wider social and political determinants, isolating

patients in a role of passive acceptance. Medically mediated
ideologies apparently depict what is natural, but actually transmit
social values. They persuade in the name of medicine, making moral
prescriptions on social behaviour - on reproduction, fertility,
family relations, the work ethic, and so on. (36) M.C.Versluysen
writes 'the medical profession has become a guardian of the social
order and a propagandist of values particularly functional to the
social and sexual relations of modern capitalism.' (37)

   We are arguing for a scrutiny of the body of institutionalised
ideas and practices which we call modern medicine - whose body is
it? And we are challenging, as the Women's Liberation Movement
does, existing (medical) ideas about who should control our bodies,
our illness and our health. This challenge is as much a political
challenge as the demands of workers to have control over industry.
We have argued that within the National Health Service these two
struggles should be seen as necessarily complementary.

NOTES

1 Nicky Hart, Inequalities in Health, Department of Sociology,
   University of Essex, March 1978, p.1.
2 Reproduced from Hart (ibid.), p.43, p.60.
3 For detailed discussion of the statistical problems, see Hart
   (ibid.), pp.12-38.
4 J.Tudor Hart, The Inverse Care Law, 'Lancet', 1971, vol.I,
   p.405.
5 See Nicky Hart, op.cit., pp.111-23.
6 Taken from a survey of recent findings by Tom Heller:
   T.D.Heller, 'Restructuring the Health Service', London, Croom
   Helm, 1978, pp.68-70.
7 See DHSS, 'Priorities for Health and Personal Social Services
   in England', London, HMSO, 1976.
8 Alwyn Smith, Priorities for Allocation of Resources, 'Royal
   Society of Health Journal', April 1976.
9 David Owen, The NHS and Public Expenditure, 'New Statesman',
   23.4.76, p.532.
10 L.W.B.Grant, The Cost of Drugs, 'British Medical Journal', 1973,
   vol.I, p.416.
11 Editorial, NHS Drug Costs, 'Lancet', 1976, vol.I, p.921.
12 R.F.L.Logan, The Dynamics of Medical Care, Memo no.14, London
   School of Hygiene and Tropical Medicine, 1972.
13 See Heller, op.cit., pp.40-1.
14 The exact nature of the financial and political relationships
   between doctors and the multinational drug industry, and the
   question of nationalisation of the drug companies are vital
   issues that need to be discussed at length. Control over a
   pharmaceutical industry which is so internationally based
   cannot be achieved straightforwardly. For further discussion
   see T.D.Heller, 'Poor Health, Rich Profits', Nottingham,
   Spokesman Books, 1977.
15 For details see: Institute of Health Service Studies, 'New
   Bottles, Old Wine', Hull University, 1975.
16 Heller, op.cit., pp.11-12.

17 Heller, ibid., pp.28-31.
18 In particular: 'Priorities for Health and Social Services in England', op.cit. and 'Prevention and Health: Everybody's Business', London, HMSO, 1976.
19 Peter Draper et al., 'The National Health Service in the Next 30 Years', London, Unit for the Study of Health Policy, Department of Community Medicine, Guy's Hospital Medical School, July 1978.
20 Ibid., p.33.
21 A good recent introduction to the notion of a social audit is Michael Barret Brown's essay, Profits and Losses and the Social Audit, in 'The Right to Useful Work', ed. Ken Coates, Nottingham, Spokesman Books, 1978.
22 Draper et al., op.cit., pp.30-9.
23 See Tom Manson, Management, the Professions, and the Unions: Power and Ideology in the NHS, a paper given to the British Sociological Association Conference, 1975.
24 A Merseyside obstetrician speaking to the Mersey Regional Health Authority Conference, Bringing Antenatal Care to the Consumer, October 1978, characterised unco-operative women patients as 'know-alls' and 'flat earthers', citing as an example a woman who insisted on conducting her labour in a squatting position. He explained that they were 'forced to anaesthetise her and deliver her baby for her'.
25 I.Illich, 'Medical Nemesis', London, Calder and Boyars, 1975.
26 S.F.Jencks, Problems in Participatory Health Care, in 'Self-help and Health - A Report', New York, New Human Services Institute, 1976, pp.86-98.
27 A.Vattano, Power to the People: Self-help Groups, 'Social Work', 17, 1972, pp.7-15.
28 David Robinson and Stuart Henry, 'Self-help and Health', London, Martin Robertson, 1977.
29 B.Ehrenreich and D.English, 'Witches, Midwives and Nurses', London, Writers and Readers Cooperative, 1975.
30 Boston Women's Health Collective, 'Our Bodies Ourselves', British edition by Angela Phillips and Jill Rakusen, Harmondsworth, Penguin, 1978, p.561.
31 M.Versluyen, The politics of self-help, 'Undercurrents', 19, 1976-7, pp.25-7.
32 Mary Ann Elston, The politics of Community Care, a paper given to the Politics of Health Group Conference, 1977.
33 R.Klein and J.Lewis, National Health Service: Brokers or Activists?, 'New Society', November 1974, p.547.
34 See the DHSS proposals on the reorganisation of the Health Service: 'National Health Service: The Future Structure of the NHS', London, HMSO, 1970.
35 'Vote for Good Health', published by the Campaign for A Democratic Health Service.
36 See Leeson and Gray, 'Women and Medicine', London, Tavistock, 1978.
37 M.Versluyen, Health Care and the Women's Movement, 'Medicine in Society', vol.3, no.3, p.8.

Chapter 10

MAINTAINING STATE PROVISION - PUBLIC HOUSING

Adah Kay

INTRODUCTION

This essay is concerned with some of the practical, political and
ideological problems posed by the mass provision of public housing.
(1) The issues raised, although fairly specific to the relationship
between local authorities, as landlords, and their tenants, have
wider applications for other areas of state provisions.

Unlike other aspects of the welfare state such as health or education, public housing has never been conceived of as a universal
provision. In its current form the British welfare state is a
partial attempt to ensure that the poorest and most exploited
sections of society have an enlarged scope for living mainly in
areas of reproductive need. These provisions represent social costs
which for various reasons the private sector has been unwilling and
unable to meet. This poses a basic contradiction for a society
which does provide for social collective needs based on use-values
within the context of an economic, political and social structure
dominated by the private ownership of capital and property. Public
housing thus reflects basic inequalities and class divisions in
Britain in which access to it has in practice been limited to those
groups which fall into the changing public definitions of 'housing',
'social' or 'economic' need.

The extent to which public housing provision is dominated by conditions prevalent in the economy as a whole and by existing social
and political relations, can be but briefly indicated here as the
necessary context for discussing the form of the landlord-tenant
relationship within the public sector. The financing of public
housing is mainly achieved by loans raised through private and corporate capital. The burden of the debt repayments, however, fall on
the revenue accounts of the various providing local authorities.
Thus increasingly, although relatively more may be spent on public
housing, as reflected in capital spending, the burden of the
spending goes to debt repayments. The construction and rehabilita-
tion of public housing is mainly undertaken by the private building
industry, largely dependent on casual and unorganised labour with a
very low productivity in relation, for instance, to manufacturing.
The rent structures of public housing reflect an increasing tendency

to be related to 'market' values mediated by a complex system of
income maintenance, split between local authorities rebates or DHSS
payments.

The extension of local authority housing provision is ultimately
dependent on the existing structure of property and land ownership.
Since the private ownership of property and land is a central ethos
in British society, local authorities are forced to compete on the
open market in order to extend their activities which again is reflected in the increasingly 'uneconomic' costs of public provision.

Historically, the ways in which state provision of services has
developed in Britain as in most other countries, is by a vast pro-
liferation of bureaucratic control. The various attempts to democratise these bureaucracies, and to ensure wider public accountability, are fraught with problems and still leave the issue largely
unresolved. These then are some of the broader issues raised by
the mass provision of public housing which can be summarised into:
the effect of collective provision on existing class relations;
the function and purpose of state provision and the relationship
between state bureaucracy and local democratic control.

Through the activities of local authorities, the 'state' is
'landlord' of more than 30 per cent of the housing stock in Britain.
However, given this extent of provision, there is still no clear
idea or coherent analysis from the left regarding the scope of the
role of the public landlord. There is a constant tension between
the demand for a better standard of provision of housing, and of
services associated with it, and the demand for more tenant control.
This tension is not irreconcilable but has arisen largely out of the
ill-defined nature of the landlord-tenant relationship within the
public sector. This, in turn, has given rise to more variations in
policy and practice. Essentially, these are issues which are raised
once public housing is provided; they are aspects of distribution
and consumption, fundamentally influenced by the type and level of
public housing produced.

Within the current political climate, it is particularly important to maintain a firm defence of public housing. There is a
disquieting consensus of opinion on the orthodox left and right regarding current formulations of what the 'housing problem' is.
Overt problems of mass housing, such as 'sink estates', ghettoing
of racial-ethnic minorities, or vandalism, are all laid at the door
of 'bad' housing management. On the other hand, the 'end of the
crude housing shortage' arguments are met with crows of delight as
an invitation to sell council housing or to move on to 'more flexible' alternative tenures. Both these arguments do, in fact, contain
elements of truth. Many local authorities have been and are 'bad'
landlords. Some estate problems are undoubtedly ignored, or even
caused by allocation policies or pressures of other work. But the
end of the crude shortage of housing arguments which applies to
certain areas is only an indication of increased overall public
housing stock. It tells us nothing about large pockets of housing
need which are a direct consequence of imbalances between individual
household sizes and their current living arrangements or about the
costs of housing.

The worrying aspect of these arguments which are gaining more
public credence is that they attack public housing from both ends -

both provision and management. Indeed the focus on the 'problem estates' as a target for action is in danger of taking on the air of the nineteenth-century arguments for health and sanitary reform. For instance, when the problems become a threat to vested or dominant class interests, formerly spreading disease, or in this instance spreading 'criminal' or 'antisocial' behaviour, then 'society' has to act to prevent the cancerous spread.

It is all too easy to capitalise on the problems of mass provision as a basis for reducing provision. Both the Labour Party Green Paper and the current Housing Bill (2) encourage the extension of owner occupation and echo early 1950s' housing policy statements. The sentiments voiced urge the return to consumer choice in tenures, with the assumption that owner occupation is the preferred tenure, and therefore that opportunities for increased private ownership should be encouraged, particularly through the mortgage-broking activities of local authorities. The sale of council housing, which is actively promoted by the new Tory administration, and even the building for sale, is now becoming common practice even in traditional Labour council strongholds.

The relative degree of complacency over the disappearance of the housing shortage which, especially in inner-city areas, coincides with a shortage of land, has been reflected in a decline of local authority new build programmes. (3)

Private renting has contracted and with previous controls under the Rent Acts again under attack in the Housing Bill proposals, the defence of a reasonably rented, well-managed public housing sector, at a time of rising inflation and unemployment, becomes crucial. What is significant is that many housing problems have shifted into the public sector and, to a large extent, are a function of the bad record of local authorities as landlords. The sorts of problems which can be mentioned have to do with bad design and construction; the use of public housing as a guinea pig for experiments in construction and design; bad, erratic, cost-cutting repairs, and maintenance and modernisation programmes; inadequate recognition and reflection of the needs for collective facilities (given the forced mass-collective consumption on large-scale estates); the abuse of bureaucratic power; lack of tenants' involvement and inadequate public accountability regarding the 'local state's' decision-making processes and outcomes.

Most of these criticisms are founded in a substance of reality, but we have to be clear that the use of these criticisms is easy fodder for the 'get rid of public housing lobby'. Thus criticising current state provision must be done on the basis of its long-term defence; moreover, in criticising public housing, it is essential to have some awareness of the consequences of the attack, and the onus it places on left critics of current state provision to attempt a more constructive reappraisal.

The types of issues that are raised in such a questioning relate to the limits of individual, collective and state responsibility and to the extent to which the 'state' should be called upon to provide an ever widening mesh of increased social support.

REFORMISM OR REALISM

What is being argued is that it is no longer sufficient to blame
either 'capitalist social relations' or 'the state bureaucracy' for
some of the issues raised here. We need to come to grips with some
of the basic choices which are an inherent function of analysing
areas of public-state policy and provision. It is no longer sufficient to hide behind a veil of 'all things being equal' in terms
of resources, for example by postulating full public provision of
everything. We have to be able to confront arguments about inequalities in rates and we cannot afford to dismiss the costs of
public provision at an ideological level. If there is a broad
political aim, then the transitional period which will enable its
achievement has to be worked through in considerable detail within
the limitations of here and now. Reformism is not necessarily a
derogatory term; it is an admission of reality, which to a large
extent is dictated by having to confront problems of 'realisation'
at the level at which they occur. Housing management, as an example
of public-state provision in action, is, therefore, a very useful
platform on which to air some of these ideas. It enables a discussion of the appropriate and most effective political responses
to the problems of state bureaucracy and breakdown in service
maintenance.
      Over the past ten years or so, these responses to inadequacies of
state provision have tended to be couched in terms of prescriptions
for increasing participatory democracy. Analysis which has attempted an appreciation from 'inside' the system, has tended to be
discounted, unless it has been directed towards the increased push
to 'proletarianising' through 'unionisation' of groups of local
government white-collar and graduate employees. The reasons why
attempts to solve problems of the existing system have been discounted are classic examples of left arrogance, i.e. the current
parameters of state provision are de facto limited, or reactionary,
since they take place within the dominant capitalist mode, financed
from the private market, reproducing bourgeois ideology. Now at a
very basic level those responses may be correct but they lead either
to totally misguided political prescriptions for change or to political inertia - waiting till the moment is ripe!
      To be slightly more precise, criticisms of the scale and inertia
of service provisions in the public sector, have undoubtedly fed the
housing association lobby, the recent moves towards tenant management co-operatives, and equity sharing experiments which are now
becoming a feature of more 'innovative' local authorities. These
experiments have, moreover, been espoused not only by central and
local government, but by tenants and their advocates. In some instances, such experiments in more collective control and management
are undoubtedly progressive, in so far as they challenge existing
notions of the family as a basic housing unit, or individually owned
private property as opposed to collectively owned property. But
they have to be viewed with caution. In the case of tenant management co-ops, for instance, they provide an ideal opportunity for a
hard pressed local authority to pass on management responsibilities
to tenants themselves, and in so doing to fail to fulfil their legal
contractual obligations to these tenants. For example, the manage-

ment co-op may well find itself responsible for the cleaning and
maintenance of common parts, without an adequate budget, or reformu-
lation of its rights vis-à-vis the local authority. In the instance
of equity sharing experiments, the development of such schemes, although again on a collective basis, is not much different from the
sale of council housing, and, of course, results in a direct loss of
the council's overall stock. More significantly, such alternatives
fail to confront the basic problems raised by mass public provision
such as standards of service, delimitations of rights and responsibilities of both parties, discrimination and abuse of bureaucratic
power. Such limited experiments do not affect the level of investment in public housing, rather they provide a convenient way of
cutting costs and transferring responsibility on to the tenant. The
reason why such alternatives are, however, being pushed both by
central government and certain local authorities lies at the ideological root of attitudes towards housing in general. Owner occupation is the favoured tenure, so by attempting to introduce certain
peripheral elements of the owner occupation model, limited financial
stakes or more individual responsibility, it is hoped that the
public sector housing will be made more palatable.

Public housing management has largely been ignored in the debates
around state activity. This is a crucial omission, since the daily
experience of tenants, and the activities of housing staff employed
within local authorities acting as agents of the public landlord,
are an excellent indicator of the limits and potential of state provision in action. Moreover, this is an uncomfortable area of
analysis, since one is faced with having to make 'prescriptive'
choices which do not fall into neat politically 'correct' or necessarily politically compatible compartments.

THEORETICAL FRAMEWORKS AND THEIR LIMITATIONS

Although housing management, or the management for that matter of
any public resource, or provision has not been the most 'attractive'
or central site for left debates around state intervention, some
formulation of the role of the state, and the location of public
housing within it, is essential as context for this discussion.

In general the formulation of Prior and Purdie regarding the aims
of state intervention, provides a useful, broad framework. They
summarise the intention of public intervention as having: (4)
    two general purposes: to stabilise the functioning of the
    economic and social system within tolerable bounds, and to
    promote the release of productive forces to achieve higher
    growth ... the specifically British aspect of state intervention
    is the heavy emphasis on stabilisation and the comparative
    failure of such productive intervention as has been undertaken.
They then go on to state that: 'state intervention is invariably
contradictory. It always contains elements which are antagonistic
to the operation of capitalism. It undermines private ownership or
distorts the operation of the market or socialises issues previously
considered purely individual.'

So far so good; we have a firm platform for the defence of
public provision, seen in terms of the role it plays in distorting

capitalist social relations and in changing attitudes and ideologies. But what about the problems which occur after whatever it is has actually been provided? Here they, along with most other people, draw a blank after having initially recognised that a problem exists:

a large state sector has evolved unconstrained by the normal disciplines and objectives of private enterprise, but at the same time not democratically linked to the requirements of the mass of people as it would be under a socialist system. It is this advanced socialising effect of British state intervention, which has emerged as a major point of current and political conflict.

'Out of the Ghetto' has been quoted since it poses some of the major issues succinctly and provides a wider frame of reference in which to consider issues raised by state intervention. The major starting point is that the socialising potential of state provision is blocked by a significant lack of creative thinking and practice regarding the development of democratic control. This, in turn, is blocked by all the other limitations of operating within a 'mixed' or 'dual mode' economy. Having said this, however, the problems are still posed at too general a level. The issues raised by the contradictions of the actual operation of the local and national state bureaucracy are not a subject of detailed consideration.

If one considers the ways in which the left has dealt with issues raised by public housing, they tend to fall into three main lines of argument. First, the state acting as an instrument of class domination, and hence the significance of class struggle around housing provision. This line of approach when applied to housing tends to concentrate on the influence of class struggle in having brought about increased state intervention. It also states that public housing is the working-class tenure and takes pains to demonstrate that public provision is always made as an adjunct to the survival of private capital. In the process of such analysis, the weaknesses of parliamentary democracy are exposed and prescriptions for different forms of political action are frequent. Such lines of argument are extremely useful in providing detailed accounts of the political and social history of the development of public housing and cases of political struggle around housing issues. However, they suffer from an overemphasis on provision and distribution and take no account of the problems which are raised by mass provision. For instance, if one views housing as an aspect of the 'local' state apparatus it is a very efficient means of social control and thus is a legitimate site for class struggle. Moreover, such arguments tend to place an oversimplistic faith in the concept of 'struggle', often rooted in fairly naive conceptions of political struggle and practice.

A second line of argument concentrates on the economic role of housing and, in particular, on the production of housing within capitalist economies. In this instance, the analysis is directed towards establishing that the role of housing production as an element in the economy is important to an understanding of the role of the state. (5)

This line of analysis basically views the role of the state in housing in terms of capital's ability to extract surplus value, which in turn will affect and determine the nature and extent of public provision. The argument is thus sometimes in direct conflict

with the first, class struggle, argument, since it essentially
focuses on the 'release of productive forces in the aid of private
capital' arguments. Public provision is viewed not as a consequence
of class conflict, but as a function of its role in assisting
private capital, and in terms of any more general role that it will
play in the economy. It is an extremely strong and cogent argument.
My main disagreement with it is that it discounts the focus for discussion here (namely housing management) as being entirely dependent
on, and in many ways irrelevant to, the economic arguments regarding
state activity. Thus although this line of analysis increases our
understanding of why the 'state' does what it does, at various
points in time, it is of little help in analysing the political and
social/ideological issues raised at the levels of both realisation
and reproduction of social relationships.

A third line of argument does fit in with 'Out of the Ghetto's
thesis of state intervention as 'economic, social and political
management', i.e. the provision or creation of conditions which
enable the continued functioning of the social and economic system.
One can thus view housing production/provision by the state as an
aid to the reproduction of labour power. Again, this view of the
scope and intention of public housing enables analysis of the
reasons for state intervention, but it too stops short at the level
of provision and distribution and fails to tackle the problems of
management and relationships between tenants and their local
authority landlords.

The main purpose in providing this somewhat brief review has been
to demonstrate a simple, but interesting, political point. The predominant and most attractive areas of thought and analysis around
state activity have tended to concentrate on macro areas such as
class relations, the economy, and the role of public provision
within it, tackling issues about the scope and function of state
provision. However, the really concrete and knotty problems of how
to maintain a quality of service once it exists, of what types of
relationships to prescribe in both social and political terms in the
public sector remain largely unexplored. The emphasis on provision
and access in housing, which highlights discrimination and abuse of
bureaucratic power has tended to lead to quite naive political prescriptions. On the one hand, more 'client' control is advocated
without thinking through the implications which this has for the
level of 'state responsibility'. On the other hand, demands are
made for 'more' state provision in the absence of any solutions for
the current problems of management and maintenance.

HOUSING MANAGEMENT

Housing management is the term used to describe ways in which local
authorities act as landlords. It is a historical product of the
ways in which public housing in Britain has developed, who has been
housed in it and consequently of the ways in which the balance of
interest, as between landlord and tenant, has been codified and defined. Since housing is one aspect of the local state's provisions,
it can call on the other resources and departments of the local
authority. This often means that there is a noticeable but ill-

defined element of social welfare included within housing management.

The list of activities covered by housing management is wide-
ranging, from rent collection and dealing with arrears, seeing to
repairs and maintenance, giving advice and assistance with problems
on general housing issues, and dealing with any other problems to do
with a council tenancy such as inter-neighbour disputes, vandalism,
or disputes with the landlord over, for instance, keeping pets or
having noisy parties. Indeed it is very difficult to pin down specifically what is encompassed by housing management in the public
sector. It is a historically ambiguous area of work and responsibility and its scope is subject to changing pressures from tenants,
local politicians, central government and local authority employees.

Until recently, with the advent of various new forms of tenancy
agreements, the landlord/tenants relationship in the public sector
was exemplified by the traditional 'Conditions of Tenancy' usually
printed on the back of the rent card. In purely legal terms, the
existence of a weekly tenancy for all council tenants did not ensure
security of tenure, and any 'contract' as such which existed between
landlord and tenant emphasised the rules to which the tenant had to
conform, rather than the obligations of the landlord to the tenant.
However, to describe the landlord-tenant relationship in the public
sector in purely legal terms is somewhat misleading. The relationship has a weak contractual basis and public housing management in
many instances goes much further than the confines of rent and
bricks and mortar. What one can say, in general terms, is that
there is a wide area of discretion for local authorities in terms
of how they interpret their responsibilities as landlords and, consequently, wide variations in standards and practices.

If one looks at the type of 'service' that tenants get from their
public landlords, it is possible to generalise that this service is,
as often as not, motivated by the landlords' interests rather than
those of the tenants. For instance most authorities have, within
their housing departments, responsibility for the collection of rent
either on a door-to-door basis or through the giro system. Whether
a tenant pays rent or not and whether rent arrears accrue is of
prime concern to housing management. Thus a large part of the work
of people in local housing offices is directed towards trying to
keep rent arrears down, to ensure that the revenue comes in to the
local authority.

In effect the state, in making arrangements for collective consumption through the provision of mass housing, has paid scant attention to the real problems engendered by collective living. Moreover, the relationship between landlord and tenant has been individualised. The net result is that tenants are individually graded
according to their behaviour and standards. They may be rewarded
for conforming to more general social standards and for conformity
to rules once they are rehoused, by being able to 'filter up' the
public housing stock into the most desirable housing. They may also
be punished for general and specific non-conformity. (6)

The other side of the coin is that local authorities have a duty
to their tenants to repair defects or to ensure that the stock is
regularly maintained - as this is included in the rent. However,
this type of work is too often largely reactive to tenants' requests

and is often out of the control of the housing department anyway.
It is definitely in the landlords' interest to make sure that they
do not have many vacant properties, both for revenue purposes and
to prevent vandalism and squatting. So, in reality, this type of
repair work will get priority over the day-to-day jobbing repairs
which are tenant-requested.

From the tenants' point of view the role of housing management
and the intervention of the landlord is often an oppressive one,
with undue concentration on restrictive covenants, for instance,
against keeping pets, having lodgers or making alterations to the
dwelling. This, as often as not, colours the tenants' view of their
relationship with the landlord. In many instances the reasons why
such covenants exist, such as forbidding pets or noisy parties in
high rise-density buildings are a logical response to the problems
of high density living. However, the fact that public provision of
housing has created for many people intolerable living conditions in
general environmental terms, is a further indication of the chain
of consequences created in the process of trying to meet housing
need through rapid and ill-throught-through measures.

However, it is all too easy to point the finger at forms of
housing management which emphasise the restrictive and oppressive
aspects of bureaucratic control and which tend to favour the landlords' interest. It is also easy to be critical of the staff employed within housing management who themselves are locked into
their own petty world of restrictive practices and limited ideologies. Often of working-class origins, they see themselves as
'better' than the tenants to whom they are meant to provide a
service. Although most of them may belong to local government
unions, this unionisation is rarely directed towards bridging the
gap between tenant and council employee; it tends to be directed
towards internal considerations such as pay or conditions of work.
The existence of these felt 'class-status' differentials combined
with the complex of the bureaucratic-administrative decision-making
process perpetuate, rather than resolve, the many contradictions of
public provision.

Thus we are dealing with a fairly complex web of social relationships, a function of historic ideologies and expectations which have
been reproduced in the course of public housing provision between
agents of the landlord and the tenant. In order to understand how
these ideologies developed we need to examine more closely the role
of public housing in meeting need, and point to some reasons as to
why it has never become a desirable alternative form of tenure to
private ownership.

STATE LANDLORDISM

(a)   The ideology of private ownership

The persistence and growth in owner occupation in Britain illustrates the dominance of values of private property and the conviction that this is the norm and indicator of a 'healthy' housing
market. The state has developed considerable regulating powers in
the housing field which affect structures of finance, standards, the

promotion of different tenure groups, as well as provision of public housing. The outcome of more than fifty years of active state intervention in housing has, in effect, led to a market split between owner occupation and public housing. But public housing has never been viewed as a fully viable form of tenure because of the basic threat it poses to dominant bourgeois values, irrespective of other arguments relating to its 'social' costs or to any contribution that public housing might make as a factor produced within the economy.

The first local authority houses were provided in Liverpool in 1869. However, the initiative for public involvement in providing rented accommodation for the 'working classes', in fact stemmed from the late-Victorian voluntary housing trust movement and the 5 per cent experiments. What is important to note here is that the initiative for providing decent homes for the urban poor derived from the health and philanthropic movement of the nineteenth century which was essentially individualistic in orientation and antipathetic to state intervention. Based in a concern for public health reform with an emphasis on self-help, the early beginnings of municipal housing were viewed as a temporary corrective to the normality of the private market.

(b)   Scarcity in public housing and changing definitions of need

Apart from brief periods, following the first and second world wars, public housing provision has in the main been selective rather than universal. One exception to this relates to people rehoused through slum clearance programmes which brought into the public sector a wider social and economic grouping. However, given the fact that demand for public housing exceeds its supply, who has been housed by the state reflects an interesting circular process from the end of the last century; a mirror of ways in which general state provision is developing currently. Poverty combined with unfit housing conditions were the main criteria for allocations at the end of the nineteenth century, reinforced by the development of public health and housing legislation. The emphasis on economic and physical criteria of need set the parameters of the 'housing queue'. Increasingly, however, given the changing climates of public opinion and fed by increased awareness of various forms of 'social disadvantage', the emphasis on allocation of public housing has shifted towards attempting to accommodate groups who have previously been denied access to public housing, because they did not qualify in terms of broader social criteria, for example, single-parent households or national minorities.

It has not been my intention to quarrel with the more 'liberal' interpretation of housing need, or with the broader cognisance that is now taken of groups who are particularly vulnerable and unable to compete on the private housing market. The fact is, however, that given the contraction of the private rented sector, in part a response to state intervention through the various Rent Acts, many more people are dependent on access to public housing. Since there has been little appreciable recent increase in the public housing stock, the pressures of scarcity give rise to the need for selection.

Although it would be unfair to compare directly the role of
public housing in Britain, for instance, with the small public
sector in the USA dubbed 'welfare housing', it would be true to say
that the increasing concentration of the poorest and most vulnerable
sections of the population within the council sector has serious implications for the landlord-tenant relationship and for the form
that housing management takes. (7) This trend will increase if
current proposals for council house sales become compulsory.

(c) Scarcity, selection and social regulation

The fact that access to public housing is restricted, and that
prospective tenants have to demonstrate a need, has significantly
affected the relationship between housing department staff and their
tenants. One aspect of this relationship, which is still dominant
in attitudes of housing management staff, is the belief in the necessity for forms of social regulation.
    Until well into the 1920s, when local authorities started to
build to a considerable extent under the powers of the Addison and
Wheatley Acts, the main model for landlord-tenant relationships in
the quasi-public sector was provided by the voluntary housing movement. This model was essentially philanthropic, despotic and rooted
in a bourgeois ideology stressing values of work, the family and
social responsibility. The element of 'proving' and 'merit need' is
very well illustrated by the Octavia Hill system of rent collection
initiated through the voluntary trust housing movement. This system
gave rise to a regiment of zealous, committed and often incipiently
feminist middle-class rent collectors.
    The rent collectors were concerned for the complete welfare of
the family. They sought to regulate and alleviate social and
economic problems through a firm, regular, but essentially kind,
supervision. Regular contact with tenants through rent collection
provided a means of access to each dwelling, to check on repairs and
on aspects of the family's behaviour. The picture is familiar,
since we now do have a fairly rich documentation of nineteenth-
century social experience. The system of Octavia Hill rent collectors depended on differential class relations as between tenant
and landlord's agent. It also was based on a relationship of dependency in which the tenant was supplicant and the landlord provider.
    Social regulation still forms a large part of the work of housing
management, and is seen to be an important indicator of 'success' in
terms of individual staff keeping their patches 'clean'! This is
evidenced by the fact that unlike private landlords, local authorities will get involved in some instances in trying to resolve inter-
neighbour disputes. They will, for instance, evict tenants who have
very noisy parties, or who keep dogs in flats. They will work quite
closely with the local police in helping check up on the use of
vacant multi-storey car parks, or will pass on information to the
DHSS regarding sources of a tenant's income if this is in doubt.
They will defer a transfer on the grounds of 'bad housekeeping', or
will arrange a transfer of a household whom they feel is 'up-
classed' by their immediate neighbours. Finally they will devote a

lot of time and energy in trying to ensure that a tenant pays the
rent by a complex series of administrative procedures which can
result in distraint and eviction. This will involve detailed investigation into a household's financial circumstances, and it is
often largely up to the discretion of the patch worker as to how
this will be handled.

The most important point to emerge from this catalogue of seemingly 'oppressive' housing management is that local authorities as
landlords do get involved in a wide range of activities and aspects
of tenants' lives. Whether they should or not is an issue to which
I shall return later - since this raises issues related to collective, as opposed to bureaucratic, responsibility. At this stage
it is important to be aware that one cannot just label the activities of housing management (which undoubtedly contain a large
content of social regulation) as being oppressive nor as just
another indicator of how distanced and repressive the state in its
local guise is.

(d)   Social support

The development of a social support role within housing management
was a second consequence of needs merit allocations. As mentioned
previously, public housing has increasingly housed certain groups
with a wide variety of economic and social problems. It is also
true that a large proportion of council tenants could buy themselves
into owner occupation but chose to remain in the public sector. It
is important to ensure that one does not fall into the trap of
labelling all council tenants as being homogeneous in class or life-
style. Increasingly, however, large numbers of households in public
housing are there because they are 'vulnerable' for some reason or
another. The reasons for this lie outside the scope of this essay
and have been amply discussed by the left's class analysis of
British capitalism. It is also a well-documented fact that high
density living, on estates in particular, have created or contributed to a wide variety of problems - such as depression, loneliness, child abuse, vandalism, domestic arguments, neighbour arguments, and so on.

The question here is to what extent should the local authority
as landlord adopt a role which includes a concept of broader 'social
responsibility' and social support for the tenants? The tradition
exists in housing management for the public landlord's intervention
in this field. The Octavia Hill approach, with its emphasis on
social regulation, also included a fair amount of social support in
non-housing matters - 'why doesn't little Johnny go to school?'.

As landlords, local authorities have always differed in their approaches to this broader welfare role. Certain authorities, particularly in the North of England, adopted a more intensive welfare
involvement, following the Octavia Hill model. Other authorities
adopted a binary system in which they isolated 'problem families'
on to a particular street or estate and then concentrated intensive
welfare-social work with the households, or left them to stew. Yet
other authorities have been quite clear that their obligations as
landlord stop at the basic legal-contractual level of collecting
rents and seeing to repairs.

One can see a wide variation in approaches, for instance, to problems of rent arrears. Large rent arrears mostly derive from low income (though this tends to be labelled by housing workers as 'bad management'). As often as not the main 'welfare' involvement of housing staff is some minimum attempt to investigate reasons for non-payment, to offer rent rebates, or check up on DHSS payments. Others will proceed to court action with minimal contact with the tenants. Yet another housing department will contact social workers, or refer tenants to more specialised welfare agencies. Finally, there are departments in which housing workers as agents of the landlord will work on a long-term case basis with tenants for whom arrears may be but one of a series of other difficulties.

Another instance of the range in practice of local authority landlords is in the case of domestic violence. Some local authorities will not rehouse or will unwillingly rehouse women who have suffered domestic violence. Others will immediately effect a transfer if they have an existing tenancy and will offer a wide range of support. Yet other local authorities will insist on the outcome of a court decision until they will take any action at all on the tenancy transfer. Again these are but two illustrations of differences in attitudes over broader social support.

The extent to which the public landlord should become involved in social regulation or support taking place on an individual one-to-one basis between landlord and tenant, is a serious issue. It raises certain questions which feed the attack on public housing and welfare state provisions in general - such as claims of pampering. It calls into question the individualisation of the landlord-tenant relationship - whereas public housing is in fact a social provision. It exacerbates the dangers of injustices in approaches to groups of tenants - who may be either penalised or given additional support both of which could be said to undermine equality of provision of services. It also lays wide open the broader issue of divisions of responsibility between landlord and tenant - such as whether in fact tenants need housing management at all. If they do not need 'management' then what are the prospects for self-management and what implications has that for the service element included in the rent?

ISSUES AND CONCLUSIONS

Ultimately any analysis of the role of state provision raises the issue of ways in which the state operates to reproduce existing class relations or to alter them. The extent to which current housing provision by the state can transcend the market (ability to pay), or can redistribute resources (the social wage), are limited aspects of changing class relations mediated mainly at the economic level. However, changing or altering existing class relations must also have reference to changes at a social, political and ideological level.

Expanding public housing

The general policy of the left is to expand public housing and bring
all housing, or at least all rented housing, into social ownership.
The arguments which are put forward in support of this are cogent.
The existing subsidy systems for housing favour owner occupiers in
the long term. Despite the fact that, even with mortgage relief,
many home-owners pay heavier costs for their housing in the early
years as compared with 'controlled' council rents, at the end of the
road many owner occupiers are living rent free. They have the
freedom to pass on their property to their children or to sell on
the open market and make a capital gain. There is an ultimate
trade-off in economic terms for owner occupation rooted in the
benefits of owning private property. The left argues that this is
unfair - that many people are unable to buy themselves into owner-
occupation and that the push to increasing owner occupation limits
the housing chances of people in the public or private rented sector
to filter up the system. The system is thus basically unjust. But
is the left really advocating an aggressive policy against owner occupation - and, if it is not, where are the gains for public housing
expansion going to come from?
   There are other spin-off arguments put forward by the left for
increasing social ownership of housing which relate to employment
policies and in particular to the role of building workers. If
there is an expansion of public housing this will mean more jobs in
the building industry for both new building and repairs and maintenance. This raises the issue of the organisation of the building
industry at the moment, in which local authority direct-labour
organisations are playing a diminishing role. These arguments have
been very forcefully put by the recent CSE pamphlet, (8) and provide
the type of detailed analysis, with broader political implications
for breaking barriers existing between council employees and
tenants, which is currently needed.
   An expansion of council housing implies more public investment.
Thus recommendations put forward for this increased state activity
must come to grips with the current structure of housing finance.
As mentioned previously, capital spending in public housing is loan-
financed from the private sector. To date, with a fairly strong
tradition of social, economic and investigative journalistic analysis from the left, we are in a position to uncover where the problems lie. We can point to the big banks, to increasing fracturing
of capital, to the shifts in investment, to the emigration of funds
abroad. We can decry central government collusion with 'big business' - but it is very difficult to be realistically prescriptive
about how the transition to increased social ownership of housing,
for instance, will in reality take place. It is, however, at the
level of a coherent programmatic approach to back up the intention
of expanding social ownership that the debate must now take place
both in the short, medium and long term.

The role of the local state and housing

Over the past few years central government policy and legislation
has favoured a broader local authority intervention in general
housing conditions within its area. This has included giving local
authorities the power to declare Housing Action Areas under the 1974
Housing Act; and to encourage Housing Advice Centres, which are
meant to assist private tenants in finding accommodation. Local
housing authorities have responsibility for administering a national
rent-rebate system, for rehousing the homeless; they can also give
out mortgages and improvement grants. These are a few of the increased local authority housing powers. In addition, the notion of
a comprehensive housing department (9) is gaining credence. Historically, many local authorities did not have separate housing departments or, if they did, then their main area of activity was
housing management. Now the pressure is on local authorities to
increase the scope of their housing functions and, as far as possible, to try to bring under one department all the activities related
to housing. Although very few such fully comprehensive housing departments exist as yet, the evidence so far points to some serious
implications for the role of local authorities in housing in general
and for the future for council tenants in particular. 'Comprehensi-
vised' housing departments appear to be moving into a situation of
acting as broker for the private sector, in terms of arranging
mortgages for potential owner-occupiers or persuading existing
owner occupiers to improve their dwellings. Although this can be
justified at the level of attempting to upgrade housing conditions
within an area in general, it raises the question, who is reaping
the benefits from this increased social, political and economic
management taking place at the level of the local state? The evidence indicates that the increase in investment and staffing is
going towards the expansion of these areas of local authority
housing activities, and it may well be that this will act against
the interests of existing council tenants.

    Although it is true that increased powers of the local state lead
to paralysing bureaucratic growth, this should not form the basis
for an attack on its broader intervention in housing issues. It is
the aims of this increased economic and political management which
should be questioned. We need to ensure that the increased powers
of the local state are positively involved and fully accountable to
local people.

Changing relations within public housing

At present, public housing tends to reproduce class ghettos through
allocation policies, and to reproduce relations of dependence and
social support demand through its management. It therefore re-
stricts social and political advance for the majority of tenants.
In effect, local authority tenants are subject to a restrictive web
of rules and regulations as individual householders. They are
forced, and will continue to live in environments which are often
admitted to be gross errors of planning. Thus, although the basis
of the individual legal relationship between landlord and tenant

creates a one to one relationship, the way in which the stock and
tenants are dealt with by management, creates the need for generally
agreed standards. This contradiction does provide the basis for
progress, since, at a social and political level, public housing is
a collective provision, enabling collective consumption and presumably collective means of control over the process - which is essentially at odds with the highly individualised landlord-tenant relationship, expressed through the legal relationship. Whether, and
how, this socialising potential can and should be extended in the
public housing sector, in a way which maintains standards and public
responsibility, but ensures democratic accountability or even
control, has still to be worked out, with reference to the long and
valid history of tenant-association activity within the public
sector. These arguments, which boil down to the relationship between service, bureaucrats and 'consumers', are ultimately questions
to do with altering class relationships at the social and political
level, and are of relevance to all state activity.

Traditionally, ways of improving conditions and relations within
the public sector have moved in two main directions. First, at the
level of the individual householder-tenant, there has been a partial
attempt, through the Housing Bill, to make the status of a council
tenant more palatable. The various restrictions which have been associated with the status of council tenants are being lifted in a
package of proposals which is intended both to make council tenure
more 'attractive' and to include the notion of tenants' rights.
Proposals range from lifting residential qualifications and encouraging wider access to groups previously denied council tenan-
cies, to giving tenants the right to alter their dwellings, take in
lodgers, have security of tenure and get involved in some limited
consultation exercises. The proposals also include a right to a
tenancy agreement in which the rights of tenants as well as those
of the landlord are set out.

There has been much detailed and general criticism of these proposals, in particular of those relating to the right to consult.
However, they do represent a noticeable advance on the status of a
tenant who was bounded entirely by obligations laid down by the
landlord. But the proposals have two basic failings. First, they
underpin the individualised relationship between landlord and tenant
and place it on a more contractual basis, bringing it, therefore,
more into line with tenants in the private sector. Second, this is
a cosmetic attempt to make council tenancy a more attractive proposition, for instance by introducing limited clauses on the right to
succession, to give a semblance of the freedoms which owner occupiers enjoy. What these proposals fail to take into account is the
social nature of council housing and the necessity to create bridges
rather than divisions between individual tenants. The net effect of
these proposals may well be to improve individual relations between
tenants and their landlords. But they also constitute a direct
threat to existing services and current, often minimal, levels of
state responsibility. They codify an individual and oppositional
relationship between landlord and tenant and, as such, should be
viewed with caution as only a preliminary step.

The traditional means by which the left has, in general, advocated ways of improving landlord/tenant relations is through the pro-

motion of tenants' organisations within the public sector. This is
no novel approach, and the legitimacy of tenants' organisations are
recognised by a number of local authorities within various, if
limited, formulae for consultation. Many tenants themselves and
some local authorities still, however, refuse to acknowledge
tenants' organisations on the grounds that they are 'politically'
motivated and 'unrepresentative'. A large body of documentation
already exists about the inadequacy of tenant participation schemes.
As yet very few examples of full tenant involvement in decisions affecting either their immediate tenancy, environment or general
housing policy matters exist. There are considerable problems with
involving many tenants in tenants' politics, precisely because they
can see the limits of their involvement or because the pressures of
their own lives make additional and unfamiliar forms of social and
political involvement difficult. Moreover, although the left has
been advocating for some time more of a coalition of tenants, employees of the local authorities and other organs of the labour
movement, instances of success are few and far between. This is
ultimately a twofold problem. First, to what extent does tenant
management or tenant control undermine the contractual responsibilities of the local authority as landlord and possibly result in a
'worse' service to tenants? Second, how can these forms of organisation be so constituted as to avoid parallel bureaucracies, and
yet to ensure comprehensive knowledge and communication with the
administrative systems which already exist?

     There are traditional problems which arise out of sectional
interests organising themselves into a coherent oppositional platform. It is important for tenants to be internally and very locally
organised themselves and the units may well have to be small to
ensure full involvement. It is also important to break down the
barriers created within local authorities between tenants, housing
employees, manual staff and building workers. (10) Ultimately
tenants both as individual householders and as a collective force
have to move towards a situation in which they have fuller involvement in their immediate domestic and broader physical environment.
Forms for this involvement and innovations are constantly emerging
from the tenants' movement but the crucial question of delimitation
of areas of responsibility between landlord and tenant still exists.

THE LIMITS OF STATISM - ACCOUNTABILITY, STATE RESPONSIBILITY AND
SOCIAL CONTROL

Current problems raised in public housing exemplify the limitations
of a form of state intervention which has failed to confront the
issues of changing political and ideological relations. Public
housing in Britain has the form, but not the substance, of social
provision and as such it is in a half-way position between market
relations and socialism. It is statism.

     However, the transition from statism in which at an economic and
administrative bureaucratic level the provision is made through
public expenditure is a highly complex one. It has to take very
careful account of the division of responsibility between user and
provider. This essay has illustrated, amongst other things, two

conflicting aspects of public provision. First, that much of the
activity of the public landlord is unduly restrictive and is directed more towards the convenience of the bureaucratic apparatus
than towards the user. Thus as often as not the tenant has to make
demands on the local authority rather than expect as of right a
level of basic services and equitable treatment which is paid for in
the rent. Second, this essay has illustrated that to some extent
public housing does operate as 'safety net' housing for the casualties of the private market and that consequently some groups who
find themselves in the public sector are in need of some form of
'social support'.

The dilemma which has been created within public housing is that
some local authorities, particularly those who have a more progressive left Labour influence at councillor level have implicitly
agreed to take on the role of broader social support as landlords.
Thus housing management staff in particular get involved with
vandalism, truancy, domestic violence, with problems of low income
or inter-neighbour arguments. The reasons for this involvement are
confused. At the explicit level of maintaining the 'landlord's
interest' to ensure payment of rent, or 'less trouble' on an estate
there is a clear reason why they should get involved. However, a
broader political commitment, as a matter of policy on the part of
certain Labour councils, to widen increasingly their net of social
support does raise the issue of over-involvement of the landlord in
many aspects of tenants' lives. The political will to make the
welfare state work at a local level and in the process to shift a
lot of responsibility which is not met by existing welfare state
provisions on to housing staff is a disturbing tendency. It is
disturbing because it demonstrates a political unwillingness to
confront the role of the public landlord and in an absence of any
clear demarcation lines to fall back on the easier solution of
letting the landlord try to meet a whole range of problems which
may be in conflict with other interests or are insoluble at that
level.

In the process of trying to resolve some of the problems raised
by state provision it is important to make the distinction between
democratic processes, public responsibility, tenant self-management
and social control. It is important to increase the level of tenant
involvement and control over the existing and future use of their
immediate and broader physical environment. But this should not be
confused with forms of current schemes for 'tenant management' which
serve to undermine the already decreasing areas of the landlord's
responsibility. Provision of housing by the state must be to high
and consistent standards as should its maintenance. At this level
the role of local councillors in policy is crucial. But major
inroads have still to be made into the problem of accountability of
employees in the public sector. Currently they are split between
seeing themselves as part of the bureaucracy of the local authority
landlord and as providing a 'service' to tenants.

Ideally state provision for 'social use' should aim for the
fullest social control by the user. But although social ownership
and state intervention do distort market processes we shall remain
at the stage of statism until the major issues surrounding state responsibility and social control are resolved.

NOTES

1   Many of the issues raised here have been discussed in the course
    of my current work in housing management in the public sector,
    with my two colleagues Charles Legg and John Mason. I am also
    grateful to Tom Kay and Langley Keyes for constructive criti-
    cism.
2   'Housing Policy. A Consultative Document', Cmnd 6851, London,
    HMSO, June 1977, Housing Bill (Bill 109, December 1979).
3   1975 New council houses started 133,661
    1977 New council houses started 92,163
    1978 New council houses started
4   Mike Prior and David Purdy, 'Out of the Ghetto', London,
    Spokesman, 1979.
5   'The contradiction between the process of production in the
    house building industry and the needs of the capitalist mode of
    production in general is a major housing problem for British
    capitalism ... and any political conclusions that can be drawn
    from them should therefore be structured around this contra-
    diction.' (Michael Ball, British Housing Policy and the House
    Building Industry, 'Capital and Class', 4, Spring 1978.)
6   Such tenants will encounter numerous obstacles in some authori-
    ties to being able to transfer into 'more desirable' accommoda-
    tion.
7   According to statistics published by the DOE in 1972, the per-
    centage of the bottom three income-groups within public housing
    had increased to 41 per cent and these percentages are on the
    increase according to more recent statistics. (Housing tenure
    in England and Wales: the present situation and recent trends,
    A.E.Holmans, 'Social Trends', 9, 1979, C.S.O.)
8   Direct Labour Collective, 'Building with Direct Labour. Local
    Authority building and the crisis in the Construction Industry',
    London, Conference of Socialist Economists, 1978.
9   'Organising a Comprehensive Housing Service', Housing Services
    Advisory Group, Department of the Environment, London, HMSO,
    1978.
10 However, it would be a mistake to prescribe a coherent united
    front for all tenants without taking account of the very real
    divisions that exist between tenants. In many instances tenants
    themselves would advocate a much 'stronger line', for example
    against antisocial behaviour than would housing management. The
    people's courts in Cuba and neighbourhood groupings in China
    point to the ways in which such 'policing' could occur.

Chapter 11

IS THE PARTY OVER?
Peter Lawrence

Ever since the victory of Lenin's Bolsheviks in Russia in 1917, revolutionary socialists around the world have held as an article of faith that a revolutionary organisation of the Bolshevik type was the key to the successful outcome of revolutionary struggle. Building the vanguard party from among the most 'conscious' or 'advanced' sections of the industrial proletariat has claimed the energies of revolutionaries in the belief that when the 'spontaneous ' struggles of the working class reached their zenith, the presence of a determined, and above all disciplined, organisation of Marxist revolutionaries would exert the decisive influence in determining the fate of the revolution. The events of 1917 were seen as lasting proof of this. Inextricably linked to this concept of the revolutionary party was (and is) a particular view of the socialist revolution as a moment when the citadels of state power are captured and thenceforward turned to the service of the working class.

In Britain, Marxists have appeared to polarise into two distinct groups on the issue of the nature of revolution and the party. On the one hand, those within the Labour and Communist parties have argued the case for a strategy of socialist revolution using the 'democratic' institutions such as parliament to gain an electoral majority. On the other hand, there are those, such as the Socialist Workers Party (SWP) and the International Marxist Group (IMG) who regard the winning of electoral majorities in parliamentary institutions as hardly relevant to the key objectives of developing soviets, or workers' councils, in which development the vanguard party plays the leading role.

More recently, Marxists inspired by the lessons of Popular Unity in Chile and by the ideas emerging from the revolutionary democratic wings of the West European Communist Parties, have attempted to develop a strategy of revolution which recognises the importance of generating organisations of popular power not only in places of work but also in the community, in order to develop a popular basis for an electoral majority in parliament. (1) The ensuing concept of socialist revolution as a process rather than a moment in time suggests that a reappraisal of the role and nature of revolutionary organisation is long overdue.

This essay is a contribution towards such a reappraisal in the British context. It will begin by arguing that the failure of the left (the Tribune group, the Communist Party of Great Britain (CPGB), the SWP and the IMG being its main components) to capitalise on the inability of successive Labour governments to carry out what they regard as socialist policies, is a consequence of its failure to provide a convincing alternative to the policies actually pursued - convincing either to the electorate or to the majority of activists in the Labour movement. It will be argued that this in turn is due to a failure to develop political initiatives which seek to build 'elements of socialism' within the womb of capitalism and so seek to demonstrate that the latter need not be the natural order of things and that there is a viable alternative to the present system. As for the groups outside the Labour party, the failure on their part to prise away discontented socialists in that party on any significant scale, is a reflection of their inability to convince, as an alternative to the Labour party, even those whose politics are indistinguishable from the politics of the smaller parties and groups. Thus one of three further conclusions follow: first, it becomes necessary to form a new party; second, one or more of the existing parties must be changed; third, the concept of the party as agent of socialist change has to be rejected.

A debate along the lines of the first and second of these conclusions has been taking place in 'Socialist Register' and this debate will be reviewed. (2) It will be suggested that Ralph Miliband, in putting forward the case for the new party, fails to show why it should be any more successful than previous attempts at new socialist groupings; that Duncan Hallas and George Bridges, arguing for the SWP and the CPGB respectively, failed, as did Miliband, to take account of the vast political space occupied by the Labour party in solid defiance of all attempts to challenge it; and that Peter Jenkins, arguing from a Gramscian standpoint for the Labour party, avoided the problem of how such a current in that party was to be organised in order to challenge for hegemony within the Labour movement. Jenkins's contribution was, however, the most helpful in that it argued for the forging of links between the Labour party and the grass roots movements which might help to turn that party into a campaigning one.

The third part of this essay proceeds to an analysis of the concept of the revolutionary party and of the notion of the momentary seizure of state power to which it is wedded. Both will be rejected and it will be proposed that what is required is an association of communists, who would perform a co-ordinating rather than vanguard role, abandoning the notion that it was the only organisation qualified to lead the struggle for socialism. It is conceivable that this 'association' might succeed in uniting all the different left forces in time, but that in the meantime those who share the perspectives associated with the concept of revolutionary process, but who have chosen to work in different parties and groups, should work together theoretically and practically to create the bonds of unity which will lay the basis for agreements between the various organisations, and in particular lay the basis for the transformation of the Labour party.

THE DECLINE OF THE LEFT

Although it has been the hallmark of left analysis that successive Labour governments' lack of political will to initiate a significant advance to socialism has led to increased unpopularity and electoral defeat, the electorate has not responded by shifting its support to those parties to the 'left' of the Labour party; indeed, the response has sometimes (though not in 1979) been as contrary a one as voting for the National Front. The 'Marxist-Leninist' parties and groupings have, however, convinced themselves throughout that they have had the 'correct' analysis, policies and type of organisation necessary to get these across to the rank and file of the Labour movement, and indeed, where they have stood in elections, to the voters; but they have convinced nobody else.

The standard response of these parties and groups is first, to argue that they have exerted an influence far out of proportion to their numbers. Second, they consistently seek to lay the blame for their failure significantly to expand those numbers at a door as far removed from their own as possible; thus it is said to be the reformism of the Labour and trade union leaders which snuffs out the revolutionary potential of the working class; it is the influence exerted by the mass media on the thought processes of the workers which obscures their realisation of the need for socialism and the necessity of revolutionary change to replace the capitalist system; and it is the predominant position of the Labour party within the trade union movement and the traditional allegiance of the working class to that party which, despite the continual 'right-wing' leadership in parliament and government, has prevented its more red-blooded members from flocking to join the revolutionary socialist parties and groups.

It is true that for the Communists in particular, the fact that its members have at various times held key positions in the trade union movement has appeared to give it an almost directing influence over its well-placed industrial militants. But in reality, the CPGB has played the role of encouraging militancy in the economic struggles, and even if willing, has been unable to give a distinct political leadership inside the trade union movement from its position of strength. Both the Communists and the SWP have always held that the development of the economic class struggle creates the basis for political development in a socialist direction. The workers are steeled for the political struggle, their levels of consciousness are raised and more cadres are won for socialism, not to mention the Party. But it is becoming a commonplace to recognise that there is nothing which necessarily links the political struggle for socialism to the economic struggle at the work-place or in the community. Indeed, the militant pursuit of economic objectives to a successful end can restore the workers' faith in the ability of the system to provide the goods. In any case, whether restored or not, there is nothing in the nature of that struggle which points the way to socialism.

There is no doubt that the leadership of the Labour party in parliament, both in government and opposition, has been and continues to be reformist, opportunist and all the rest of the familiar epithets. Why so? Why has it been able to survive and take the

majority of the movement with it? Why has the media been so
successful in subverting the onward march to socialism? Is it
really a matter of thought control as the revolutionary left have
always implied? Are the members of the movement so many empty boxes
waiting to be filled with ideology, but with bourgeois ideology
getting there first and leaving no room for the socialist faith?
Is the Labour Party's continued political dominance within the movement really the consequence of a false consciousness on the part of
these empty boxes? Such a view of party and movement cadres, a view
which underlies political discussion on the left, is clearly con-
temptuous of the men and women who, much as they might like to see
some alternative set of policies pursued, and some alternative
organisation to help push them through, have not been convinced that
any of the existing variants, either of party or policy, are likely
to get us any nearer to socialism. Better to stick with the party
which has achieved governmental status rather than move to a party
which cannot even muster one MP. Better to retain some channels to
the powers than go into political oblivion.

A NEW PARTY?

There are, then, three ways of proceeding from a conclusion that the
revolutionary left has failed to provide a convincing alternative to
those on the left of the Labour party. One is to argue the need for
a new party which will convince people to join it and to vote for
it. The second is to argue for convincing changes within the
existing parties. The third is to question the concept of the
revolutionary party itself. A starting point for discussion of
these questions is to take up the debate which has been going on in
'Socialist Register' in 1976 and 1977 on the Future of the Left.
Miliband began the discussion by arguing for the formation of just
such a new party; one which would have a 'serious implantation in
the working class movement', that would command sufficient electoral
support to give it political legitimation and that would have an
internally democratic structure. He rejected the Labour Party on by
now well-rehearsed grounds: reformism, right-wing domination, the
futility of entryism and so on; the CPGB on the grounds that it was
wedded to the fallacy, shared with the Labour left wing, that it
could win the whole Labour party for socialist policies; and the
'ultra-left' (his term) parties and groups on the grounds that they
were committed to the 'Bolshevik model' and to 'democratic centralism'. Now is the time to 'move on'.
    Given the arguments which Miliband puts forward for the formation
of a new party, such an event has been long overdue. 1976, twenty
years after the watershed year of Hungary, Khruschev's secret speech
and the large exodus from the CPGB, is, to be sure, an appropriate
year to reiterate the regular plea for a new left, but it has been
tried before and found wanting. The May Day Manifesto group, the
Radical Alliance and currently Socialist Unity, have in various ways
represented attempts to establish a party of the sort Miliband demands. Yet no party has got underway to challenge the hegemony of
the Labour Party within the movement and within the British socialist tradition.

No doubt Miliband felt the influence of the apparent break up of
the two-party system in the two parliaments of 1974-9, but the 1979
General Election has confirmed the trend towards a return to bi-
polarity evident in earlier by-elections with the decline of the
Nationalists in Wales and Scotland, setbacks for the Liberals, and
the disappearance of the Scottish Labour Party, the latter being a
significant test for any 'breakaway formation' from the Labour
Party. The Tribune left's loyalty to the Party has been guaranteed
not only by the failure of all previous breakaway attempts, but
further by the fact that it does not wish its socialist reputation
tarnished with the accusation that it has made the political tasks
of the Conservatives easier by splitting the Party. Such considerations weigh heavier with the left than the sacrifice of its version
of a socialist platform required by rallying round the leadership.
Though Miliband is probably right to argue that the Labour Party as
presently constituted cannot fulfil its socialist purpose, he is
unable to come up with an answer to the problem of how that party
is to be removed from its dominant position, precisely because of
the belief of its sincerest socialists that it is the only alternative and that it has to be changed from the inside.

Miliband can reject the CPGB for the very reason that it has what
he regards as the illusory strategy of helping such a change within
the Labour Party to take place. The new model of the 'British Road
to Socialism' (BRS), the policy statement of the Communist party,
states that 'the next stage of the revolutionary process' is to win
a 'new type of Labour Government' to begin to carry out left policies. (3) The constituents of these policies differ little from the
Tribune group's own demands. The CP's conception of political development is that of gradual shifts to the left, with successive
Labour governments carrying out increasingly redder programmes. A
concomitant of this process would be an increase in influence and
support for the CP as the party leading (or pushing) the leftward
drift. Whether this series of shifts occurred 'would depend on the
closeness of the relationship [of the left government] with the mass
movement, and their ability to move at a pace which would strengthen
the broad democratic alliance'. For Miliband, of course, once such
a strategy is predicated on a shift inside the Labour Party, it is
lost anyway. But a more serious objection is to argue that once
such a shift has taken place within the Labour Party, there is
little need for an organisation separate from the Labour Party, such
as the CP. If, in order to effect such a leftward shift, the CP
sees its role as wagging the Tribune dog, then why does it not
simply disappear into the Labour Party and help organise the Tribune
faction?

For Miliband, the SWP, or other 'ultra-left' groups, is no
alternative either. In rejecting these, he clearly rejects, not
only Lenin's vanguard, democratic centralist party, but also the
pre-eminence, within the strategy of these groups, of factory
struggles. He stresses the importance of working through the admittedly inadequate but generally accepted democratic institutions.
That is, he clearly accepts the need to operate from within the
local and national 'parliamentary' system (and in that differs
little from the 'British Road to Socialism'). This means recognising that our given political environment is 'capitalist democra-

cy' and that political implantation in the institutions of that
democracy 'at local level, first of all' should be put on as important a footing as struggle 'at the point of production'.

Miliband's new party is to be grouped from members of different
existing parties, people who have come to realise that their groups
would not become the agencies of socialist change and who have
worked together in various kinds of political activity at the grass
roots. Such a party would be a loosely-knit, federal organisation.
Based in the Labour movement, it would have to contest elections effectively, secure some representation locally, and offer a coherent
political programme which appealed to people at work and in the
community. So indeed it would. But how is this party to secure
such support? On this Miliband is silent. Demonstrating the inef-
fectiveness of one political organisation does not automatically
bring support for an alternative. There is no reason why any new
party should be any more effective than any of the older alternatives to the Labour Party, nor for that matter any less so.

Thus, on the basis of Miliband's arguments for a new party, it
was not difficult for Hallas and Bridges to propose that their
parties were what Miliband had in mind and that his reasons for rejecting them were mistaken. Hallas was able to argue that the SWP
had become an active workplace, community and electoral force (in
that order) of some 3-4,000 activists and could become bigger and
reach the magic 10,000 figure if only the left could see how effective it is already. For Hallas, Miliband's mistake was not
merely to underestimate the credentials of the SWP but to reject
revolutionary struggle. His objection to the SWP's 'Bolshevism'
represented a misplaced faith in the parliamentary/peaceful road
and clearly, if he could overcome this defect in his thinking, he
would see more obviously the attractiveness of the SWP as the agent
of socialist change most likely to succeed. Yet Hallas's problem is
the same as Miliband's; he cannot face the fact of the dominance of
the Labour Party in the movement and can provide no reason why this
situation should not continue. Any amount of agitational attacks by
the SWP press and activists on the 'traitorous Labour leadership' is
likely to do no more than cement Labour party and trade union loyalties rather than lead to internal division and major political
change. Thus how the Labour Party and movement is to be approached
is answered by Hallas, to say the least, in an unsatisfactory way.

What of the SWP itself? A rather damaging blow to Hallas's confident assertions of SWP maturity came from an account of the
history of the IS/SWP published in 'Socialist Register 1978' by a
former member, Martin Shaw. For on that account, Hallas had argued
the case for a party which was formed on the basis of the International Socialists (IS) in a highly undemocratic way, and which
has degenerated into a centralist organisation on the Stalinist
model. As Shaw concludes, (4)

> The SWP is in fact much more sensibly compared to the CP at
> various times in its history. ... Ideologically, of course, it
> is still anti-stalinist and revolutionary socialist, but there
> is a close resemblance to stalinism in the way 'the party' itself
> has become the ideological reference point for all work ...
> Central political control, affecting the decisive areas of work,
> is firmly entrenched in the hands of the small Central Committee.

A party which claims to have one set of political practices but
which follows another, is hardly likely to instil confidence in its
members; as has in fact happened, they are more likely to leave in
large numbers.

Bridges's response to Miliband reflects the general position of
the Gramscians within the CPGB. They see in the 1977 BRS a change
in the conception of socialist revolution as a process rather than
a break, and the important position given in it to the Broad
Democratic Alliance, a reflection of the party's realisation of
the necessity of developing democratic and socialist forces in order
to establish working-class hegemony in civil society. If we are
then to assume that the Gramscian wing is on its way to establishing
hegemony within the party, then clearly such a party would come
closest to Miliband's conception. If, as Bridges argues, the CPGB
is losing its Stalinists and is innovating new political practices -
the People's Festival, the Communist University and so on - and
above all is initiating a serious critique of the 'socialist'
countries, then as he himself suggests, Miliband need look no
further. But the question of whether a revamped Communist Party
can make any impression on the dominance of the Labour Party still
remains unanswered.

In any case, is the CPGB really making the theoretical leap
claimed for it by its Gramscians? The programme does talk of a
'revolutionary process' and the concept of broad democratic alliance
does recognise the importance of struggles other than those on the
factory floor, but nowhere else does the concept of challenging
'capitalist hegemony' in the sense of the people's consent to the
capitalist order as the natural one, find expression in revolutionary tactics and strategy. This is because the BRS cannot show why
engaging in a whole series of struggles should show to those engaged
in them that socialism is a credible alternative and a real possibility. The very conception of 'road' to socialism militates against
this. The inhabitants of capitalism set off on the road to socialism (and eventually to communism); the journey is a long one and
there are several stopping points on the way, staging posts which
when reached, enable people to refresh themselves before setting off
on the next leg. There is no return trip as, once on the road,
nobody will want to go back. But why should anyone want to set off
on such a journey at the outset? And, if they have found life in
capitalism wanting, why should they set off to socialism and not to
fascism? Mobilising the mass pressure to move on once the journey
has started presupposes what is not proven, namely, that there is
mass pressure to start the trip. The concept of process suggests
that no long-distance journey is in order. To translate, the concept of process insists on creating the experience of socialist
organisation and life wherever possible, within the heart of capitalism. Demonstration that such practices can work is the most
powerful means of combatting capitalist hegemony. The latter is
constantly strengthened whenever the societies of Eastern Europe
and the USSR are referred to as 'socialist', so appeals to the
superiority of the existing 'socialisms' are no alternative.

The CPGB does not articulate such a programme. It decisively
marks off three time periods: the heightening struggle, the election of a left government, and the achievement of socialism. What

is struggled for in the first period, that is now, or at least some optimistic projection of 'now', does not relate at all to what happens under socialism. Thus *now* the Communist Party opposes workers' participation in non-nationalised enterprises, *then* workers' control will exist because such enterprises will be publicly owned. So now, only those workers in the nationalised sector can discover what workers' participation might or might not mean; they can develop the socialist experience, but what of the others? Equally with incomes policy; *now* it is to be opposed, *then* it will exist and 'excessive differentials' will be reduced. How will this happen? What is there about wage bargaining *now* which suggests that workers can agree differentials? Plainly, not enough to suggest a workable arrangement *then*. Now the Communist Party opposes membership of the EEC; then Britain will seek to develop 'all European co-operation in all important spheres'. With the possibility of twelve European countries in the EEC by the end of the decade, the logic of opposing the highest form of co-operation in Europe to date because it is not yet 'all European' is the logic of the 'road'.

A party which can provide a realistic alternative in which its members can see that certain practices fundamental to socialism are being developed and are working, is a party which will gain credibility and generate popular socialist consciousness. Miliband, and to a certain extent his critics, elevate the party above the programme, thus begging the question of why the party should be supported. But the BRS on the other hand, charts a programme and a strategy but fails to demonstrate the need for a party such as the Communist Party to carry it out. For once the elements of its programme become acceptable to the Labour movement as a whole and result in a new kind of Labour government, then that government and party will carry it out. Given the present difficulty of distinguishing between which policies are those of the Labour left and which those of the CP, the programme really does away with one or other party. As the programme recognises a long life for the Labour party, suggesting that it will always remain the major working-class party, then the purpose of the CP is almost argued away. For those within the Communist Party who wish to give it a character and purpose distinct from the present one, i.e. one which generates, or rather helps to generate, a process, rather than acts as a travel agent, then the question which remains is whether the struggle which they have to mount is one which is best carried out in the CP or in the Labour Party itself.

For Communists, this question is supposedly resolved by the quest for affiliation to the Labour Party. There have, however, always been two major obstacles to CPGB affiliation: first, the Soviet connection, and second, the contestation of elections by the Communists against the Labour Party. Set up with the encouragement, if not at the instigation, of Lenin, the CPGB's subsequent subjection to Comintern policy, increasingly framed according to the needs of Soviet foreign policy, cannot have helped it in its attempts to affiliate to the Labour Party. The latter was rightly suspicious of what the 'Soviet system' meant for Britain, especially as the fate of the non-Bolshevik parties became clear. That the socialist revolution meant, or appeared to mean, the effective elimination of parties other than the Communists decisively affected

attitudes to the new-born CPGB. Such attitudes were to be confirmed
with the labelling of social democratic parties as 'social fascist'
between 1929 and 1934 and this could hardly be repaired by the
Popular Front *volte face* in 1935. While there have been considerable attempts by the CPGB to distance itself from the Soviet Union,
particularly after the revelations of 1956 and the invasion of
Czechoslovakia in 1968, this distancing involves merely a criticism
of the use of 'administrative measures' rather than a thoroughgoing
investigation of the claim that the Soviet Union is socialist or
even building socialism. The non-Stalinist majority of the Labour
Party are unlikely to be convinced of the Communists' democratic
credentials unless such an investigation is made. (5)

As for electoral competition against the Labour Party, it is
clear that arguments as to the necessity of a separate vanguard
party, as to the inadequacies of the Labour Party and thus for the
contesting of elections to take support away from that party cannot
help the cause of unity through affiliation. Left unity is the aim,
but only, it would appear, on the basis that it is the Communist
Party which understands how to achieve socialism and which, therefore, must take on the vanguard role. The CPGB appeal in 1978 for
a British 'Union of the Left' exemplified this approach, apart from
exhibiting extraordinary delusions of grandeur.

THE LABOUR PARTY

Both the failure to replace, and the attempts to affiliate to the
Labour Party in themselves testify to its central place on the
British left. Peter Jenkins's response to Miliband was indeed the
most persuasive in its arguments for the Labour Party. This was
because it did try to show how the concept of revolutionary process
related to the Labour Party, that is, how different political practices within the Party and related to it might lead to hegemonic
change both within the movement and within the society as a whole.
The notion that major political change depends upon the 'leftness'
or 'rightness' of the Labour leadership in parliament is gone.
Rather the question is one of the generation at the base of 'organs
of popular power' which can give support to a 'leftward shift'. The
necessary electoral change is a consequence of changes at the base
and the process of change involves one of complementarity and interaction between government and 'popular power'. In engaging in
struggles to build popular power at the grass roots, socialists of
this 'orientation' can, by trying to engage the Labour Party in
these struggles, turn it into more of a campaigning party, rather
than the electoral machine which dominates its official energies.

Of course, the Labour Party is not, as Jenkins admits, the party
which fits Miliband's description, but it is the party which occupies such a large part of the socialist terrain that the question
for revolutionary socialists can only be one of how to intervene in
that terrain, first recognising the position of the Labour Party and
then creating the links between it and the grass roots movement
which will be the starting point for changing the political character of the party. Jenkins argues for revolutionary socialists to
work inside the Labour Party to create the links with tenant com-

mittees, shop stewards' committees, the women's movement, anti-racist and minority groups, environmental and other community groups, which will create an interdependence between popular movements and the Labour Party, which in turn will force a Labour government to pursue policies which assist the development of these movements and lay the basis for grass roots democratic control. It is Labour Party members who are responsible for their leaders, and while they see no alternative which makes sense in the light of their experience, then the majority are unlikely to change the leadership. Rather, therefore, than engage in a fruitless struggle to get 'left-wingers' into key positions, this strategy of entry is distinguished from classical entryism by its emphasis on the forging of links between the party as a whole and the popular movements.

However, it is not at all clear that the Labour Party is fitted for even this more appealing strategy. It is not the old question of the relationship between the parliamentary Labour Party and the Labour Party Conference which suggests problems here, but rather the relations within the Labour Party itself, reflected in first, the weakness of the constituency parties and second, and indeed the other side of the same coin, the domination of the large trade unions in conference decisions. The Labour Party is a mass party only on paper. Indeed as Hindess has observed for Liverpool: (6)

> It is not an easy matter to discover the precise membership of
> the Labour party in many parts of the city. The membership
> lists, where these exist, are often unreliable. They contain
> the names of people who are dead, have long since left the area,
> are no longer members, and in extreme cases do not even know they
> are in the party.

Furthermore, of this paper membership less than 10 per cent attend ward meetings. The trade unions have an equally low activity rate. Thus, even when, as often is the case, the Labour Party Conference shifts to the 'left', this reflects the changing view of a small minority of activists. It is therefore not surprising that the PLP leaders can claim that they represent a wider constituency among the membership, individual and trades union, because rarely does the political activity of the left activists extend to forging alliances and movements which will convince the PLP leaders that they need to change policies if they are to retain popular support.

The failure of the left in the Labour Party has been the consequence of directing all its energies to party transformation by getting left delegates to conference, left motions passed, left MPs into parliament and into key positions in the shadow cabinet or the real cabinet. But the majority of the PLP has always been able to hold sway precisely because it knows that in the last resort the left will never split the Party. The left itself has never built up the support at the base necessary to give it the strength to challenge the right-wing leadership of the PLP.

The foregoing is not to negate the importance of left voices in the highest echelons of party and state. As Geoff Hodgson has pointed out, it was Tony Benn who stimulated the UCS workers to take up the struggle for a workers' co-operative and the Lucas Aerospace workers to take up the idea of a plan for socially useful production. These ideas were taken up partly because they were given support by individuals such as Benn, and they could in turn

help to reinforce the position of such figures inside the Labour
Party and eventually in the government if the workers were able
successfully to wage their struggles for a socialist alternative.
It would then become increasingly difficult for the leadership to
ignore the groundswell of popular opinion for different forms of
organisation and this would cause a leftward shift in the party as
a whole. Socialism would then increasingly represent greater
control by the mass of the people over their own lives through popular democratic structures, or organs of popular power. As it is,
the left maintains as its central plank a commitment to an extension
of the role of the state, and to a view of socialism as a state-
inspired objective. In the given economic conditions, as Coates has
observed, this can only lead to the incorporation of the state into
the economy and a cementing of a managerial private and state capitalism. (7) It cannot lead to socialism.

Trade union strategies for socialism lay equal emphasis on the
role of the state and the question of worker and community control
is low on their agenda. Even if the left as a whole was to shift
its struggle towards increasing links between the party and the
popular movements, the trade union hierarchies will endeavour to
maintain the Labour Party as the political arm of their predominantly defensive struggles. Their effective control of the Labour Party
Conference will ensure that, until the balance of forces within the
unions changes, economism will be in the forefront. As we have
witnessed over the winter of 1978-9, the failure of the trade union
movement to bargain for a real shift to the left in exchange for
another phase of agreed incomes policy effectively sealed the fate
of the Labour government. The re-election of a Labour government,
which at least keeps socialist objectives on the agenda, if not on
its agenda, was subordinated to the competitive demands of the
labour market, reasserting the competitive ethic of capitalism dear
to the heart of the subsequently elected and militantly right-wing
Conservative government. Trade unions now return to doing what they
are best at - defending their position and the living standards of
their members, and leave alone what they are deeply suspicious of -
workers' participation and incomes planning, both of which would
have to be major features of a socialist economy. The struggle to
revive the Labour Party is also a struggle to reorient the trade
union movement.

Revolutionary socialists persuaded of Jenkins's arguments will
not be deterred by the knowledge that the task of engaging the
Labour Party as a party in the struggles of popular movements is
going to be a very difficult one. After all the right and much of
the left will argue away the need for the Labour Party being involved in any popular struggles: lobbying MPs and ministers will
do. In this they will be supported by the trade unions at the official organisational levels. The question that is not discussed
by Jenkins is how the revolutionary democratic orientation within
the Labour Party and trade union movement is to come together in
some recognisable way in order to co-ordinate activity and create
links between different grass roots struggles and between those
struggles and the Labour Party itself. Thus we return to the
question of organisation.

REVOLUTIONARY ORGANISATION: THE CONCEPT OF THE PARTY

The seeming impossibility of changing the Labour Party from the
inside has been the main justification for those seeking to replace
it from the outside.   Such activists have been persuaded of the
virtues of the Leninist theory of revolutionary organisation, of
the concept of the revolutionary party.   In its classic formulation,
this concept is of a vanguard consciousness bearer, disciplined,
organised, custodian of the revolutionary truth embodied in the
party line.   Its principal function is to give leadership to the
struggles of the class - the working class - but its relationship
to this class is a complicated one, more often than not existing
outside of the class rather than as a part of it.   This is the party
organisation of Kautsky and of Lenin's 'What is to be Done?'.   Whatever changes Lenin made in his formulations about organisation after
the 1905 revolution, the basic features of his party remained. (8)
The problems of the party which had developed prior to Lenin's
death, associated with the rise of Stalin as General Secretary, with
bureaucratisation and increasing centralism at the expense of democracy, were to be overcome by changes in leadership - an infusion of
workers into the higher party organs and the removal of Stalin. (9)
The vanguard party was therefore to lead the class, and the correct
vanguard of the party to give leadership to the vanguard of the
class.   The success of the Bolsheviks in winning state power in the
peculiar conditions of Russia in 1917 universalised the revolutionary party as agent of change.
    The Bolshevik victory also universalised its organising principle
of 'democratic centralism'.   In practice, centralism continually
triumphed over democracy, not only in the so-called Stalinist
communist parties, but also in their later 'Trotskyist' and 'Maoist'
variants.   This produced a deadening effect on the development of
party theory and practice as well as, of course, upon the development of Marxist theory as a whole.   In the so-called bourgeois democracies, the restraining demands made by 'democratic centralism'
upon the individual party member have been judged to be inconsistent
with the degree of freedom of expression and democracy that operates
within the wider society.   To counterpose the hierarchical discipline of the Tsarist police force with a disciplined centralised
political organisation is one thing, but to continue to advocate
some variant of this organisation within the framework of societies
where many basic democratic liberties have been fought for and won
by popular struggles is another matter entirely.   It is, therefore,
not surprising that such parties wither away or stagnate or are
forced to become more open, at least in outward appearance.
    However, the vanguard party dies hard.   In Britain, while the ap-
parent hopelessness of the Labour Party seems to emphasise the need
for a single-minded revolutionary organisation committed to socialism, developments within the large number of small organisations
claiming this characteristic drive socialists back towards the
Labour Party.   This latter trend has been reinforced by the recent
developments in theorising the transition to socialism and the
nature of the state, and in particular the argument that a transformation of the structures of capitalism is possible by predominantly peaceful means from within, rather than by a violent seizure

of power. Avoiding the misleading polarity of either the parliamentary path or the extra-parliamentary path, the theorists of
what has come to be known as 'Eurocommunism' argue, with different
emphases of course, for a necessary combination of the two strategies. Commitment to extending democracy in economy and society does
suggest more open and democratic political organisation within
socialist and communist parties to match the commitment to pluralism
outside.

Classic Leninism, represented forcefully in current debates by
Mandel, retains its view of the state as an increasingly centralised
authority enforcing capitalist class rule. Mandel is highly critical of the view that the state can be transformed rather than
'smashed' or 'dismantled', to use a more recent concept; transformation certainly cannot take place via parliamentary political activity and neither can it take place as a consequence of popular
struggles alone. Such struggles have to be co-ordinated towards the
ultimate seizure of state power. Therein lies the need for a revolutionary vanguard party: (10)

> The Leninist concept of the party is not the only possible one.
> It is however the only possible concept of the party which as-
> signs to the vanguard party the historic role of leading a revo-
> lution which is considered, in an intermediate or long-range
> sense, to be inevitable.

And further: (11)

> To fully grasp the profoundly revolutionary nature of Lenin's
> strategic plan, it must be approached from yet another point of
> view. Any concept based on the probability, if not the inevita-
> bility, of a *revolution* occurring in the not-too-distant future,
> must inevitably deal with the question of a direct collision with
> state power, i.e. the question of the conquest of political
> power.

Given the inevitability of revolution and given the need to dis-
mantle the state apparatus of capitalism, an apparatus with increasingly centralised powers, then, the argument runs, an equally
centrally organised revolutionary vanguard is required to seize the
moment, to unify the spontaneous struggles of the increasingly dis-
enchanted workers and so to give the leadership necessary to overthrow the state machine. But it is not simply a question of organisation, but one of the content and method of the organisation: (12)

> The difference between a 'workers' party' in general (referring
> to its membership or even its electoral supporters) and a revo-
> lutionary workers' party (or the nucleus of such a party) is to
> be found not only in programme or objective social functions ...
> but also in its ability to find a suitable pedagogical method
> enabling it to bring this programme to an ever-growing number of
> workers.

It is important that such a workers' organisation is kept small,
that it is a 'combat unit based on the selection of only active and
conscious members'. In such a 'combat organisation ... the possibility of finding independent thinking is actually much greater' as
'differences of opinion will be resolved less in terms of material
dependency or abstract "loyalty" than according to actual substance'. Such a revolutionary grouping then keeps plugging away,
encouraging struggle at all times by the advanced working class,
the industrial proletariat: (13)

The relation between the revolutionary organisation (a party
nucleus or party) and the mass of the workers abruptly changes
as soon as an actual revolutionary explosion occurs. At that
point the seeds sown over the years by revolutionary and
conscious elements start sprouting. Broad masses are able to
achieve revolutionary-class consciousness at once. The revolutionary initiatives of broad masses can far out-distance that of
many revolutionary groupings.

The foregoing constitutes a very coherent argument. It sets out
the kind of political organisation consistent with the political
conclusions arrived at, namely that the state and its apparatus have
to be overthrown in a revolutionary explosion, during which moment
the party (or nucleus) is ready to take state power in the vanguard
of a fully conscious working class. Quite apart from the dream-like
assumptions about the instant mass realisation of revolutionary
consciousness, there is Mandel's characterisation of the state, a
characterisation which is completely opposed to more recent Marxist
theorising. In criticising Poulantzas's view of the state as an
arena of struggle, Mandel is, however, forced to acknowledge first,
that the state employees can struggle for a more democratic practice
within the state apparatus, and second, that such a struggle would
be an important factor in altering the balance of political forces.
(14) Mandel also cannot deny the possibilities of controlling state
activity through the development of popular organisation in the
community. His only basic objection rests on the view that the
democratisation of the repressive state apparatus, the police and
the armed forces, is impossible because it is inconsistent with
their coercive role. Yet in the end Mandel allows for the possibility of such change: (15)

If one encourages in every way the introduction of the political
and class struggle 'into the state apparatus' - including the
army - then one promotes a decomposition of the old structure,
which can ultimately be replaced by new structures generated by
revolutionary mobilisations and self-organisation.

What is at issue here is whether dismantling old structures is to
be a consequence of the vanguard storming Whitehall or a consequence
of democratic structures being won by public sector workers and
community organisations. Mandel denies that the latter course will,
by a process of attrition, lead to the dismantling of old structures, though he is not opposed to alternative structures being the
object of struggle in the state apparatuses. There is, according to
Mandel, a limit to what can be granted under the system: sooner or
later this limit will be reached and with it the realisation that
the system has to be overthrown, because what is being demanded is
unobtainable under capitalism.

However, it is a long way from recognising that a demand cannot
be met to seeing the need to overthrow capitalism. The working
class has won major victories under capitalism, and this through
consistent economic and political struggle. Having won victories
they are none too easily convinced that the storming of Whitehall
is necessary to their winning further ones. As a consequence of
their victories, they have far too much invested in the existing
order to risk an upheaval. To tell them that this upheaval is inevitable because eventually the system will collapse is to utter

some futuristic fantasy for which there is no current evidence.
Mandel gives the impression that when capitalism is made to give way
to a demand, this is pure illusion, a devious tactic on the part of
capital to reinforce capitalist relations. If such a demand can be
granted then it cannot be a revolutionary, transitional demand. If
such a demand is not granted then it must be a revolutionary demand
and have revolutionary consequences if there is a revolutionary
party to teach the masses, with the right pedagogical method, the
revolutionary lesson. In fact, of course, many demands regarded as
transitional forty years ago by the Fourth International are now
reality, even to the extent of the trade unionisation of some West
European armed forces. The degree to which changes laying the basis
for socialism can be initiated within capitalism should not be
underestimated.

These very changes must lead to the questioning of the other
great concept of socialist revolution linked to the leading role of
the party, namely that of the leading role of the working class, or
more specifically the industrial proletariat. However, in Britain,
as elsewhere under advanced capitalism, workers on the factory floor
comprise a minority of those who sell their labour by hand and by
brain. In Britain, the total working population in manufacturing
is less than one-third of the total working population. With the
increasing integration of economic activity, there is nothing about
manual workers in factory production which elevates them above
technical 'white collar' workers, or scientific workers such as
design engineers, other than their ability to stop production. If
it is to be argued that it is their industrial muscle which puts
them in the leadership role in the struggle for socialism, then a
connection is being made between industrial militancy and socialist
potential which is, to say the least, unproven. A conception of
socialism which emphasises the development of non-commodity production under popular democratic control must address itself to the
importance within economic activity of such sectors as housing,
health and education, indeed to the fact that one-third of the
working population is employed in the public sector. When, for
example, Mandel argues that 70-90 per cent of the population of
Western Europe is strictly working class he clearly recognises the
changes that have taken place. But his insistence on the article of
faith of the leadership of the industrial proletariat shows a
failure to follow through the logic of his own discovery. (16)

The foregoing discussion, then, argues for the rejection of the
insurrectionist seizure of the citadels of the state as a strategy
of revolution. As a corollary of this it is necessary to reject the
concept of the revolutionary party as a disciplined, vanguard,
quasi-military combat unit. A rejection of the necessity of the
industrial proletariat as revolutionary vanguard of the working
class requires further rejection of the revolutionary party as vanguard of this vanguard. Arguing for the equal importance in the
struggle for socialism of the myriad of popular struggles outside
the arena of industrial employment, suggests that we must argue for
a different concept of the 'party'. Not only, therefore, does a
questioning of the historic necessity for a democratic centralist
revolutionary party arise from the historical record of such
parties, but from an argument for a different revolutionary logic.

AN ALTERNATIVE CONCEPT?

Such considerations suggest a party which is a co-ordinating body of communists and socialists working in different areas of life, involved in different struggles (indeed, if applicable, organised in different factions), providing an organisational framework which allows maximum debate and discussion in order to provide a unifying theme for these struggles and in order to generate policies which such an 'association' (rather than party) can place on the agenda of the Labour movement, in which communists would play a full part. Once the primacy of the party is rejected, its role, organisation and relationship to the Labour movement (and the Labour Party) would exemplify the co-ordinating/policy-making function of a democratic socialist movement and in its functioning would help to generate similar developments within the Labour Party itself. Such a political organisation might provide a home for many who have engaged in political struggle outside of Marxist revolutionary groups because they have felt that little importance has been accorded their particular concerns, the Ecology Party being the most recent instance of this phenomenon.

Writing in the very different context of the German Democratic Republic, but conceptually concerned with many of the issues raised here, Rudolf Bahro has put forward views on the question of the party which are extremely relevant to West European experience and deserve even brief reference in this essay. In his important work, 'The Alternative in Eastern Europe', he calls for a different communist organisation to the ruling party - a League of Communists - which 'must be organised as the *collective intellectual* which mediates the reflection of the whole society and its consciousness of all problems of social development and which anticipates in itself something of the human progress for which it is working'. Such a party seeks to 'bring together the various interests of different strata and groups, where these diverge, by always making the standpoint of the higher synthesis prevail'. Of the relationship between party and state machine, Bahro writes that the party 'must organise the social forces in such a way that these confront the apparatus on a massive scale as autonomous powers, and can force it into progressive compromises'. There has to be a separation of state and party such as allows for the 'subjugation of the state apparatus to society'. (17)

This latter question of party-state relations is a critical one not only in the countries of 'actually existing socialism' as Bahro calls them. It relates closely to the notion of a party as both one of struggle and one of government, a formulation of the Italian Communist Party which has been considerably criticised by left critics of 'Eurocommunism'. For it is important that a communist or socialist party can as a mobilising and campaigning force effectively challenge a government in which that party may have a minority or majority position. It is precisely in order that a party of communists can become both a party of struggle and of government that different structures must prevail within the party such that loyalty to the party cannot be invoked through democratic centralism as a means of stifling debate and independent political organisation and mobilisation. Such a change in concept is merely a long overdue

recognition that state machines tend to ossify and take governments
with them.   Thus pressures for change have to be organised from
below, in conjunction with those individuals or groups within party
and state that seek to generate further change.

The possibility of an organisation of communists without a firm
line raises problems for its members, many of whom join because they
feel a need to be told what to do.   The concept of leadership inherent in the 'Marxist-Leninist' party generates followers who reinforce the position and claims of leaders.   There is thus an important psychological dimension to the individual's need for an organisation to which to belong and from which to take instruction.   The
psychological analyses of fascism have provided us with some understanding of this need, but we have yet to admit to ourselves the
degree to which socialist organisations and parties satisfy it too,
thus providing the basis for degeneration within the parties as
leaders are able to rely on pliant members who have learnt rather
than understood the line.   Clearly we need to examine this question
more thoroughly than can be done here.   However, if such leadership
manipulation of individual psychological need is to be undermined,
the concept of a correct 'line' and of an omniscient and wise
leadership which both feeds on and feeds the individual member's
need for leadership must go.   The recognition of different answers
to problems and of the claims of others to have alternative strategies towards a common objective can only undermine these psychological attitudes.   The expansion of internal debate, the continuing
questioning of all concepts and decisions in the light of experience
can only encourage the development of a more independent membership
subversive of leadership hegemony.

Where does all this leave the debate about 'Which Party'?   If the
Leninism of the SWP or IMG is rejected, then 'revolutionary democrats' have the choice of working in the Labour Party which occupies
the crucial space on the left, or in the Communist Party, which occupies an important one, and though rather small, will not go away.
Its very custodianship of the title 'communist' and its links to the
important developments taking place in some European parties, gives
it significance in the context of a growing, though as yet inadequate critique of the 'socialist' countries, and, therefore, in redefining for their own societies what socialism must mean.   The very
fact that a communist party takes such an approach could be of
enormous significance for the attitude of the Labour Party in co-
operating with communist parties in the EEC political system, thus
helping the process of CP unity with the Labour Party here in
Britain.   Within each of these two parties struggles for similar
objectives go on at the present time.   Members of both co-operate
in the grass roots popular movements and bring to their parties new
ideas and approaches from these movements.   There is a great deal of
scope for the expansion of such co-operation between 'revolutionary
democrats' in each party, thus forcing in time the changes necessary
for a closer relationship at the official level.   As regards the
'Socialist Register' debate, there can be no specific conclusion
drawn in this essay of the kind drawn by each contributor to this
debate.   It can, however, safely be concluded that the struggle for
hegemony within the Labour Party and movement will itself be a long
process requiring patience on the part of revolutionaries;   a group
not usually known to have a surfeit of it.

NOTES

The author would like to acknowledge the helpful comments on an earlier draft of this essay from Geoff Hodgson and Mike Prior.

1 See, for example, G.Hodgson, 'Socialism and Parliamentary Democracy', Nottingham, Spokesman, 1977; D.Purdy and M.Prior, 'Out of the Ghetto', Nottingham, Spokesman, 1979; F.Claudin, 'Eurocommunism and Socialism', London, New Left Books, 1978.
2 R.Miliband, Moving On, 'Socialist Register', London, Merlin Press, 1976; D.Hallas, How Can We Move On?; P.Jenkins, The Labour Party and the Politics of Transition; G.Bridges, The Communist Party and the Struggle for Hegemony; R.Miliband, The Future of Socialism in England, 'Socialist Register', 1977.
3 Communist Party of Great Britain, 'The British Road to Socialism', March 1978. Subsequent quotations are also from this edition.
4 M.Shaw, The Making of a Party?, 'Socialist Register', London, Merlin Press, 1978, p.140.
5 See M.Johnstone, Early Communist Strategy, 'Marxism Today', September 1978; S.R.Graubard, 'British Labour and the Russian Revolution', Oxford University Press, 1956; Hodgson, op.cit., ch.4; also M.Prior, Communist Labour Relations, 'Marxism Today', February 1978.
6 B.Hindess, 'The Decline of the Working Class', London, MacGibbon and Kee, 1971, p.57ff.; see also, D.Coates, 'The Labour Party and the Struggle for Socialism', Cambridge University Press, 1975.
7 Coates, op.cit., p.217.
8 See, for example, V.I.Lenin, The Reorganisation of the Party, 'Collected Works', vol.10, pp.29-39.
9 See M.Lewin, 'Lenin's Last Struggle', London, Wildwood House, 1973, ch.9.
10 E.Mandel, The Leninist Theory of Organisation, in R.Blackburn (ed.), 'Revolution and Class Struggle', London, Fontana, 1977, p.78.
11 Ibid., p.92.
12 Ibid., pp.102-3.
13 Ibid., p.105.
14 See E.Mandel, 'From Stalinism to Eurocommunism', London, New Left Books, 1978, and the PCI's Pietro Ingrao's discussion with Henri Weber 'EuroCommunism' and the Question of the State, 'Eurored', no.9, in which Weber takes up the Mandelian cudgels against, and Ingrao produces an eloquent defence of, 'Eurocommunism's' state strategy.
15 Ibid., pp.177-8.
16 See Mandel's Leninist Theory of Organisation, pp.113-14, for an explanation of why workers in large factories are likely to be more receptive to revolutionary ideas and organisation; on the definition of the working class with the industrial proletariat as vanguard see Mandel, 'From Stalinism to Eurocommunism', pp.209-10.
17 R.Bahro, 'The Alternative in Eastern Europe', London, New Left Books, 1978, ch.9.

Chapter 12

THE WEANING OF HOMO SAPIENS
Steve Bodington

> 'We are all born in moral stupidity, taking the world
> as an udder to feed our supreme selves.'
> George Eliot, 'Middlemarch'

A DISCUSSION ABOUT SELF-ORGANISING STRUGGLE FOR A CLASSLESS WORLD

'Organon' is Greek for tool. Human beings make themselves collectively into, 'organise themselves' as, instruments to aid the
tasks of living. Human societies are, that is, structures in which
relationships are assigned to individuals. Individuals 'classed' by
occupations and duties (related often to birth) are the elements of
these structures. For some four or five thousand years human societies have been in rapid flux - rapid, that is, against the time
scales of biological change, for, within a mere matter of centuries,
again and again structures of domination have crumbled and given
place to new structures of domination: great empires have been won
only to decline and vanish, 'Sceptres and crowns have tumbled down
and in the dust been equal made with the poor crooked scythe and
spade.' Throughout these millennia of social change, viability and
decay of systems expressed the discovery and then the working to
exhaustion of new modes of material freedom - for some fed by surpluses produced by others. These were class societies - using
'class' in the narrow sense of classes of exploiters and exploited.

Language, a craft-adapted hand, a large brain and a creative
imagination gave homo sapiens peculiar advantages. The making of
fire and agriculture (cattle-raising and crop-planting) were the
early milestones along new pathways of human history. But men
turned control over nature also into control over other men and
women. Human beings were now capable of producing surpluses over
and above their barest needs for survival. It was these surpluses
that some few found ways of appropriating from the many that produced them. Social structures were organised for war (external
domination) and class privilege (internal domination). The wealth
of the few and the unremitting instability of struggle - defensive
or offensive - for or against domination generated energy and in-
ventiveness that from century to century enlarged the human potential for social knowledge and environmental control, but, albeit
in changing forms, continually reproduced social instability.

In so far as the social dynamic was struggle by human individuals
and social groupings to dominate other human beings, social stability could hardly be an expected outcome. But the transmitted intel-

lect of the human species which this turbulent history so sharpened
and enlarged, began asking questions about itself. Some formed the
view that human wisdom was not God made flesh, but was itself the
outcome of processes of life and material evolution preceding its
existence. They discovered too that thoughtful and conscious
creativity was frustrated by socio-economic structures over which
human will and human intellect had lost control. Human society
existed as a thing apart from human wisdom, outwith human control
as if it were governed by forces of nature. And this is where we
are today.

Awareness of this situation - and awareness is, of course, far
from universal - takes many forms. The problems of human existence
in general cannot be mastered until the intellectual powers of homo
sapiens - which are social - are brought under control. The first
problem is human control over the structures of human organisation
itself. This has escaped the conscious will of the totality of
human individuals who are its elements.

Where human intellect is used to establish domination over other
human beings whose intellects are being used to turn the tables and
win domination over the would-be dominators, the outcome can only be
an unforeseeable resultant of these conflicting purposes. Some may
dream - indeed have dreamed - that one grouping of elite human
beings may be able to establish a structure of permanent domination
over all other human beings. The fallacy of this line of thought is
that the dominant, in order to permanently and ineradicably establish dominance, must eradicate the humanity of those they dominate -
but in doing so they, of necessity, also eradicate the very qualities that they seek to exploit for their own advantage. Solutions
for some by means of exploitation and domination over others can, on
the time-scale of history, be no more than transitory. For this the
historical testimony is ample. The logic of human control over
human (social) faculties must ultimately imply relationships between
human beings other than those of dominator and dominated.

The latest structural format that overshadows all parts of the
world, supplanting the earlier political structures of hierarchical,
monarchical, military-imperial and feudal power, is that of capitalism. Capitalism universalises and extends domination through the
agency of the market and money-based relationships organising production as well as distribution. In this structure alienation (in
the sense of a social system that has an existence independent of,
'alien to', the conscious aims of the human beings whose social
existence is organised by it) reaches its most extreme form. The
economic and hence the social development of the human species
throughout the planet appears to be governed by economic laws that
operate like natural forces outwith human control. The very termi-
nology used likens the economic behaviour of what is, after all, a
social system, the system of rules, criteria and property rights
governing the production and distribution of goods, to storms, to
blizzards or prosperous growth, as if the economic phenomena were
in fact phenomena of nature.

In the seventeenth and eighteenth centuries this self-regulating
market system was backed as the great liberator with which to break
down in the name of humanity the bulwarks of aristocratic authority
and monopolistic reaction which were unaccountable to reason or

democratic will. The diffusion of property was to provide the democratic will with a material power basis. The new property system of the market indeed provided a new material power basis and indeed liberated new initiatives and a vast expansion of human experience and knowledge so that collectively more and more human energies were poured into the enlargement of social powers to explore and change the environment in which our species lives.

However, these new forms of property and the new political and economic relationships that became established with them, did not in fact diffuse and democratise the material basis of power peculiar to the market/money system, namely, control over capital; it did not create a power base for the alienated many. Instead it concentrated world-wide economic power for a dominant few. We end up again with a world-wide social structure outwith the conscious control of human will, dominated by dominators whose power base is control over capital by the agency of which social production and distribution is organised.

This situation is intolerable not only because the dominated resist the domination that oppresses them; it is also not biologically viable because (a) the vast potentials of human knowledge available for use in struggle for domination make mutual destruction in nuclear war or by other scientific horror so real a possibility that the species may totally destroy itself in this way, and (b) the automatic pursuit of the market/profit-dictated aims of capital, being outwith deliberate social control and competitively motivated to expand capital limitlessly, may as a by-product destroy the human ecological habitat of which its motivations can take no regard, and (c) finally, the nervous and mental systems of individuals are exposed to strains that they cannot support; richness of imagination and sensitiveness of intellect are confronted by social processes that cannot accommodate them and over which their actions as individuals exert no control.

Today's struggle against domination is more than a struggle of the oppressed against their oppressors. It is a struggle for human survival since the world scale of internecine struggle for domination is now armed by knowledge (by 'science') of devastating potency. This same knowledge could also produce means of survival and leave for all ample surpluses of time to be spent on human activities of their own choosing. Such a world of human freedom has, however, to be struggled for as also the dangers of species destruction have to be struggled against. Laws of social development continuing to operate independently of conscious human purpose will destroy humanity. If the human species is not to perish, it will be because human individuals combine to act to see that it does not perish.

This imposes upon any individual who wishes for survival a need to consider how her/his conscious acts may increase the chances of species survival and make way for the changes that she or he desires. Reluctance to think in such terms stems from the feelings of impotence that class societies foster; for in such societies human beings struggle to weaken others and wish others to feel themselves impotent. But ending domination must make human destiny the concern of every human being.

Big ambitions, you may think, for one small creature! But where

except in the heads of small creatures such as ourselves, does human
consciousness reside? Certainly it does not float disembodied in
the atmosphere. But what can one single human being on his/her own
do? So one may feel, contemplating the dismal tides of history -
but the question is not well framed. One is not on one's own. One
is part of a species and what will survive for the species is those
modes of action that many share in common. So the individual in
seeking his/her individual course is seeking also a course that can
be that of many others at the same time. When the new mesh of
social relations is fine enough intensively and its network reaches
widely enough extensively, the single individual will no longer be
in isolation and no longer without social effect.

In 'concern for human destiny' there is an aspect which is,
biologically, entirely new. No species before has *consciously*
devised a 'strategy for survival'. Some species have survived and
some have not. They have adjusted themselves to their environments
and changes, in inidvidual genetic structures and in collective
group behaviours, have occurred. Where they proved favourable to
survival, those species and individuals that were their vehicles
have survived and where in the hard school of history they proved
unfavourable, they have not survived. Conscious species purpose was
not a factor in survival; the art of living was learned in a more
pragmatic way. Why now should it be otherwise? Because, I think,
there is no possibility of species survival unless the peculiarly
human faculties of imagination, communication and conscious collective purpose begin to be used collectively for the species as a
whole (not just for individuals and groups within the totality of
the species).

To make this demand is to suggest a sharp historical break from
the processes of historical evolution so far, in which conscious
social purposes have played second fiddle to cruder logics of survival. One might compare social history to the biological history
of living organisms - requiring a time-span of perhaps some thousand
million years to find the passage from unicellular life to the
subtle structuring of the many interrelated cells that make up the
living animal. Must not the social unification of the species likewise grope its way by failure and success through innumerable
contradictions?

Whilst the biological analogy in several ways illuminates the
problems of social change, it should not be pressed too far. The
dangers of species annihilation are too close in time for evolution's slow learning by doing. The patience of history is no longer
a virtue. Moreover, there is available an instrument of species
survival - consciously co-ordinated human action - that immensely
accelerates the learning process. In it experiments in the social
imagination - which is what social consciousness is, namely a means
of anticipating social purposes in imagination - are conducted with
a rapidity that far exceeds the generations of deaths and births, of
successes and failures, which shape the blind learning processes of
historical evolution hitherto.

The argument so far does little more than define and justify an
objective - namely the elimination of relationships of domination
and dominated to be achieved by *consciously co-ordinated* activities
of all who seek this objective. The problem is how to root such a

general aim, such an uncompromising ideal, in the tangible present of social and individual activities, tightly structured as now they are by routines and vantage points inherited from the past. How can the future inform the present? How can desired future relationships give direction to the practicalities of the present?

'Ideas of the past' are much more than just ideas. Counter-ideas may destroy their spiritual status, but yet they live as organisers of practice. 'God will punish you' you may not believe, but the code of practice ascribed to God's command will still, for want of any other code, organise relationships of men and women. 'Let us organise,' we say; we then set up a hierarchy of authority because practice has taught us no other way of organising. Though we have long questioned the principles of authority by virtue of which aristocrats have claimed their right to rule, we have not progressed much further than substituting for appointment of commanders by divine right, appointment – again of commanders – but instead by periodic democratic vote. That is, the machinery of authority remains with us as an apparatus of social organisation because practice has not taught how socially to use forms of organisation to replace 'hierarchical chains of command' – if not for all, at least for many social purposes.

That is not to say, however, that humanity has not in the course of historical struggle been trying to discover alternatives to arbitrary oligarchic power – the democratic assembly, democratically voted representation, recallable representatives, codified law, property rights, civil rights, participation in decision-making and much else are moments in this long struggle. Nor is the whole story to be found in social machineries, customs and constitutions. These are ideas of the past externalised, so to speak, as social practice. Ideas of the present also have a social-practical existence as 'public opinion', 'sense of justice', 'political or social consciousness' and, as such, when from the inside of individual heads they somehow or other visibly display numerical strength and spiritual energy, they become social forces in their own right capable of seizing hold of and rapidly transforming situations. But, of course, how they come to display themselves and declare their social-practical feasibility is the hardest thing of all to understand.

From all this there are many conclusions to be drawn and they are of varying weight and kind. Perhaps the drawing of these conclusions is for us the main substance of politics and social morality.

First one needs to be alive to the power of the past. The past is lord of all the territories that we have not conquered for the future. If we say: 'Act decisively against our enemies' fifth column' what do we do? We set up a secret service in ways learned from our enemies, on the same pattern. Long and bitter experience alone teaches us that by imitating our enemies' ways, we have in fact – ipso facto – installed our enemy in the very heartland of what we claim as our own territory. As 'intelligence' and secret police power is not a territory we have conquered for the future, it remains a territory controlled by the past, de facto by our enemies.

It is the same with organisation; we say 'organise' and set up

a hierarchical chain of authority. We are in territory that has
only partly been conquered for the future and all the time we run
risks from many pockets of resistance remaining from the past. We
need to be acutely aware of these risks, but not to be alarmed by
them.

Consider in this context the concept of 'party loyalty'. We
become alive to the situation we find ourselves in. We join the
army of the future to do battle against the armies of the past. We
dedicate ourselves to fight the good fight and preach loyalty to all
our comrades. So inspired the battle goes well. But the moment of
agreed singleness of purpose passes – and to what then is the dedicated individual loyal? To his commander? To the apparatus that
organised his struggle? Clearly to neither of these – but only to
his own purposes, his own aims, his own freedom to control his own
circumstances and his own actions. The 'army', the 'party', the
'organisations' that his own actions in the first instance may have
'freely' created become no more than a feature of the historically-
given social environment. They must be reassessed realistically for
their ability to contribute to social change but the assessment must
be critical in so far as the original apparatus will by the very
nature of things comprise features over which the past is lord.

Hierarchical organisations cannot possibly suffice as instruments
with which to eliminate hierarchy. But organisations of the present
are a part of the reality of the present and as well as bearing increasingly heavy burdens of the past, they may be capable of still
embodying something of the future they were meant to serve. The decision that political judgment and social morality has to make is
always a two-sided one – critical awareness of where the past has
its main strongholds and realistic, undogmatic aliveness to the
multiple forms in which the future may find habitats within the
present.

There can be no rules differentiating good organisations from
bad – except in some negative senses. 'Put not thy trust in
princes' – nor in organisations. In the last analysis the individual's own judgment is the ultimate court of appeal. This follows
from accepting the aim of 'no domination'. If an organisation is
mightier than individuals, it – or rather those who control it –
dominate these individuals. The practice of organisation without
domination has as yet largely to be learned, to be discovered out
of struggle and imagination. To strive critically to understand
de facto domination and to discover and enlarge means of de facto
democracy is the essence of the struggle for humanity's future.

Invention of socially viable forms of human co-operation from
which domination has been eliminated is the lodestar of political
action and social morality. It is never easy to move away from
hierarchical and authoritarian structures, but the conscience of
humanity is becoming more and more committed to this goal and the
defenders of hierarchy more and more take refuge in deceit and
demagogy. So within many structures (industrial, social, governmental, party-political, trade union etc.) it becomes possible to
claim rights to grass roots control, to challenge or at least bring
into debate its autocratic procedures in decision-making and in
control over information (its analysis and communication).

There can be no set rules for what can or can't be done; it will

be discovered by exploration - imaginative intuition, trying out
possibilities and learning from experience. But certainly - for all
their obvious inadequacies - existing organisations are necessary
frameworks for many forms of social action. Trade unions are an
obvious example; their defects are easy to list, but in industry
nothing can be done unless with them and through them and at the
same time nothing can be done unless against them - that is, in
struggle against deeply established practices. Devolution of industrial control directly challenges the trade union official who
sees himself as paid to take burdens off the rank-and-filer. Bureaucratic and ambivalent as central organisation at national level
may be, it is none the less essential. National policies, legislative frameworks and so forth are necessary to create space for
new forms of grass roots control and developed activity; but
national policies and national organisations tend to suppress
initiatives at the base. So in many ways 'trade union loyalty' and
'solidarity' are in uneasy partnership with critical transformation
of outdated structures and notions.

The fact that political strategies at national and international
level are indispensable to social and political change, should not,
however, excuse the propensity of theorists and practitioners to
spend too much time 'playing God', that is, imagining strategies
to lead the enslaved peoples out of their captivity. In fact,
national and international politics can only be secondary to the
power and articulation of political consciousness and activity at
the base. The question is what national and international policies
are needed to give these forces space in which to grow and what
policies, by force or persuasion, can constrain leadership policies,
can compel hierarchical power to create growing space for non-
hierarchical power.

Some theorists will say this is absurd; hierarchical power never
'surrenders'; but the same theorists in their next breath may
champion 'leadership strategies', in effect, to replace 'bad hierarchical power' with 'good hierarchical power' which presumably
means hierarchical power that will surrender its power. But will
it? History suggests it may not. So is not the first necessity the
development of consciousness, organisation and power 'at the base'
in order to constrain and compel the power 'at the top'. Certainly
it will help to have opponents of hierarchy in the hierarchy; but
supposing people in the hierarchy are against hierarchy they have no
power to act against hierarchy without the strongest support 'from
the base'. So the first priority is always organisation and consciousness at the base.

The democratic logic that accords overriding priority to enlarge-
ment of power at the base is, once stated, simple and compelling.
But it calls into question long-accepted conceptions of socialism.
Socialism has long been equated with state-directed enterprise.
Socialism has been so presented in the writings and practice of the
Webbs, Morrisonian nationalisation, the Soviet economic system,
Keynesian socialism and elsewhere. Socialism, in contrast to
laissez-faire, has been seen as planning, as rational co-ordination
by the state, to correct the anarchy of the laissez-faire market.

In Britain and other countries state enterprise is constantly
expanding with an economic logic of its own but so far from elimi-

nating irrationality it goes hand in hand with massive unemployment, extreme centralisation of political and economic power and unwieldy bureaucratisation. It is defended and attacked as 'socialism', but to those who experience it as a lived-in socio-economic structure it does not 'feel like socialism' if socialism has anything to do with a shift of power towards the base.

What happened? The first yearnings towards socialism and communism were libertarian - a social order in which the oppressed would be freed by sharing of resources and throwing back the oppressive power of 'have's' exploiting 'have not's'. So that we may be free to use resources freely, we must change the economic system. So the argument started. The next step would then be to *transfer ownership of means of production* from private hands to public authorities who would then *plan* use of resources. Then the argument - and the practice - got stuck. The objective of freedom from oppressive power by the devolution of power got lost from sight, being obscured and so replaced by the suggested means of attaining it.

The emphasis now needs to be brought back to the base and the role of 'state direction' needs to be seen in terms of governmental provision at national, local and international level necessary to liberate and facilitate co-ordination of social forces at the base or to create an interface between continuing market forms of economic activity (which in places will long continue) and new forms of using resources generated by activity at the base.

Not so long ago talk in these terms would by many have been dismissed as meaningless; but today initiatives in industry against redundancy define necessities for governmental buying (or guaranteeing) socially useful products and for financial support and for monitoring use of resources by new criteria. These needs and possibilities in industry can be defined very concretely, as the much quoted Lucas Aerospace example illustrates.

Analogous provisions are also necessary in support of community initiatives to tackle local employment problems and make better social provision for co-operatives, cultural centres and many other grass roots activities. The problem is not one of hand-outs from the public purse but of differently administering and financing public social service and cultural activities under grass roots control.

All this has moved far from the anarchist Utopias of everyone doing their thing. Required is co-ordination of action by grass roots groups but not only co-ordination: required also is the working out and discussing of socio-economic theories about new structures and the paths by which they may be reached.

Ideology too is an organiser. Imposed dogmas determine patterns of action for the faithful; they are significant instruments of domination. Struggle against domination implies self-determination in thought as well as in action and would suggest that opponents of domination are debarred from enjoying the organisational benefits and the social unity that adherence to a common doctrine gives. This is a matter that needs to be deeply explored, but, whilst the dangers of subordination through the agency of doctrinal conformism are clearly real, there is every reason to believe that the unifying benefits of shared theoretical concepts can be enjoyed without loss of intellectual independence. In the first place, a sharing of aims

and concepts of social relationships from which domination has been
eliminated is necessary to give unity to some broad co-ordination of
human activity directed towards social change. It is, moreover, not
just a question of unifying activities; intellectual co-operation
needs to be approached in new ways so that social knowledge more
directly and more deliberately serves aims of social change.

'Division of labour' has played a lop-sided role in the evolution
of human society. It has socialised human knowledge but has permit-
ted control over the direction of its use to remain with dominant
minorities. The structures and motivations of a commodity society
encourage the specialist to deepen his/her understanding of a narrow
area but discourage study of possibilities of self-managing, non-
hierarchical co-ordination in the use of social knowledge. Such
non-hierarchical co-ordination is not only necessary for struggle
against domination; it opens up huge possibilities of enlarging the
power and effectiveness of forces opposed to domination. It still
calls for a high degree of specialisation on the part of human
beings whose training and experience makes them what Henri Laborit
(in 'Decoding the Human Message', Allison and Busby, 1977) calls
'monotechnicians' but - and this is what most human beings today are
not - they must also be (again Laborit's term) 'polyconceptualists',
that is, people concerned about the totality of human knowledge and
action of which each speciality is but one element. Division of
labour in a commodity-structured society is integrated by the commodity system. The specialist sells his speciality to a system over
which he has no control, which to him as an individual is an alien
system. Polyconceptualists themselves co-ordinating their own
functions as specialists will need to raise to the level of consciousness the social meaning of their specialities; social responsibility will enter into the activity of human beings as
'scientists' - and 'polyconceptualism' may well also imply that all
human activities will acquire a 'scientific aspect' - that is, all
social activity will feed and be fed by the sum total of social
knowledge (which, when sophisticatedly integrated, we today call
'science').

The argument - necessarily - has led me to seek somewhat distant
ideals as compass points for present actions. The present actions,
however, are the important thing and these are not at all easy to
work out. The potential of forces eager to struggle against exploitation, domination, privilege and obscurantism, for peace, for
better use of resources and knowledge, is considerable. But this
potential is not harnessed. The apparatus of domination has always
been skilled in the techniques of 'divide and rule'. The conclusion
to which opponents of domination have jumped has been 'we need a
strong clear-headed leadership to unite our forces'. Points already
made suggest why this line of argument must fail. If we try to use
the same weapons as our enemies we run the risk of finding these
weapons turned against us. We need to unite the intellectual and
material strength of all who are opposed to domination, but to do
so we need to discover some collective means of integrating our
ideas and actions.

As one of many possible illustrations one needs only to look at
the failure of the French left to marshal strength enough to deal
with Giscard d'Estaing, Gaullism and their variegated consortium of

the right. French democracy badly needed to shift the log-jam of
politics that blocks its way. There is a great potential to be re-
leased but the Communist and Socialist organisations displayed such
sclerotic foolishness in defence of their separate programmes that
an electoral victory of the left - that would have had far-reaching
significance far outside parliamentary politics - for the world as
well as for France - was, quite simply, thrown away. Basically
there was not enough political vigour transcending the organisational myopia of hierarchically dominated party apparatuses. It proved
impossible to realise joint action based upon wider possibilities f
for initiatives at the base - and this really should have been the
central objective of the alliance. Instead energies became focused
on programmes conceived by political chiefs - meaningless programmes
since their elements were achievable only in so far as political
muscle was generated at the base. The essential objective was joint
action itself - democratised outward-looking joint action by all potential elements in an alliance of the left.

There is too much hierarchical dogmatism from the past embedded
in movements hoping to travel to a new future. Such failures are by
no means peculiar to France. British Labour, 'the British left',
'democratic elements generally' or whatever one should call the
whole spectrum of progressively inclined people in Britain are similarly failing to seize opportunities through inability to make
common cause about essentials and to respect the seeming contradiction between well-founded disillusion with the political apparatuses and the necessity also of action through political apparatuses
to facilitate other forms of action.

Arguments for giving paramount allegiance to one or other of
existing organisations, or for that matter a new organisation, carry
no conviction. The problem is not one of leadership but of dis-
covering common purposes and unifying forms of action that spark
natural enthusiasms. Unifying ideas are very important but they
live in and develop from joint activity, the activities of discussion, yes, but, more significantly, doing things together for
one's own as opposed to externally imposed purposes. The problem is
to find such forms of action that 'take on', that in a living way
win credibility and draw into activity the many who in most different ways respect other human beings and hate oppression.

The assumption has always been - analogously perhaps to the
equating of socialist economics to planning plus public ownership
of the means of production - that the instrument to unify political
action is the political party, the new socialist and communist aims
requiring a 'political party of a new type'. Obviously the area of
politics is a field of hard-fought actions in which real social
forces find themselves in burningly actual conflict with other
social forces. Without underestimating the gigantic power of well-
thought shared ideas, it would be utter folly to think that forms of
political organisation and alliance are not essential and not to
recognise that such alliances and organisations must engage in hard-
headed political actions to win specific objectives which transfer
power from those who now exercise it.

In the changes currently being witnessed in Iran, ideas have
acted significantly as an organising force, but alliances, organisation and co-ordinated action have been their means of implementa-

tion; without them the ideas would have had no cutting force. So
what's wrong with 'the party' provided it sets itself the right objectives? 'The party?' *Which* party? That is one problem. Of
course, existing parties, trade unions and other organisations of
the people can play most important roles in political actions to win
specific objectives - and individuals through their activities in
such organisations stamp on the present actuality of history an important part of themselves. But to say this is also to say these
organisations are different and must - and indeed should - come into
conflict in the working out of social forms that truly express a
multiplicity of 'freedoms' at the grass roots.

All, however, is destroyed if some one of these organisations
decides to elect itself the supremo to shape the world's future for
all. There is today all too much evidence in blood that differences
alone without also forms of unity, leave international and inter-
organisational relationships exactly where they were before the
goals of socialism and international peace had been conceived. So
beyond the desirability of political action through existing organisations and the desirability of new organisations in particular
circumstances for particular purposes, there remains the underlying
problem of alliances, of unity amongst the multiplicity of social
forces that are in some sense against oppression, domination and exploitation and for classlessness, equality and freedom in some sense
or form - in senses and forms maybe yet to be evolved.

How unite? How define a basis for alliance? The essential
failure of communist parties is that organisation has always dominated the multiplicity of individuals. So slyness and singleness
of purpose have enabled 'apparatus-men' to prevail against the
social pooling of original thinking, and individually desired purposes. The old ways of hierarchy prevail against new explorations
of collectivity. The once hoped for international co-ordination of
great armies of progressive human beings dedicated to social change
proved an empty and rather sick dream; bad legacies of organisational stubbornness prevailed and are still very much with us.

Those of us who see these problems from different angles cannot
do more than try to float some ideas out of which discussions grip-
ping the social and political realities more closely, may develop.
The whole line of argument presented above opposes proselytising
for any one movement. This is a hard thing to say since all movements need members, so why not recruit? This is so. The point
rather is that one cannot pre-elect any organisation as humanity's
one chosen instrument to open the door to salvation. Organisations,
to be sure, are needed - but what organisations, new or old, and how
they are to be used, must be the choice of people themselves in the
light of their own aims, their own views, their own situations, the
particularities of their own circumstances and their own desires.
This means necessarily that social change will continue to generate
many organisations differing because people's interests, circumstances and views differ. Some will cover new particular interest
areas, some will be pre-existing organisations, some may be new
organisations experimenting with non-hierarchical structures and so
forth. All will contribute experience from various fronts of
struggle.

The problem is how can the huge numbers of people opposed to domination and concerned for social change match the centralised hierarchical power of their opponents? The forces of democracy are organisationally weak. 'Democracy' exists only in the form of footholds from which to oppose privilege and domination, footholds in law, in public consciousness, in structures of limited scope and purpose, in freedom of expression and communication. We need to look for keys in present reality to association that widens in many senses and directions the span and vision of democratic struggle - in arts and entertainment, in community living, in intellectual discovery as much as in the arenas of political, economic and military confrontations.

One individual can only most tentatively suggest steps towards some needed new associating of interests. Means of richer discussion and communication may be the first thing to tackle.

Who can tell how or where those who hate oppression will first discover bonds with the myriad humanity who differing in so many other ways share this hatred so actually as to be able to act together. It is hardly likely that any of us can anticipate in imagination what in the end can become actual - but reality may be learned only by exploration of doing. In attempting to suggest exploratory doing one might follow various lines of thought. One central idea provides a basis for unity - that is, dedication to the aim of a human society from which relationships of dominator and dominated 'as between both individuals and groups' has been eliminated. We need practical facilities for any individuals, groups or organisations subscribing to this overriding aim, to meet or communicate as and when need for support or joint action is felt. The mere statement of this practical need to be able to get together and communicate with others defines a problem about which there is a need to get together and communicate with others - how to do just this! Who should be approached? Their names and addresses? How define the range from which to draw participants? Geographically? Industrial employment? Field of special interest? Our concern is to associate people, individuals at the grass roots, not hierarchical representatives in committee. So there is a double problem: (1) association of people and groups at the grass roots; and (2) how associations of grass roots activities are to be mutually linked.

There is an organisational form - 'the standing conference' - that may have relevance here. People come together in conference, but when they have conferred they do not then simply disperse; they remain 'in conference' but 'adjourned'. That is, they are ready to come together and continue to confer whenever next the possibility or the need arises. The practicalities of such arrangements are a 'here-and-now problem' to be worked on; but one somewhat unusual principle of procedure suggests itself as necessary - such conferences should, whenever they so wished, recommend courses of action, record those in favour and those against, but *never* should such 'decisions' be binding upon conference participants. Courses of action worked out would simply and solely indicate potentialities for united action. When the desire for unity was strong this desire in itself would impose a discipline on participants, but never should the organisation of the conference be in a position to exert organisational power over participants. Their power would

consist solely in the working out of ideas and the power of these
ideas themselves to carry conviction. The carrying out of actions
must be determined by participants (as organisations or as individuals) for themselves.

Such 'standing conferences' would provide a machinery for collaboration and communication, a sort of enrolment of like-minded
people whose getting together would also be the means of working out
the rules of their own discussion. That is, people and groups or
organisations of people would arrange to meet in such ways as they
found convenient, stimulating and fruitful to their central purpose
of generating practical and intellectual support against the social
apparatus of domination.

A structure to give unity to the diverse forms that opposition to
domination takes, in contrast to centralised organisation 'from
above' to which we are so accustomed, may need to grow more like a
crystal, self-extending but strongly linked, transmitting old experience and acquiring new experience. Theory needs to find
channels of connection to the practicalities of life.

Perhaps the formality of 'standing conferences' - the atmosphere
of public proprieties that infects the politics of an alienated society - would in practice leave too little room for the humanity of
human beings. It could be that the brotherhood or sisterhood of
human beings opposed to oppression individually as well as group-
wise would find itself in forms closer to those that have developed
in the contemporary women's movements or in new forms of artistic
and cultural expression rooted in the involvement of people in protest against the oppression they themselves most feel. Who is to
say? Or how to find out but by trying whatever seems to hold some
promise? One thing seems certain: communication and contact of
people doing things for themselves is a necessary - though maybe not
a sufficient - condition to generate and sustain wider political
forms of unity. People need to unite to hold back threats of reactionary dictatorships or trends towards militarism and war. They
need also to unite to make progress towards social change; but here
the economic and social achievements of unity cannot be anticipated
in programmes of unity to be subscribed to in advance. Rather it is
that unity needs to precede so that strengthened by it people may
for themselves fashion their own achievements in their own priorities. The essential economic and social objective is, therefore, a
simple one: to create more space for more people to do things for
themselves.

Democracy in the sense of power in peoples' own hands implies a
social morality that, in demanding freedom of action for individuals
and their immediately associated groups in life and work, responsi-
bly defines relationships to the social environment in such ways as
may similarly advance the freedom of others. The problem is to discover viable social relationships to others who share the broad
ideal of democratic freedoms - no oppressors and no oppressed. The
discovery will come from trying out possibilities that respect the
actuality of society as it is. This means nurturing and giving
strength to developing forms of interhuman relationships that point
towards newly structured human futures; but it means at the same
time intervening politically in the political realities of the
present so as to create growing space for the new.

NAME INDEX

SUBJECT INDEX